Living amongst the beasts

The rise and fall of the Grendon experiment

Terry Ellis

Edited by: Chris Alston

Photography by: M. Rahman (Tittu)

Copyright © 2020 Terence David Ellis

All rights reserved.

No part of this publication may be reproduced, stored in a retrieval system, or transmitted, in any form or by any means, without the prior permission in writing of the author, nor be otherwise circulated in any form of binding or cover other than that in which it is published and without a similar condition including this condition being imposed on the subsequent purchase

ISBN-13 9798468815300

A note from the Author

Thank you for taking the time to read my book.

HMP Grendon has been at the forefront of therapeutic/psychiatric intervention since 1962, not that the therapy offered has been successful, one such therapy in the early days was aversion therapy.

Writing this book was a way for me to express my own personal experience of HMP Grendon, not to say what does or does not work.

Therapy alone will not stop offending and reoffending, in purchasing this book what you have done is help contribute to me being able to continue to take my story to people at risk of crime and to those already caught up in crime, people who can or would like to be swayed away from the path that I took, perhaps even for me to influence policy makers within the justice system to seek a more comprehensive approach to rehabilitation.

A lot of people have written a lot of things about HMP Grendon, some champion it, some argue it is an expensive waste of money, it is not for me to try and tell you what it is or is not. I will let you make your own minds up but what I will say is this:

In 2018 - 2019 (which at the time of writing, was the last full year the office of National Statistics had published for) self-inflicted death in custody accounted for 27% of total deaths, over 60,000 prisoners self-harmed and there were over 34,000 assaults. These figure have been rising year on year.

One of the only UK prisons that doesn't see numbers that match this trend is HMP Grendon. I am not saying there is no violence, no self-harm and no suicide, I am saying that the figures for all of these are much lower in Grendon than those in mainstream prisons.

Living amongst the beasts: The rise and fall of the Grendon experiment

CHAPTER ONE

Gavin's first community meeting started just like any other, but the temerity of the man was absolutely breath taking, the arrogance of a man who accepted he had done no wrong. As no sooner had we finished our introductions than he started to recount every sordid detail of the crime that he had inflicted upon the naive and innocent mind of a young girl.

As his words so cruelly rolled off his lips the enormity of what he had just said reverberated around the room like a psychological sledge hammer. That inflicted a wave of indignation that only a deviant of his species could elicit, even his degenerate peers were utterly incandescent with rage at the severity of his actions against his own six-year-old daughter. Such moral outrage by the deviant collective had rarely been seen on the wing since I had arrived at Grendon. But what made it worse was his denial of any culpability in her brutal slaughter, then add this to his admission that he had killed her because she wanted to die, so she could be with him when he went to heaven, was for us the straw that broke the camel's back. So, we as a community took the beast to task.

This is my account of living amongst the beasts. It is really the only way I can truly describe the two years I spent at Grendon, a therapeutic prison in Buckinghamshire which holds 240 B category prisoners. The title I hope will become especially poignant when you consider that most of my fellow Grendonites, as we were called, were made up of serial killers, child murderers, paedophiles, rapists and all other manner of despicable deviant acts imaginable, and me the token recidivist, or Terry as I like to be known. I am doing a 16-year 9-month sentence for robbery.

Over the years many of my fellow prisoners and family have asked me frequently why I went there in the first place and what I gained from my experience at Grendon. Well, that is a difficult question to answer, but I will try my best, in my inevitable way to explain the circumstances that brought me to Grendon in the first place and eventually what I got out of it.

CHAPTER TWO

I was arrested on the 16th September 2008 in Luton following extensive enquiries to trace me, as I had been on the run due to the fact that my friends or co-defendants had been arrested some 9 months earlier for a number of robberies and because we were life-long friends I was implicated as one of the ring leaders in what the papers eluded to was the 'the real Ocean's Eleven style Heist Gang'. We were responsible for a number of multi-million-pound robberies. Our biggest one to date was Verizon. We had used police cars, police uniforms and even taken a German shepherd dog with us. So, the name the papers gave us was like putting a noose around our necks as now every copper in London wanted our heads for a trophy on his mantel piece. All because we had robbed Verizon business, a global telecommunication and IT company based in St Pancras Way, Kings Cross. The company hold IT kits for most of the major banks including JP Morgan and is one of the largest data centres in Europe. The Verizon website boasted of its security saying it had 24/7 uniformed guard service with interior and exterior closed-circuit television surveillance, electronic access at all data centre entrances including biometric hand scanners. Also, electronic key racks for over 100 rooms full of IT computer hardware including motherboards and processors.

But there was a flaw in their system which we exploited, as apparently checking police ID cards was not part of their security measures, so, we took the opportunity to just walk in on the 6th December 2007 using no violence. Just our intellect and 16 pairs of handcuffs and as it was my birthday on 9th December it will always be a birthday I will never forget.

Then fast forward to the 16th September 2008, I am now spread eagled and face down in the dirt with my hands cuffed behind my back with 20 or more old bill talking into their radio saying "we have got the bastard" as they slapped each other on the shoulders, then I was taken back to Kentish Town police station where I am greeted by all the plods to a round of applause. Then I am banged up in a cell for 3 days as we go through all the

Terry Ellis

bollocks but I give them the normal 'no comment' statement before I am carted off to Pentonville.

Pentonville is a cockroach invested shit hole where I spend the first week in the block as I refuse to share a cell with anyone. I am then put in a single cell on D wing next to the visitor's entrance, No 1 cell which is right opposite the screw's office. The cell is infested with cockroaches, so I spend the first week catching them and putting them into a large see through HM Prison bag which I have hung up on my wall. To date I have managed to bag 120 of the fuckers as I have been waiting to tip them over the Governor's head. My reason for doing this is when I complained to him when I was down the block the cheeky fucker told me not to tell anyone as they would all want some and then he shut the door in my face, then he and his screw mates laughed as they walked away.

So, today was payback. As the Governor was just outside my door sitting against the pool table with a large group of Prisoner Inspectors, mostly women, so I took the bag off my wall with my little friends inside, I looked through the crack in the door so I could see all the screws who would normally guard him and as luck would have it there was only 3 with him today and none of them looked on point so I took a deep breath and made my move. I slowly opened the door then walked up behind him and tipped half the bag over his head before I threw the rest over the Prison Inspectors. The Governor screamed like a little baby as he jumped up and down and tried to brush all the cockroaches off his head, while all the women ran for their lives down the landing screaming blue murder. As for me I just stood their laughing just before I was jumped on by all the screws and carried off to the block for a bit of retribution screw style.

Two weeks later I was put on a production order and requested to appear at Kentish Town police station where I was questioned about a number of robberies. But once again I gave a 'no comment' statement before I was taken to Islington Police Station. But once we were outside there we were told that Islington was shut due to building work being carried out so after twenty or so minutes sitting in a car it was decided that we were now going to St Anne's ID suite for me to go on an ID parade and take a photo of me. So off we went, me and three plod in a van and 4 plain clothes bringing up the rear in an unmarked police car. As we were driving along I was aware that one of my handcuffs was a bit loose and after a bit of persistence from me, I was able to free one of my hands but the other one wouldn't budge, no matter how much I tried to force it. But not to worry because at least now one of my hands was free.

There was still about twenty minutes travelling to go before we arrived at St Anne's in Tottenham. But all I could think about was how good it would feel to escape from these mugs and be free again. But first I had a mountain of obstacles to overcome, the first one being that I had to somehow overpower my guards. Secondly, I had to get enough distance between me and my escorts and thirdly I needed to get a good enough run up to wall to make my escape. Fourthly I had to do all that without someone jumping on my back. So, my timing had to be right, it would also ultimately rely on a bit of Ellis good luck. But most of all a lot of effort on my part which meant me banging out a few plod something I wasn't keen on doing, as the last thing I needed was a GBH charge. But I had no choice as my escape depended on me overpowering one or more of my guards. I had the bottle to do it, in fact I had an abundance of bottle so there shouldn't be too much trouble as for me making my move.

The journey seemed to be taking for ever, so I took the opportunity to put my captors at ease by making some small talk and to be honest they were a bit receptive to a bit of old chat as one of them even offered me a deal if I could grass my mates up. They even offered me 6 years if I owned up to a few more robberies. But I told them to fuck off as I had made my own plans for that night as I was thinking about breaking out of the van and fucking off home. My joke seemed to make them all laugh and one even quipped back at me saying 'it is going to be a long time Mr Ellis before you see the light of day again". I smiled at his sarcasm as I believed my freedom was just around the corner and in a few minutes these mugs would have a rude awakening.

As we pulled up to the gates I noticed that the wall was about 15-foot-high, but the gate was only 10 foot which looked easy enough for me to get over. All I needed was a good run up or maybe if I had to go over the wall I could use the car parked up against the wall. A part of me really wanted to do this but there was another voice inside my head saying don't be such a fucking idiot. It felt like a battle of good and evil and evil was definitely going to win today as it kept shouting at me "you can fucking do this Tel". Then the gates opened and my adrenaline started pumping and this mixed in with the butterflies in the pit of my stomach was all I needed to get me ready as I kept telling myself "this is it Tel, get ready son".

The car following us parked up against the wall, and as I looked over at them I noticed that none of them were getting out. This was my first bit of good luck. Maybe they thought their job was done. Then the other driver got out and walked over to the back entrance. He then buzzed on the bell and went in. My second bit of luck and if I am honest it felt good to see him go in as he was a big fucker. I was now on my own with my two escorts, both in their late 40's who I hoped wouldn't be a problem to me. Just as I thought about nutting one of them in the back of the van, the one nearest to me slid the door open and stepped out while the other one just sat there. What luck, so I made my move. I jumped

Terry Ellis

out of the van, spun round and banged the copper on the chin which put him on his arse. Then I started running towards the front gate but as I looked up I could see two uniformed old bill coming through the fucking gates, who were now blocking my escape, at the same time as I looked around I could see 6 or 8 plod pursuing me. I then jumped up onto one of the car bonnets then ran up the wind screen onto the roof before leaping to the wall grabbing it with both hands. I fucking made it, see you later mugs, I'm on my way to freedom. All I had to do now was pull myself over, but then I felt a whack in the middle of my back, then one across my head, then someone grabbed hold of my legs, then another one on my back with his arm around my neck, choking the life out of me. Then I lost my grip before all three of us fell to the ground with my head in the dirt again, spread eagled on the ground with my hands once again cuffed behind my back, before I was frog marched to the van with a load of relieved coppers. I got three busted ribs, a sore shoulder and a swollen eye for my troubles.

But just at that moment my solicitor turns up shouting at the old bill, demanding to know what was going on. So, plod had no choice but to stand me up again so I could talk to him, so I showed him my hands cuffed behind my back, at the same time telling him that I had just been jumped for no reason. Telling him that I had just got out of the van with my hands cuffed behind my back and these fuckers had just jumped me. How can I defend myself against all this lot I tell him? Then we have a few more protestations from the plod that I am lying. I am then placed in the back of the van face down and taken back to Pentonville with sirens blazing and blue lights flashing.

Well at least I tried and as I have always been told, God loves a trier

Once I am back in Pentonville I am charged with attempted escape and put in the yellow and green stripe suite as it will distinguish me from the rest of the other prisoners. As someone who has tried to escape I am also referred to a prison psychologist, a good-looking woman called Melanie and we meet once or twice a week for about 6 months. And seeing her helps. She takes me to some dark places which bring back memories of my time in care as a kid. She discovers that I have abandonment issues and suggests I try therapy, so with a seed planted I start to believe that Grendon might be a place for me to make some fundamental changes in my life. So, we send off for one of its brochures which lists all of its amenities such as gym most days, an hour's exercise, keys to my room, sky sports and open all day. So, I sign on the dotted line believing I was on the way to therapeutic utopia.

However, nothing could ever prepare me for the eventualities of my stay and the mental scars it would leave on me, good or bad while participating in this exploratory and intrusive

Living amongst the beasts: The rise and fall of the Grendon experiment

study into my psyche. Nevertheless, as I said, I will leave it up to you to make your own minds up based on all the actual events that took place there. The therapy I underwent, my fellow Grendonities crimes, the notes I made at the time in what I believe was an extraordinary experience, that I for one will never forget.

Terry Ellis

CHAPTER THREE

It all started for me on 16th July 2010. The day I arrived at Grendon. As Grendon is one of only a handful of establishments that believe confrontational therapy and behaviour cognitive therapies can change a recidivist behaviour. This challenge to change is another reason I filled in the questionnaire some 8 months previously. But even though I have now been accepted, I was still surprised that my application had been recognised at all, as it is widely believed throughout the prison system that Grendon only accepted the really deviant criminals as the accepted face of Grendon. Also because of their shame it made them more manageable dictating that they automatically got through the induction process. So, believing in this I had to prove that I had what it took to be here. Not just for me but for the sake of every guy in the prison system who had missed out on the chance to change, just because they were not deemed deviant enough.

As we pulled up to the gates of Grendon, I could feel the butterflies in the pit of my stomach doing somersaults. And this combined with the nervous tension I was feeling put me on edge. I always get this way when moving from one prison to the next. And today was no exception. I believe that everyone experiences this, some sort of trepidation when moving, it doesn't matter who you are or how long you have been away. Every move is different but always starts with their journey. First there is the excitement of the move, mixed in with the sadness of leaving friends behind. But once you are in the sweat box with only your thoughts for company, it is then that all the little niggles start. This foreboding of the unknown mixed with apprehension is enough to get your adrenaline rushing to the pit of your stomach. It is a feeling that you cannot submit to, it is only those that have been through a similar experience can possibly understand. All I know is once this feeling kicks in my defences go into overdrive which is weird because at the same time I'm the picture of equanimity, a defence I have mastered over the years, as god forbid you should show any signs of fear in prison. Especially when your first port of call

Living amongst the beasts: The rise and fall of the Grendon experiment

is the prison reception area as it is run by the screws who are old hands at spotting any signs of weakness in your armour and exploiting it to their own advantage. Which normally means putting you in a cell with someone with mental health problems and bad hygiene, which I am sorry to say has become common practice over the years, due to the fact that all the mental hospitals have been shut down and turned into flats under the guise of care in the community. Which leaves prison the only sanctuary for anyone with mental health troubles to live. You could also be placed in a cell with a junkie, who for his needs for drugs at any cost would sell your trainers the moment your back was turned. But the normal scenario in these cases was you would most likely be put in a cell with broken windows, a busted TV, no pillows or sheets and because it would be so cold in there you would need to block up your window with the only blanket you had. Unfortunately, this is the norm in some prisons, especially Pentonville as it is also running alive with cockroaches. An infestation it has had for years.

It is a lottery who you get banged up with, but starts the second you open your mouth in the reception area. They call your name, then the games begin. You are given a number. You are asked your date of birth and then the million- dollar question 'have you any medical or mental issues?' The question is irrelevant as the only real concern is putting you in a double cell as space is paramount, a premium in prison, even if it is at the cost of your own mental health. They don't really care about a little thing like that. However, if you can't share or you refuse to, you will be referred to the prison doctor who will pretend that he can't speak English as he is under strict instructions on pain of death not to give you or anyone else a single cell regardless of your real state of mind, or any other excuse you might give him. But if you are new to the prison system you will take what the doctor says at face value. If not, you can hold out and protest but you will then be threatened with being put down the block i.e. segregation unit. Also, you will be placed on basic regime which means that throughout the whole of your sentence you will be discriminated against, as you will be unable to get a job of any significance. You will have limited association and be paid the minimum wage of £2.50 per week, which doesn't go very far especially if you are a smoker. You will also be placed on the high-risk register making it harder for you to progress through the categorisation process. And given this option most will choose to be banged up with someone regardless of the consequences, other than their own peace of mind that they have made the right decision.

As for me I always choose the block as peace of mind is worth its weight in gold even if it is at the cost of a few days down the block.

However, Grendon was a different kettle of fish, as the atmosphere of the place seemed calm and relaxed. As we entered the reception area I saw that there were 3

Terry Ellis

officers behind a 5ft counter, one female and two males. They were standing on a raised platform which gave them an elevated position to look down on any new arrivals such as myself. To the left of the counter was a BOSS chair, a chair with an electronic sensor built into it to detect anything metal. When you sat on it anything such as a mobile phone or knife could be detected. If anything is detected the chair will beep and one of three lights will indicate on which part of the body the offending article could be found. At the same time notifying the officer standing behind you, who would then jump on you with as much gusto as he could muster before being joined by his colleagues, who would then handcuff you before marching you to one of the strip cells where you would be searched and then left in an observation room until the item had been passed.

I was now standing in front of the counter with my two escorts who had accompanied me from Rye Hill. One of them handed over my movement papers which seemed to be the signal for the induction game to begin, as one of the screws came down from behind the counter and introduced himself. His name was Patrick, he was quickly joined by his colleague a 6' 9" giant called Dean. Dean asked for my date of birth, then my prison number before he took off my handcuffs. I was then asked to sit on the BOSS chair which beeped for some fucking reason. I was taken to the strip cell and once there they were satisfied that I didn't have anything on me. I was asked to return to the front desk where I was asked a few more questions and once they were satisfied I was who I said I was they welcomed me to Grendon.

I then said goodbye to my two escorts then officially signed over as a new Grendonite. I was given a new number; a new photo was taken which was very flattering which I was told I had to wear at all times. As failure on my part would result in me being put on an adjudication or if it was deemed necessary I would be sent back to Rye Hill. Once these terms were explained to me, it was time to check all my stuff in which normally takes an eternity as everything I owned had to be checked against my property card, from colour and make of shoes, jean sizes, tee shirt makes, the lot. Even the serial number on my radio. My toiletries also had to be checked for drugs before being refolded, rebagged and reboxed, which again took the best part of an hour. Once I was finished I was told to put my gear on a trolley as we were now being taken to F wing.

F- Wing is where all new prisoners are quarantined for a period of 12 weeks or more depending on whether or not they make it through the selection process. As we were about to leave the reception area the third officer came down and joined us. Her name was Jackie, she was about 60 with blonde hair, big long finger nails, big ego and a big mouth. My first impression of her wasn't good as she was quite condescending but nothing I couldn't handle.

Living amongst the beasts: The rise and fall of the Grendon experiment

The journey to F wing took us through the healthcare waiting room. And as I pushed the trolley through the gates, I noticed there were 5 guys sitting around a small magazine table. They all gave me the once over, so I returned the favour with added veneers then carried on following Dean through the next set of gates which led us to a short corridor. At the end of this corridor was the Arts and Craft room and the Education Department. We turned right and as we walked along I read a few of the door signs library, OMU, security, chaplaincy, MDT room, and piss test unit. Halfway down this corridor there was a left turn which I was told by Jackie was called the M1 as it was a long corridor with access points to wings A, B, C, D and G. Also access doors to the main kitchen and main exercise yard.

We then came to the prison Chapel which had two large doors. To the right of the entrance was a book stand with the usual God paraphernalia, then another 20 feet we were at the gates of F wing and my new deviant hell for the next 3 months.

Once through the gates Jackie gave me my cell number, then called Steve, Jock and Alan who were tasked with showing me to my new abode. Jock had a look of a man who had been on drugs for all of his adult life. He was about 50 but looked much older. Alan on the other hand looked about 30 but was actually 23. He was a peculiar looking chap who looked the part of deviant. He had a goatee beard and glasses and gave me a strange look. He also had something wrong with his hand as it was pressed up against his belly, like a broken wing on a bird. He gave me the horrors as he and Jock helped me up the stairs. When we got to the 2s landing there were two corridors, one went to the right the other was my landing to the left which was dimly lit and painted lime green. There were 3 cells in this section. My cell was the middle one which was aptly number 2 as it was a right shit hole, nothing like the brochure had depicted. The walls were filthy, the floor was greasy and round the toilet there were piss stains everywhere. The place was fucking disgusting and as I stood there shaking my head in disbelief, Jock told me not to worry as the cell was only temporary as I would be moving round the other side as soon as a cell became available. So, with this new information I reached down and picked my jaw up off the floor, at the same time I decided not to unpack. I just made my bed and put my shower stuff on the sideboard. Alan went back downstairs but Jock stayed and gave me the lowdown on the place and some of the guys here. The normal bonding advice as he tried to become my new best friend. He also told me not to trust anyone as most of them are just deviant scumbags. He then volunteered to dish the dirt on bird hand Alan, which was a bit disturbing as I had only been here for 5 minutes and now he wanted to pollute my head with some depravity. For that split-second I wondered if I could handle this much information regarding my new comrades without beating the fuck out of them. But before I had time to ask him to stop he regurgitated bird hand Alans offence. Alan had been walking along the canal and had bumped into a young girl out playing on her own. She was only 9 years old, so he started talking to her. She wanted to go home but he insisted she stayed and played. .So, with the innocence of a young 9-year-old she played the morning away not realising Alan had taken her acceptance of him as them now being boyfriend and girlfriend in his warped head. He tried to kiss her but she started to scream which panicked him and scared that he might get into trouble he picked up a rock and hit her over the head. But she still kept crying and so he put his hands around her neck until she passed out. Then he threw her lifeless body into the canal believing she was dead and that he was out of trouble. But thanks to a passer-by who had seen this spectacle unfold before his eyes, he quickly jumped in and retrieved the body as Alan ran off. It was only by the grace of God the young girl started breathing again. Alan was caught the same day but due to him having learning difficulties he was only given a 10-year sentence which I thought was a joke but that's life.

It was now time for me to go back downstairs as Jackie wanted me to sign the wing contract stating that I would comply with all F wing regime rules. Jackie was still sitting behind the desk when we got there. In front of her desk were 3 soft blue chairs of which one was occupied by a young guy called Nick who was preoccupied reading the daily papers. There were also 2 other daily papers on Jackie's desk, the Sun and The Mirror. I was told the papers were not to be taken back to the cells as you were only allowed to read them in the office under the watchful eye of the screws. To be honest I found the thought of reading the screws papers perplexing because for as long as I could remember, the screws office is and always has been out of bounds. And as for reading their papers, this was definitely taboo, a no-go area.

Once again Jackie read my mind and decided to explain the concept of reading in the office. She said it was supposed to help all new arrivals integrate better with the old foe the screws. Also mixing with other Grendonites would bring us together as a group because like most of the guys here who had lived through the old prison system many were still well and truly anti authority. A bit like myself, we still saw mixing with the enemy as sacrilege and strictly forbidden but now I was being asked to mix with not only with the screws but with the deviants as well. All because I was at Grendon and because they encouraged it. You could say that it was an absolute necessity if you wanted to advance yourself through to one of the main wings, which if you can't accept the officers that were running the therapy groups then you might as well not be here. Which I could understand as it wasn't really rocket science. As even I could see that eventually given 12 weeks on this induction wing it would break down some of the many beliefs that I held.

Living amongst the beasts: The rise and fall of the Grendon experiment

As I pondered the merits of this radical new approach to rehabilitation, Jackie raised her head from behind the magazine and gave me a smile that would have brightened up the darkest hour. At the same time, she asked how I liked my new accommodation, which made me wonder if she had deliberately put me in that cell to see how I would react. But I didn't bite because I could see it was her job to be antagonistic.to everyone as she was constantly pushing buttons, or was it just me? She then asked me to listen to Nick and Jock as they would be giving me a lecture on the wrongs and rights of Grendon and what was expected of me whilst I was here. I could see that by giving them this responsibility it was her way of boosting their self-esteem and confidence, as making them part of the process would encourage and reinforce in them Grendons ideology. It's a popular technique used by some religious cults like Scientology but there is always a downside to this approach as brainwashing people to affect their radical transformation of their beliefs and behaviours is that there is no room for free thinking as free thinkers are normally demonised and portrayed as trouble makers, which I only hoped was not the case here at Grendon.

As I was listening I could see Jackie eyeing me up and at the same time I could see how proud she was of her blue-eyed boys and the wonderful job they were doing. Their conversion to the dark side of this new doctrum was paying dividends. When they finished I was asked to sign the wing compact which stated I wouldn't use violence or bully anyone. Also, I had to adhere to all the rules and regulations laid down by Grendons constitution as failure on my part to do so would result in me being kicked out, so I signed on the dotted line with a new belief that my life was about to change for the better. But before I could digest this information I was told it was dinner time and because I was the new boy on the wing, I was given a sandwich and a menu to fill out so that I could get my food ordered for the rest of the week. The menu guy also told me that another way of installing responsibility in us was to make every wing responsible for preparing and cooking all its own meals. Every wing had its own cooking team, made up of 3 inmates. The No 1s job was to cook all the meals, the No 2s job was to make sure the right amount of food came over from the main kitchen and the No 3s job was to do the washing up and cleaning.

Each kitchen area was called the pod. They were all fitted with the latest mod-cons such as a chip fryer, combi oven and large double fridge. And to make sure the pod chef did his job correctly a member of staff was tasked with checking his work. There was also a complaints book specifically for any discretions regarding the quality of the food. Also, all the wings had dining areas and all inmates were encouraged to sit together at meal times in the belief it would improve their social skills. Another great idea, I now had to sit and eat with all these dribbling fuckers.

Terry Ellis

As I sat in my cell over the dinner period, I decided to clean my cell as I couldn't live in this shit hole, even if it was only for a few days, so I got down on my hands and knees and cleaned the floor. I cleaned all the piss stains from around the toilet then I attacked the walls with a bit of sponge bobs and a bit of elbow grease. I spent over an hour doing it and when I finished I was thinking that I really needed a shower. So, when the senior officer opened me up at 2 o'clock I had my towel in my hand but before I could go he wanted to welcome me to the wing so I spent 10 minutes talking with him. He told me that if I wanted to make it through the induction process I had to prove that I could mix with everyone regardless of their crimes, as any ill feelings I held towards them had no place in Grendon, as truth and honestly was paramount if I wanted to do therapy. I thought what he was saying was a bit deep as it was only my first day. I had come here to change but now I was being told to hide my feelings towards these deviant bastards so much so I thought for honesty. I must admit I was angry, I had met a child killer this morning, I had been served a sandwich by a rapist so my nut was all over the place, but he was right and he was talking sense, so point taken. I would try my best to hide my dislike towards them. So, it was chin up, chest out and a big smile. John the SO ended our conversation by saying I shouldn't hesitate to call him at any time if I ever needed help, so I thanked him and headed for the shower.

The shower room was a surprise as it was spotless unlike my cell. Plus, it didn't smell. All the walls were tiled white. There were 5 wash basins with mirrors, 2 sit down toilets, 3 small urinals and 2 standing showers with privacy curtains. I jumped into the shower and washed away the day's woes. It felt so good. After about 15 minutes I felt brand new again and fighting fit to take on Grendon, but first I wanted to look around my new surroundings.

The wings were arranged over 2 floors but were practically identical. The ground floor had a kitchen and dining area. There were 4 offices, a laundry room and one small washing machine and drier. The phone was also on the ground floor along with 14 cells and a large community room that could easily fit 40 people. A pool room, small. A TV room, small. 2 therapy rooms and a store room. On the 2s landing by the stairs, there was an assortment of potted plants that wouldn't have looked out of place in Kew Gardens. Every window and window sill had curtains and potted plants, which looked quite chic, especially when you considered where we were.

It was now teatime and someone downstairs was ringing the bell which I was told by Jock was a signal for everyone to grab their plates and head down to the dining room. I followed the guys with my new plates and plastic cutlery. I was starving, as I had only had a cheese sandwich that morning and I hated cheese, so I ended up eating just the 2

Living amongst the beasts: The rise and fall of the Grendon experiment

slices of bread. As I entered the dining room all the guys gave me the once over. So, once again I flashed my veneers. After a minute or so they all went back to their conversations. I then took my place in the queue still wondering what the fuck I was doing here. I had done some crazy shit in my time but this was by far the most off-key move I have ever done. As I looked at the faces I was surrounded by, it was becoming apparent that I was well and truly out of my comfort zone, as they looked a motley old crew.

It took about 5 minutes to get to the front of the queue, but it was really worth it as I walked away with chicken and chips, 5 slices of bread, a cake and custard and a proper glass of milk. At least the food compensated for the shit I was surrounded by. I was famished and with my bounty in hand I made my way to the only empty table in the room by the window. But my peace was short lived as bird hand Alan and a black guy called Julian sat down next to me followed by a young guy of about 20. They all seemed nice enough but at the same time it felt a little weird being in their company.

But still I had to make the effort by introducing myself. It felt a little bit surreal sitting there like a mug and going through all the normal pleasantries hoping they wouldn't notice the disdain I actually felt for all of them. But I hoped at the same time that by me sitting here it would send out a message that I wasn't a threat to anyone. As I was here for me and me alone, I wanted to change. That is what I had to keep telling myself. Hoping that eventually this reinforcement would help me cope, as what's the point of me coming here for if I didn't at least try to change. So, I had to integrate with those murderers of women and kids and it was imperative, especially if I wanted to get through this first week, as I would be under scrutiny from Jackie and everyone.

After tea I went up to the pool room and had a few games of pool with bird hand Alan, Sam, Jock and Chris who all made me feel welcome. I was starting to relax in their company. But there was still a part of me that resented the fact that all of them might be deviants of the worst kind and sooner rather than later I was going to find out. Which I knew would definitely have an adverse effect on me and the way I would eventually interact with them. It was a daunting prospect to say the least. But first I needed to talk to Kelly and the kids, as I knew that talking to them would cheer me up, and maybe after talking to them it might help me get back on track.

I tried to phone the kids most nights as I know they worried about me. This would be the first time that I had spoken to Kelly about trying to change my life. Even though I had raised the subject with the kids, I knew that Kelly would not believe me, especially when I told her where I was and who I was surrounded by. This was going to be a fucking nightmare conversation. It was now my turn to use the phone. The kids were fine and understood right away but Kelly just started laughing and said I was just going through the motions of change. And as the pessimistic cow knew me better than anyone else I couldn't blame her for laughing her socks off. So, I just laughed along with her wondering at the same time if I was really capable of any real significant change at the age of 46. So, I said goodnight to my girls and made my way back to my cell and 10 minutes later the bell rang out as it was now bang up.

As soon as the door was shut I just sat on my bed and reflected over my day and the enormity of the task ahead. But with Kelly's words and my kids ringing in my ears I had to win this battle, even though I knew there was worse to come. I had to remain positive.

I couldn't sleep all last night. I kept wondering if this was worth it coming here. I know that I am a tolerant person and especially tolerant to others. I have endured everything life has thrown at me other the years but this was different as I have never been in the company of rapists and child killers or any Jimmy Saville merchants before. It's a line I have never had to cross or for that matter ever had to, as my attitude has always been one of total disgust for these people. But now I was being told that my rehabilitation was dependant on it.

The door opened at 8:00 sharp so I took the opportunity to have a quick shower and a bit of breakfast. Two toasts, some Weetabix and a large cup of bromide. It felt strange sitting there on my own in the dining room but at the same time pleasantly surreal. The room was adorned with pictures which made it feel quite homely. There was also a small fridge in the corner that I hadn't noticed the day before which had a sticker on it that read cold drinks and butter only. The window ledges were also covered with potted plants and part of the floor space at one end was covered in plants. And as I sat there I expected Ray Mears to pop his head out and start talking about the great crested newt at any moment.

CHAPTER FOUR

It was now approaching 9 o'clock which meant for me the start of my first full day at Grendon.

It was also my first community meeting. God I was feeling anxious which I hoped would pass as I didn't want them to think I was a nervous wreck.

At 9 the bell rang out so I followed the guys to the community room. I took the seat right next to the door hoping I would get a look at all the guys that I had missed the day before. As they entered the room I could almost sense their unease and I wondered if it was because they had to recant their offences, as it is part of the process as Grendons mantra was openness, which was a good idea as it would stop any ambiguity. Over the years I wasted many a time with a lying mug as I have had many a selective conversation with people I knew were lying to me. So, to know who my fellow Grendonites were would be a refreshing change.

As the room began to fill up I counted 20 inmates, two officers Jackie and John and the wing phycologist who I named Mr Bean as he had the same mannerisms and dress sense. His real name was Richard. They all welcomed me to the wing. I was also informed by Mr Bean that all the community meetings were held by the inmates. It was also their job to delegate all the community jobs from ordering the wings supplies and chairing the meetings. Each wing had its own chairman and vice chairman. Today's meeting would be chaired by Andy and Nick with Nick taking the minutes and Andy directing. As I was the new boy on the wing it was customary that everyone introduced themselves to me, whilst at the same time giving me the short version of their offences and sentences. Now I understood why some of the guys looked apprehensive, which felt narcissistically pleasing as I enjoyed their discomfort. So, I sat back and listened as one

Terry Ellis

by one they offloaded their deviant shit. I could only assume that the whole exercise was supposed to make me feel at ease, that my fellow Grendonites were being open and honest believing in turn I would follow their example. One other objective regarding this outpouring of horror was to see my reaction. As for me I was indignant as I found the whole experience cold and emotionless as everyone was so matter of fact. It made me feel repugnant as some of the guys accounts were quite cold and graphic whilst others were short and to the point.

Andy the Wing Chairman was the first one to speak. He said "my name is Andy, I am doing a life sentence for the murder of my boyfriend who I stabbed and killed after we had a drunken argument. I dismembered his body and dumped the remains in a rubbish bin. Welcome Terry". Andy was about 55, 5' 8", 13 stone and a northern accent.

Next up was Sam. "Hi I am Sam. I am doing 6 years for child cruelty against my 6-week-old baby girl. Her Mum went out for the night with her friends which made me angry. So, when the baby started crying I just snapped. I pushed her legs over her head which fractured her hips and back, also broke her legs and 4 ribs. Welcome Terry". He then started crying to elicit some sort of sympathy as if it would absolve him of his crime. I found it hard to comprehend but at the same time compelling. Sam was about 20, 6', 12 stone, he made me wonder how a human being could do such an act of depravity on an innocent helpless child. He was supposed to protect her.

I was now in a dark place and finding the whole experience overwhelming, but I had to sit through another hour of these atrocities.

The next one out was Nigel who started out by saying that he lived on a canal boat and used to travel the length and breadth of the country raping women. Adding that the women were mainly old as they were easier to handle. He said he was doing a life sentence. "Welcome Terry" he said. Nigel was about 65, 6' 12 stone and a miserable looking old git. But at the same time, he looked just like any other old granddad and not your typical rapist.

Chris was the next guy up. I had played pool with him the night before and he had come across as shy and never said much. He said he was doing a life sentence which meant he had to prove himself fit to leave prison. Which I hoped he never would as this was the second time he had been in prison for rape. He was about 6'2", skinny about 30. He wasn't just a rapist he was a fucking nut job, which became apparent the moment he opened his mouth. He said he phoned a prostitute and when she came around he smashed her over the head with a hammer, beating the shit out of her. Which he said was the bit he really liked because it excited him as it was the only way he could get an erection on so he could masturbate over her. He said he thought he had killed her as there was so much blood but she had only passed out and when he left the room she had the fortitude to escape, raising the alarm. Chris came across as a cold-blooded killer with not one ounce of compassion or empathy. He also had a God complex. As he was speaking I wondered if this really was supposed to be a bonding exercise, because I really wasn't feeling it. But what I was feeling were thoughts of eradication as he was the scum of the earth.

Mac was up next. He introduced himself, he was about my age 46, 15 stone 6', a white South African. He was doing 36 years for killing his friend, who he said was a drug dealer. He had robbed him then tortured him, then shot him in the head. Then he burned the body, a classic case of overkill. He came across as a bit of a prick. I didn't warm to him straight away as I know a lot of drug dealers and none of them deserve to die over a few quid. He came across as a proper mug.

Mick was up next, he was a Scouser doing an 8-year IPP for GBH. Mick was about 40, 6', 13 stone. He looked and came across as pretty intense as he talked. He said he was walking his dog in the middle of the road one day when a guy pulled up beside him and asked him to get out of the way. But as Mick had been drinking he reached in through the car window and cut the blokes throat. He was arrested 3 days later. To this day he insists that he can't even remember doing it. He had a blackout which in turn made him angry. Mick was also a manic depressive and hyperactive. He talked a million miles an hour but came across as an OK guy.

Unlike Steve. Steve was about 50, 6' and 20 odd stone. He had a big lump on his head the size of an orange. He looked like Uncle Fester. He was a grotesque human being especially when you put him together with his crime. He was the only one so far who looked exactly what he was, a fucking rapist, who I nicknamed x2 because when he introduced himself to me he said "I am in for rape x2". He was so nonchalant about it, it made me sick to my stomach especially when he carried on with his story. He said the last time he was released for rape, they put him in a hostel believing he had been cured after spending 10 years in therapy, which we could all see hadn't worked. His neighbour in the hostel was a young girl who he had befriended. One night he knocked on her door asked her for some sugar and as soon as her back was turned he jumped on her, beating her into submission, doing all sorts to her that I can't write down. All I can say is he was a sick deviant who stunk to high heaven and God only knows what that poor girl went through at the hands of this fucking beast of a human being.

Terry Ellis

As I said I still had to listen to the rest of them and if I thought that it couldn't get any worse I was wrong, as a fat guy called Mark was up next.

He was about 40, and as big as an ox, 20 odd stone. He had a big fat neck, 5'6" of northern scum, who like x2 looked like a rapist. He really was a slimy bastard who had been raping women all his life. As soon as he started talking I just switched off as I had had enough of all this shit.

I just wanted to go back to my cell, but I couldn't, as I had to do my duty as a new Grendonite, which meant listening to the rest of them. What a fucking nightmare this was turning into. All I could hear was I am a murderer, welcome Terry. I am a rapist, welcome Terry blah blah blah until we came to the last one, Andy from Clacton

He said he was doing a life sentence for GBH (Grievous Bodily Harm). He said one night he had gone out looking for a prostitute and once he had found her, he asked her to get into the car. He then drove to a quite spot where he couldn't be disturbed. He then parked against the wall so she couldn't open the door. He said they spoke for a few minutes before he asked her to close her eyes and poke her tongue out, which she did believing it was his fetish. But the bastard just bit off her tongue and spat it out of the window. He then dragged her out of the car and beat her senseless before leaving her for dead. The hell that poor girl must have gone through as Clacton Andy was a scary guy. He was about 20 stone, 5'9", he had massive hands and was built like a brick shit house. He was also one ugly bastard of a man.

It was now my turn to face the music, as I looked across the room I could feel the deviant's eyes on me, willing me to be one of them, so that we could all be united by our own acts of depravity, and even sharing each other's misery. The whole mad situation felt surreal. I had actually come to Grendon to find some guilt or even shame regarding my life of criminality. But today all I felt was how proud I was to be a robber and not like them, who were parasites, rapists and murderers of women and children. I wanted to shout out "I am the only normal one here, you deviant bastards". Which again was crazy as I was supposed to feel guilty about letting my kids down by leading this criminal life. The whole situation was making me angry and I just wanted to get out of there, but I had to say my bit. So, I just said I am doing 16years 9 months for a few robberies. I then thanked them all for welcoming me to the wing.

Mr Bean then thanked me, then Andy and Nick called the meeting to an end. I just sat there until everyone had gone. I felt as if I had just come through a baptism of fire, or I

Living amongst the beasts: The rise and fall of the Grendon experiment

had been surrounded by evil. Everybody is this place seemed off-key and to listen to them all speak of their crimes with no empathy or guilt made me wonder if any one of them had the capacity to change.

As for me it was too late to quit, as I had all their stories in my head, so leaving now would be a waste of time. I had to listen to them for over an hour. Also, I had listened to the most- vile acts any human being could do to each other. So, to walk away now would be a failure on my part, which was not an option I was willing to take, as I had every right to be here. Plus, I wanted to make some real changes in my life on this sentence, as I knew I was a product of my environment, so knowing this I believed I could change.

But first I had to get through the next 12 weeks of the induction, which meant keeping up the pretence of what I had heard here today hadn't affected me. Because it had, as the world as I knew it had changed for ever. It had just become a darker colder place.

It was now time for some exercise, so I queued up with the rest of them, hoping that none of them would latch onto me as I wanted a bit of 'alone' time, especially after the morning I had just had.

The exercise yard was small however the sun was shining and the sky was blue. It felt so good to be outside in the summer heat with only my thoughts for company. The only down side was that I had to go back in after 1 hour.

Once inside Sam informed me that I would be joining his small therapy group which was group 2. These Small Groups were held on Tuesdays, Wednesdays and Thursdays from 9 in the morning until 10 o'clock. Then from 10 to 11 after all the small groups had finished, we would all come together in the community room for what was called feedback. A feedback would give all the 4 groups the opportunity to discuss any small issues that might have come up on any of the groups. Also it helped to see within the Groups who was struggling. Attendance for all of these meeting was compulsory as I found out the next morning, as Sam had been sent to get me.

The officer in charge of our group was Keith who was an ex-serviceman. He banged on quite a bit about his army career before telling me he was the group's main facilitator. He also said if I was ever late again I would be winged for a whole week. Even though Keith was a screw, he came across as an OK guy, who I warmed to straight away as I could see by the way he spoke about Grendon that he genuinely believed in therapy. He also told me not to go into too much detail about my life and background as the purpose of these groups was to see how we got on with each other. Also, how we communicated,

Terry Ellis

as the real therapy would start when we got over to the main wings. But for now, it was up to us what we talked about. As for me I wasn't too bothered as I had heard enough about rape and murder for one week.

CHAPTER FIVE

There were 5 of us on group 2, 6 if we counted Keith.

First was Howard who was doing a life sentence for killing his wife. He was about 50, 6', 18 stone. Then Faz, a young guy of 30, 6', 15 stone. He was doing 12 years for kidnapping. Mark who killed his boyfriend was a lifer. Skinny, he wore glasses, about 45, 5'6". Then Sam who was doing 6 years for child cruelty on his 6-week-old baby girl. He was 20/ 20 odd, 6'.

Howard started the group by saying he used to be a DJ and a mini cab driver, jobs that kept him out most nights, which led to accusations of him womanising and drinking too much, which in turn made him angry. The night he killed his wife he had been out with another woman, he had been drinking and when he got home his wife noticed there was lipstick on his shirt. He tried to deny it but she got angry and attacked him, so he knocked her to the ground. The more she tried to get up the more he beat her down. Then he put his hands around her neck and squeezed her until her eyes went dead. He said he then panicked and phoned his mate for some help but his friend phoned the police. He then said how much he loved his kids and the devasting effect it had on them. He then started crying and all I wanted to ask was why he had killed her as it was *he* who was having the affair. And if he really loved his kids then why kill their Mum. You selfish prick I thought but I couldn't ask as he looked so pitiful and I honestly felt sorry for him. While there was a long silence Keith asked him how he was feeling. The reason for this question was because most of the guys who came to Grendon have never spoken about their crimes or thoughts or feelings before. I could see from the relief on Howards face and from his demeanour that this was the first time he had ever spoken about it. It was important that we all saw this as it would give us the courage to open up within the group. Giving us a chance to share our thoughts and feelings, thus hopefully releasing years of pent-up emotions and frustrations.

Terry Ellis

As I played over what Howard had said in my head I could actually see the darkness in his eyes as he relived every moment of her murder. I could also feel his torment which was confusing for me. Keith and the guys asked him a few more questions which seemed to upset him. So once again I held back as I didn't want to frighten him off from opening up again in the future.

Keith then turned to me and asked how I was feeling so I said it felt strange to listen to someone talk so openly about killing their wife, especially regarding their feelings of guilt about depraving their kids from their Mum. I said the whole experience had normalised Howard in my eyes, as I no longer saw him a just an animal that kills women, but as a man who was trying to make sense of his crime. But no matter how much I tried to reconcile with Howard's thoughts and feelings in my eyes he would always be nothing more than a disgusting low-life.

These conflicting thoughts and feelings were driving me crazy, as one moment I felt empathy for Howard and the next nothing. I was living in the madness and for the first time in my adult life I didn't know the answers.

After 2 weeks in my shit hole of a cell I was finally given my own cell on the 2s landing as one of the guys had moved over to the main wing. So, I packed my stuff and got my new key from the office and waded into cell 206 my new home for the foreseeable future, which meant I could come and go as I pleased. The whole idea of having my own key felt somewhat surreal. The cell was small, 8' x 8', with a low ceiling which I could almost touch with my head, however, the view was amazing as I could see green fields, trees and a couple of cows in the distance. My little bit of utopia in what was a den of iniquity. At least now things were looking up.

I spent a few days getting the cell right, cleaning from top to bottom. I also met a few of the guys on my landing, my next-door neighbour was Kevin who was doing 6 years for child porn. He was about 50 and was going through a trans-gender reassignment period. Opposite him was Richard who was a 5' hobbit with facial hair down to his waist, who was doing a life sentence for murder. Next to him was manic Mick, the Scouser who was doing an 8-year IPP for cutting some guys throat. Then Mac, the white South African who was doing 36 years for murdering his mate and torturing him. Followed by Nick the Greek who was doing 10 years for robbery. He had robbed a security van. He was about 30, slim build. Then Norman who was a lifer who had killed his 17-yeasr old girlfriend. He was about 35. And Nigel who was about 45, he was a rapist and murderer. Thank God he was a lifer, he was a proper nut job, Next to him was a black guy called Gummy. He was about 40. He had nicked an old ladies handbag and car and as he was driving away he had run her over putting her in hospital for 6 months. He was doing a 6-year IPP. Which only left Howard the wife killer who was next door to me. Which made 11 of us, an odd-ball lot to say the least.

I missed my Group this morning as I had to go over to the Health Care Department as I had pretended that I had a headache, as I was sick of the group already. However, as I had missed my group I had to stay in my cell until all the groups had finished. So, while I was waiting I decided to watch a bit of TV, make a cup of tea and put my feet up. As I was lying there Patrick the reception screw popped his head round the door and politely asked me to turn my television off as it was wing policy that all TVs had to be switched off throughout the day to stop people like me skiving off and too it was hoped that we as a community would mix more which in turn would help us develop better social skills. I could see the logic behind it so I switched the TV off, as rules were rules and I was here to change even if it meant mixing with my new compadres.

As Mac was my new neighbour and lived opposite me we found some common ground as we both loathed the rapists and wife killers. And though I didn't warm to him at first as he was self-opinionated, aggressive and had all the traits of a bully who didn't tolerate fools, I actually decided to like him, as he was a lot like me as I won't take any nonsense from anyone. I also hated the world. Mac was also a very intelligent guy who was doing a degree in politics and over those first months we spent a lot of time together, as he had spent years in therapy over the years, so he had a wealth of knowledge when it came to psychology. Which helped me make up my mind about continuing with the therapy, as I was finding it hard being around these people. But Mac helped me understand that it wasn't about them, it was about me and the rest of my life. Another thing I liked about Mac was he never once talked about crime, a topic I was bored to death with, as I had come here to challenge myself intellectually which meant finding the answers to the meaning of my life, and by talking to Mac over those months it helped me realise what a journey I was going on.

He also helped me see what a waste my life had been. In fact, both our lives as he was doing 36 years and I 16 years 9 months for a few poxy criminal endeavours. Well that was our past which we couldn't change, but what we could change was our future and the way we wanted to live it now.

Howard was my other neighbour. He acted quite differently on the landings compared to our small group. In fact, most of the guys here did the same as they were like Jekyll and Hyde's when it came to the wing meetings. They portrayed themselves to the staff and psychologists as victims of their crimes and even victims of their circumstances or

Terry Ellis

incarceration. But I saw their bullying, their intimidation, their manipulation, the racism , the misogyny, the jokes and behaviour towards the women officers which were perpetrated daily behind their backs, mostly under the guise of Howard jokes. Such as the one Howard was telling today. Even I was amused which made me feel awkward. Not just because they were misogynistic jokes but because the jokes were being told by a wife killer. Someone I normally wouldn't mix with.

Over the weeks my defences had been breached as I was having deep conversations with fat Mark, Phil and nutty Chris who were all rapists. I was even speaking to Howard regarding therapy methods. It felt so normal but at the same time disconcerting.

At 2: o'clock my intercom came on and I was summoned to Mr Beans office, which surprised me as it would be the first time I had spoken to him regarding therapy or why I was here. As I entered his office I noticed that Keith my group facilitator was also there. So, I took a seat in front of them waiting for my interrogation. Which Mr Bean seemed to pick up on as he told me not to worry adding that they just wanted to know how I was feeling and how I was coping being around the other guys. This went on for about 20 minutes before Mr Bean passed me a diary which he then asked me to write down all my thoughts and feelings in as it would be helpful to me. It would be a way for me to start expressing myself. Also, a way for me to release any frustrations I may be having. And with that I thanked them both and left the room.

I found out over the next few weeks how good it felt expressing myself in this way. It also helped me reflect over my thoughts and behaviours, which gave me a renewed enthusiasm that I was finally doing some sort of therapy. And at the same time, I felt the weight of the years of missed opportunities fade into the background. But if I was to move forward I had to leave my ego at the door as it was holding me back as I was still being judgemental of others, who I still thought of as deviants. This was still a massive stumbling block for me which I had to overcome as I had to bring the focus back to me and concentrate on doing therapy, as the deviants distractions would make it impossible for me to reach my goal of making it through to the main wings where all the real therapy was being done.

CHAPTER SIX

So, enough was enough. I had to listen more to these guys and learn from their past mistakes as well as my own. I would also try to address my own behaviour because over the last few months I too wasn't really being myself, because on the outside and to the rest of the community I was polite and civility seemed to ooze out of me. But inside my thoughts were dark as I character assassinated everyone I met which included the screws who were being open and honest. It was like I was at war with myself. I was also fighting an internal battle with the good side of myself who was reasonable and understanding, also kind and considerate.

But then there was a dark side, not necessary the dominant part of me but the side I have always relied on to keep me safe, as I could always rely on the dark side of my ego. But now that I was at Grendon there was no place for it. I could only assume Mac and the other guys were in the same predicament, as how else would everyone here be so friendly with each other, especially when you consider their crimes. Or was everyone playing the same game all because they wanted to get through this selection process at the cost of who they really were.

The hypocrisy of the situation was overwhelming because if everyone here was starting their therapy off with a lie, then who could we really trust. Because if everyone was acting contrary to their real character or normal behaviour, then what was actually real about the selection process. And would only those who were smarter. and more manipulative be the ones to go through. Making dishonestly and manipulation the order of the day. Which made me wonder how many had slipped through the therapeutic net and were a danger to others and me.

I was now into Grendon routine as I was running every morning. Small groups and the community meetings were going well and I was even asking some sensible questions and

Terry Ellis

generally accepting that I was in the right place to make some fundamental changes in my life.

I was also given a job which brought me down to earth, it was probably the reason why I was given it in the first place. The job was to clean the toilets twice a day. And after cleaning them I had to find Chris, the rapist, as he was the wing foreman whose job it was to check my work and sign me off if I did it properly, which was humiliating to say the least.

The next morning after our group a few of the guys went down to read the daily papers, but I was still reluctant to join them as it still felt awkward with them and the enemy. Even though I promised my group I'd try , I still couldn't get my head around the fact that for years back in the system I had been brutalised in the segregation blocks, beaten by grown men who were all ex-army and who should have known better. But the stupid fuckers believed they could rehabilitate us by giving us a good kicking. And now I was being asked to forgive them. It just felt so wrong.

I'd also been questioned about using the shower after bang up as using them after lock up was strictly forbidden due to health and safety. I had also been told off for playing my music after 10 o'clock at night and for smoking on the landing.

This place had so many poxy rules, which if broken by you, meant you had to be punished by doing a manual forfeit, which in my case was to read the papers in the office for a week. Also hoover every morning, clean the windows and water the plants. All forfeits were therapeutically based and as I hated going in the office, my punishment was adequately chosen with that in mind.

These punishments also stopped me from taking showers in the middle of the night and playing my music. Also, I stopped smoking on the wing landing. So, in some small part Grendon was already changing me. I was also asked by Keith and some of the officers to stop calling them 'Guv' as everyone, even the officers, were all on first name basis with each other. I even found calling them by their first names awkward. But I promised to try my best. It took me a few weeks to become more accepting of them but I persevered and by week 3 I was starting to realise they were an OK bunch, with one exception, Jackie, as she was still trying to push my buttons at every opportunity. Which was becoming so boring as I knew what she was up to and even she knew that I knew. But she kept persisting.

Living amongst the beasts: The rise and fall of the Grendon experiment

I remember one particular morning while I was on exercise, she started talking to me. She started by asking what I was in for. So, thinking she was up for a sensible chat, I told her I was in for robbery. But no sooner had I said it than she quoted a freudism at me by saying a man's gun is an extension of his penis. So, I said "I never used a gun plus my dick is party sized". Then I started laughing and informed her that for the best part of Sigmund Freud life he was addicted to cocaine and I can only imagine that when he wrote that penis quote he must have been off his tits. And I turned around and headed back inside.

I could see she was a little put out about my comment. She called me back but I ignored her. Plus, I was half-way through the door. I also didn't want her having the last word as the last thing I needed was her quoting bollocks at me. However, I'd fired the first shot, so now the psychological war between us was on. It was round 1 to me.

The next morning when I walked into the office Jackie was on duty, so I said good morning and picked up the copy of the Sun and sat down next to Craig, a guy of about 35. And like me he was in for robbery. He was also on Jackie's 'I must rub up the wrong way' list.

Another guy on the list was Julian. Julian had passed his induction and moved to D wing 2 days earlier but because he taken his TV aerial he had been returned for theft and he like the rest of us was learning fast that to lie or break rule was unacceptable. Even those most of us on the wing believed that the punishment was disproportionate as it had taken him 17 weeks to get through to one of the main wings. On the wing we felt he had been treated unfairly. But before he could even sit down and read his paper Jackie said that she couldn't believe that he had been so stupid. She asked him what was he thinking of, he knew the rules like everyone else, he knew that all aerials must stay on the wing in their assigned locations. Which in his case was his own cell, so why did he take it? Julian just said he had already explained the whole situation to Mr Bean the wing psychologist and his punishment for nicking the aerial was he had been brought back to F wing, and as far as he was concerned the matter had been dealt with. So, could she please drop it as all he wanted was to read his paper in peace.

Jackie seemed a bit put out by what he had said, so quipped back "Julian you acted like a moron" adding "you have got less brains than a gibbon". With that Julian just walked out of the office. So, I said "that was a bit harsh Jackie and if I am honest it's a little bit racist. And if I were you I would apologise for those remarks". She told me to mind my own business. So, I said again "your remarks were demeaning and borderline racist and it is only because you are wearing that uniform that you think you can get away with that,

Terry Ellis

because if we were in main stream prison you would never have gotten away with it. Just because we are at Grendon you think you can bully everyone who can't defend themselves under the guise of therapy. It's you who is a fucking joke" I said. And she said it was for his own good that she was on his case. And she was only doing it and saying it because she was the one that was being honest and that it was me that who had over-reacted to the situation. "I can't believe that you are throwing it back on me" I said adding "just face the facts, your comments were ill-timed especially as Julian's black". She then told me once again to mind my own business adding I should leave the office right now to think about my reactions. The bitch I thought as I got up and walked out now believing that I might have lost my chance of getting through to one of the main wings. All because I had spoken up for a rapist who never had the balls to fight his own corner.

I am such a mug when it comes to speaking up for the under-dogs. All my life I have got myself in trouble for reacting against bullies. Maybe it has got something to do with me being in care or maybe I should see it as one of my issues, when and if, I start therapy. I just have to wait and see what happens over the next coming weeks.

Mac came into my cell earlier this morning to tell me that he was moving over to C wing. At the same time, he pleaded with me to help him down with all of his gear. He also mentioned that Jock was moving over to G wing. As Mac said this his mouth twisted into a grimace as G wing had a reputation for being disruptive as it had only recently opened, so the inmates, staff and wing psychologists were going through a transition period which made for a very volatile environment, especially on their small groups, as the friction could clearly be heard and seen most days on the exercise yard.

As Mac left, I promised that I would stop winding Jackie up. Also, I would stop standing up for any more mugs, especially the fucking rapists. We then wished each other well. As the door shut behind him the news that everyone had been waiting for filtered out, that Mac was gone. Which brought about a collective sigh of relief in the guise of some silent clapping from the deviant population, who disliked Mac immensely as they believed his presence on the wing was intimidating.

As soon as he was gone the place seemed to come alive as the deviants came out of the shadows. Even those guys I hadn't spoken to before started popping their heads around the door. But the happiest guy on the wing was Andy ,the wing chairman, as he despised Mac with a vengeance as Mac had torn into him a number of times about his moralistic attitude and his God complex.

Living amongst the beasts: The rise and fall of the Grendon experiment

Even though he didn't like Mac, I got on with Andy as I found him to be an OK guy. He was also good company. That was until you got onto the subject of God as you couldn't get a word in edgeways. He like most of the murderers turned to religion hoping for some sort of redemption. But even so he was a kind old sod and I warmed to him.

I remember the day I packed up smoking. He had come into my cell to cast out the devil in me as he believed smoking was the devils vessel to my soul. So being the nut job he was, he asked me to kneel down in front of him as he placed his hand on my head as he exorcised the bad spirit within me. At the same time, he asked me to repeat what he said as we both asked God to free me and give me the courage to pack up smoking.

I couldn't believe I was doing what he said, I only hoped none of the screws walked in as I was on my knees. I felt embarrassed enough but I didn't want to offend him as he meant well. It also felt good, a bit like being baptised. As soon as Andy finished he went down to his cell and when he came back he had a bible which he promised would change my life. He said he would give it to me if I promised to accompany him to church on Sunday and like a mug I caved in again and said yes.

I had been here for just over 3 weeks now and I am starting to get a handle on the place and what I believe is expected of me. But just lately our small group is in danger of being hijacked by Howard, who was becoming somewhat tiresome, as all we seem to do is talk about him. He is a proper needy fucker. He puts written complaints in the box every day and then repeats the complaints to us on the group and what he believes should be done about it. This normally takes an eternity and always ends with him threatening to taken Grendon and the Prison Authorities to court. Which in his case isn't an idle threat as over the years he's managed to extort over £30,000 out of the various establishments, whose misfortune it's been to have been on the receiving end of his acrimony regarding procedural matters. His addiction to complaining was one of the many reasons he was referred to Grendon in the first place. As he like most wife killers I have known need an outlet for their own self-loathing, so they take it out on the prison or their staff by taking them to task, believing every victory they win through the courts makes them a feared adversary. It's a distraction technique used by the beasts as they believe that by belittling the screws and the way they run the wings they can hide their shame and cowardice under the guise of fighting for all the prisoner's human rights. It is absurd but characteristic of the deviant mind and no matter how much I agreed to try to help him and persuade him to concentrate on changing his behaviour he wouldn't listen. He was more interested in the pursuit of a pound note and hiding behind his shameful charade. Which in turn drove us round the bend and also made going to the group mundane, which is turn made going to therapy a boring place to be.

Terry Ellis

I was also finding it harder to fill up my days with positive things to do, as we had so much free times after finishing our jobs. The days really started to drag. Also, Grendon's regime of not being able to watch our TVs throughout the day whilst the cells were open only added to the misery. Despite the fact I knew the process was designed by the psychologists for the process of seeing how we handled boredom, however it still drove me to distraction like most of the rules did. But I realised very quickly there was always a method behind the madness. So just like experimental rodents in a therapeutic maze we adapted. And just like the mice we not only found the way out, we found the cheese. Meaning we learnt new coping strategies. We started talking to each other which in turn helped with our social development. We also began to work harder by dragging out our jobs. Which answered the question 'why was it so clean and tidy here'? and why were there so many plants scattered around the place. It was due to boredom. This cleaning phenomenon was seen as a break through by staff on our quest for therapeutic enlightenment, and another step brought about by self-introspection, which again was its aim. So, another lesson learnt by these epiphanies.

CHAPTER SEVEN

Boredom makes men do some strange things, as even I started to mix with the deviants. My first incursion to the dark side was to help x2 Steve repot a few plants. I had even shown him how to take cuttings and repot them, an art I have learnt many years ago, as I had done a few grow rooms for hydroponics or flood and drain as we used to call it.

I learnt how to do it from my Mum as she used to work part-time over at our local park. She used to take me into the greenhouse for hours on end, showing me her craft, and as there were a thousand baby saplings to choose from I really enjoyed our time together, as it is one of a few memories I have of her before I was put into care.

Until I came to Grendon I had all but forgotten any good times I had with her or my brothers and sisters. I know there were many because she was a good Mum and we were a close family until I was taken away and banged up in a community home that is.

After being taken away, things would never be the same for me ever again, as I felt abandoned. And that is why I have cut them out of my life for years as I was jealous that they had all stayed together and the resentment I felt for years is palpable and something I need to resolve.

My psychologist Melanie believes my abandonment issues are the reason I am able to walk away from any relationship without a second thought. It is a defence mechanism I have put in place against people I love who I believe will let me down. It is also the reason I am able to turn my empathy on like an on/off button enabling me to be a caring father one minute and the next a ruthless criminal.

Terry Ellis

However, if I felt that helping x2 was betrayal of all that is sacred to me then my next incursion should be seen as me jumping into the deviants den feet first. As tonight I had gone to bingo, something that should never be spoken of. But because I am writing this for my girls I've got to put everything on the table.

So, when the bell rang out for bingo I went down with the rest of them. As I promised my group that I'd start fraternising with my fellow Grendonites, as it would be seen by all of them as an olive branch of me and my acceptance of them.

The dining room would be the venue for tonight's extravaganza. On each of the tables I could see 4 bingo cards laid out, all laminated and by their sides sat a felt tip pen, all different colours. On the main table sat a white spinning basket with green numbered balls. Beside the basket sat tonight's prizes, Skittles, peanuts, Twix's' and an assortment of chocolate bars, 5 bottles of Coke and 3 Pepsi's and a large bag of assorted sweets. It looked like an Aladdin's cave of goodies or a customised paedo abusers kit straight out of Willy Wonker's Chocolate factory, which was now being used on me as I was now being regaled by this brightly coloured mountain of confectionary, in what I could only assume was the belly of the beasts lair, disguised for all to see as a bingo hall.

Andy, the Wing Chairman would be calling the numbers out and his side-kick Nick the armed robber would be giving out the prizes. Mixed race Lewis, rapist Chris, Julian and gay Mark who had chopped up his boyfriend were sitting on table 1. On table 2 sat wife killer Howard, scouse Mick, x2 Steve and kiddie porn Nigel. Table 3 sat mad Dennis the schoolgirl killer, Richard the Hobbit whose claim to fame he said was killing a rapist, (a claim that still had to be verified), sat happily at his side was Phil and fat Mark both vile rapists. The table was a contradiction in terms. I sat at table 4 with Craig the armed robber, bird hand Alan and child cruelty Sam. Table 5 sat Clacton Andy and Gummy a black guy who liked robbing old women, he was doing an 8-year IPP for nicking some old dears handbag and her car and just for good measure as the scumbag was making his getaway he ran her over. Opposite him sat a longhaired drip Norman who had killed his girlfriend . Which left old Pete another rapist who had killed his victim. On table 6 and 7 sat the staff. Dean and Mark on table 6 and Jackie, SO John and Mr Bean on table 7. You could say a full house of horrors, pardon the double entendre.

As we all waited for Andy to shout out 'eyes down', I wondered what the outside world would make of all this. Grown men playing bingo. Men who had raped and murdered. The whole situation felt ludicrous as we were now being punished with kindness and chocolates.

Living amongst the beasts: The rise and fall of the Grendon experiment

It was now time to concentrate as Andy shouted eyes down, adding that there would be a prize for a line and a prize for a full house. He then started picking numbers with all the enthusiasm of Michael Barrymore and the comic timing of Rolf Harris. And add the zeal of a professional bingo caller into the equation then we were in for a good night.

The first number out was Kelly's Eye number 1, then 2 fat ladies 88, on its own number 4, 3 and 2 32, round the bend number 10, then one bunch number 5. Craig shouted a line with a big smile on his face. As for me when he shouted line I automatically reached into my pocket for a rolled up £20 note before Nick came over to check the numbers, before shouting them back to Andy. 88, 6, 32, 1, 5, 4. Once the win had been verified he handed Craig a bar of chocolate and a large bag of sweets.

Then the game commenced and after about 5 minutes I was waiting for one number for a full house. As I sweated over the possibility I might win a bottle of Coke, my heart started beating, then my number came up. Key to the door 24, so I shouted "house". It was the first time I had ever won anything, so my jubilation was palpable, but short-lived as Richard, the Hobbit and fat rapist Mark had also shouted 'house'. We all looked at each other expecting the other to say they had made a mistake, everyone looked bemused. Mick collected the offending cards before Andy checked them and discovered we all had the same numbered cards. A printing error and a genuine mistake and in the fairness of the game we were all given new cards and all paid out for our win. I was given a large botte of coke, a Mars bar and a mixed bag of sweets. The others had the same with the exception of Richard who chose Pepsi.

The evening seemed to fly by and slowly over the hour, the mountain of chocolate was divided up amongst the guys and staff who were now starting to leave as their pockets were full of goodies. Just as the bell sounded for lock-up my thoughts on the night had changed dramatically as I really enjoyed the experience as the contrast between the draconian methods of rehabilitation by the antiquated prison regime of 23 hours a day bang up and no productive work, compared to the way Grendon went about changing heart and mind was like night and day.

So, with my belly full and the last glass of coke gone, I patted myself on the back believing I had made the right choice about coming here, and with a smile on my face I turned the light off.

The accumulation of the week's events ended on the Friday with Karaoke night as it had been organised by bird hand Alan, who by the sound of things was doing a good job because I could hear the Tom Jones classis Green, Green Grass of Home being

Terry Ellis

slaughtered by Clacton Andy who had just started singing it. As I entered the community room with Craig whose face had just turned into a picture as he was transfixed by bird hand Alan dancing around in a circle like a demented retard on acid, as his side-kick Sam bopped away beside him with a large pair of ear-phones on. Clacton Andy tried his best to look cool as he swayed his hips back and forth, gyrating them hypnotically to the music in the direction of Jackie, hoping his efforts would be rewarded by her turning her head towards him. But his display of sexual magnetism fell short, as it was like a Trojan Horse, 'wooden' but the rest of the guys seemed not to notice this car-crash moment, as they cheered him on with all the enthusiasm of a paid-up member of the Susan Boyle fan club. It was a sight to behold but one that would be repeated several times over the next two hours, until that was I had a go. I started signing Engelbert Humperdinck's 'please release me, let me go for I don't love you anymore'. My vocal rendition was aimed at my old foe Jackie, who I could see was now going red in the face as I stood in front of her before going down on one knee and taking her hand as she squirmed with embarrassment as I pulled her up onto her feet before we both started dancing around the floor. Cooling, I hope, the psychological war between us, as she smiled at me for the first time since our little disagreement, which in turn let me see her in a different light. We'd both had our differences but I'd never resorted to profanity or lost my temper which showed on my part I could get angry but at the same time keep my composure. Just the right attribute Grendon was looking for. Guys who could articulate their thoughts and feeling through words. So, all in all the karaoke night was a success for me as I'd buried the hatchet with Jackie and the deviant's believed I was one of them and actually I'd enjoyed myself, which is a rare thing, especially in prison and especially in a place like Grendon.

Living amongst the beasts: The rise and fall of the Grendon experiment

CHAPTER EIGHT

On Monday a new Grendonite arrived called Paul. He went into Mac's old cell right opposite me. He seemed an OK geezer, who I'd heard tell Howard he was doing an IPP sentence for robbing a security van. He looked the part, was about 40, 5" 8", well- built and seemed to mix in well straight from the start, but for some reason he kept his distance from me, but was always polite. He knew Craig from another prison, so I assumed he was one of the boys. But I could see there was something about him which I didn't particularly like, but like most things in prison the truth eventually comes out and behaviours start to make sense.

It took 3 weeks before I found out why he didn't want to speak to me, because he knew I'd see right through his bollocks. As it came to light he wasn't in for robbing a security van, he was in fact in for robbing his own mate. It seems Paul used to be a crackhead, and one night when he was out of his head, he'd gone around to his friends flat, who it transpired was looking after his young daughter. But Paul still put a knife to the guys throat and marched him and his daughter down to the cash point machine, making the guy withdraw £60 before letting the guy and his little girl go. A scumbag move.

Craig told me all this one morning. He also asked me not to repeat it, then said he had been walking around the exercise area when Paul had slivered in beside him and told him he had a sure-fire way of getting through to one of the main wings. So, I asked him 'how?'

He said Paul was going to pretend that he had been sexually abused by his Mum and that she had also broken his arm as a kid. And by claiming this he said Paul would endear himself to his small group and at the same time it would prove to his facilitator he was ready to talk about anything. Which in turn he thought would fast track him through to one of the main wings. Even Craig said Paul was off-key. He even told him that he thought it was an ill-advised idea as there were guys here at Grendon who had been

Terry Ellis

abused, and who would see though his deception. But Paul just laughed and walked away. The next morning when I went into the showers Paul was standing there in his pants shaving his legs and as he looked over to me I could see he knew that my card had been marked by Craig, and that his dirty secrets were now out.

At 9 o'clock I entered the community meeting and like most mornings I'd just made it before the door was closed. Mr Bean and Jackie gave me a disparaging glance as I took my place near the window, just as Andy started taking the minutes.
The first minute was taken by Howard who complained about his private spends. Nick took the second minute to complain about Howard's typewriter, as the noise of him banging about at night was keeping him awake. Howard counter-claimed stating he needed to work on his court papers. Mr Bean worked out a compromise which considered Howard's need to write out his complaints and Nick's right to sleep, with the out-come being that Howard could only use his typewriter until 10 pm most nights, Case closed.

The next to take a minute was Richard who complained about Gummy's music being too loud and his bass was driving him mad. Gummy agreed to be more considerate.

Then Norman who had killed his girlfriend, said someone had been stealing tobacco out of his cell and could the thief stop.

Sam also said he had had tobacco stolen, also Andy, Nick and Lewis had been targeted. Mr Bean then asked the whole community who they thought might be the culprit, but no-one ventured their opinion. But their gaze betrayed them all and as one by one they all looked towards Gummy, who pretended he didn't notice.

Then Craig took a minute about being piss tested every week.

Then Andy thanked everyone who came to bingo night. The same was said about karaoke night by bird hand Alan.

Then Sam said gay Mark had been picking on him, but wouldn't elaborate on the matter. So, when Mr Bean asked Mark what was going on he refused to answer any of his questions, adding he didn't think Grendon was the place for him adding that Sam was a lying piece of shit.

Then Paul put his hand up to take a minute and in front of the whole wing he said that he'd had a conversation with me over the weekend and he now believed I was at Grendon for all the wrong reasons.   The manipulating shit I thought, the bastard wanted me out because I knew his little secret. My adrenalin started pumping. I wanted to punch his face in, but I knew if I go up and threatened him I would be thrown out and he knew that, the shit. However, I was still new to Grendon and I reacted by calling him a fucking lying cunt, I also said I knew his game, but because I'd promised Craig I'd keep schtum, I couldn't tell the room why he had said what he had. So, I just called him a few choice words until Mr Bean asked me to stop before I said something I would regret, adding I had over reacted to what Paul had said, and in future I should look at my behaviour with my group members, so I bit my lip and said I was sorry for my outburst. I also apologised to Paul who was now looking at me and grinning. At least now I knew how far the deviant's would go to manipulate their way through therapy. It was a good lesson for me to learn so early on in therapy. A lesson I would never forget, a lesson never to trust anyone again.

The next morning Paul said good morning to me. So, I pulled him to one side and whispered in his ear. I said if I don't get through to one of the main wings I was going to come back and cut both his fucking ears off. And if I ever saw him in the system, I was going to break his little fucking neck. Paul just looked at me and went white. We never spoke of the situation again

The next day started as normal, I spent an hour in my small group talking about my thoughts and feelings regarding my outburst yesterday and if I thought that by talking my anger towards Paul would dissipate. I was wrong as it had only worsened, as I had taken it out on Sam and Howard all because they'd asked me some probing questions about my anger. And like a fucking idiot I had retaliated by bringing up their offences, when all they wanted to do was help me. So now I'd ended up hating and pissing off three deviants instead of just one, Paul. Keith had also tried to help but by the end of the group he too had gotten on my nerves, which again made me realise that if I really wanted to make it through this induction period, I had to grow up.

I had to be more disciplined. I had to find some coping strategies. It had taken me just over a year for me to get here, 6 months of talking to Melanie, 6 months of filling in forms and just because I can't control my fucking temper I was now in danger of losing my place here. I needed help. I needed some divine intervention which came just after we finished our small groups, as I was asked to accompany Dean to the MDT room, Mandatory Drug Test; voluntary. Once we got there he parked me up in the waiting room, then he went back to the wing, leaving me in the capable hands of two willy watchers, who were preparing their room for the inevitable onslaught of piss testing that takes place most mornings at Grendon. So, like a good boy I take my seat and waited. The room was bright and airy, there was a little coffee table with magazines on. Six plastic brown backed

Terry Ellis

chairs and a large cabinet occupied about 6 feet of the room. The cabinet displayed confiscated drug paraphernalia. Also, there were written descriptions on the pitfalls of taking heroin, speed, cocaine and weed. The substance list was endless. There was also a shelf full of pamphlets describing the consequences of abusing drugs. At one end of the room there was a large window, the view from it was stunning as I could see lots of trees, a well- manicured lawn and flower beds.

I could also see the prison front gate and the parking areas. While I was waiting, I picked up one of the holiday brochures but before I turned the first page the general alarm sounded over the screw's radio which sent one of them bolting out the door, while the other one locked the doors as he too disappeared along the corridor. Leaving poor old me sitting there twiddling my thumbs for what would be an hour and twenty minutes of pandemonium.

The screws came running from every direction. I could see security screws all dressed in black running across the lawns. In the corridor I could hear keys and radios. I could also see officers coming out of every wing. Even Dean, Jackie and big John from my wing had joined the affray, and I could see them through the little window in the door. They were definitely panicked, I could feel it in the air, as this many screws were not normal.

Then a woman Governor came running past, followed closely by two male Governors and six senior officers. Then like clock-work three of Grendons' best turned up fighting for their breath. The three out of shape health care staff with medical kits and defibrillator also disappeared through the door.

I then heard an ambulance siren. So, I moved over to the large window to get a better view. Just as the main gates opened I saw the ambulance drive through and park up next to the reception entrance. Four medics got out all carrying medical bags slung over their shoulders, two of them pulled out a 'ferno gurney' and placed their medical kits on top as they pushed it through the reception gates. Then I saw a police car pull up. One male and the other female both carrying notepads. They like the ambulance guys were joined by even more screws

I then moved back to the door to get a better look and right on cue the four medics and screws came flying past on their way to G-wing. About 5 minutes after a female screw and one of the women psychologists came out. The young screw was really crying and I could also see the psychologist was distressed as she put her arm around the young girl to comfort her.

Living amongst the beasts: The rise and fall of the Grendon experiment

Just then the vicar came running past them and quickly vanished through the gates and for him to be called, someone was either dead or dying. But whatever had happened it must be something ghastly as even the screws looked mortified.

After about 10 minutes one of the ambulance guys came out chaperoned by a screw both disappeared down the corridor.

I then heard the rota-blade of a helicopter, but I couldn't see the fucking thing. Then the main gates opened again and 3 helicopter crew came walking through. It looked like a slow-motion scene from Top Gun, as all the guys had dark glasses on and wore helmets. All were dressed head to toe in orange. All were carrying matching shoulder medical kits and they looked the real deal, very professional.

As they came through the gate they were met by the ambulance guy, who was speaking frantically and gesturing with his hands as he and the screws guided them back past me and onto G-wing.

As they went through an old screw came out and started walking up the corridor towards me. He had a blank expression on his face. Then he stopped and looked out the window then back again before he leaned up against the wall. He looked bewildered, the poor old fucker.

Four more screws came out. They too rested their backs against the wall. One even put his head in his hands as he went down on bended knees, they all looked confused. Then more came out and started standing round in little groups with their backs pressed against the wall as if the strength had gone out of their legs. I could see one of them was weeping.

Then the vicar came out shaking his head. He walked straight past me. He was followed by the health care workers who were ash white, all walked with their heads down.

There were now police cars everywhere. Three of them were parked in the car park. They were all holding clip boards and a few were wearing forensic white suits.

Then one of the medics came out with two screws carrying yellow documentation bags, which they handed over to the police. They too all looked visibly shocked. The Security Department were now out in force, but I could see and feel the pace of the emergency had tapered off and replaced with despondency.

Terry Ellis

It felt like the calm after the storm. I wanted to ask someone what had happened, but I didn't have the heart as they all looked so dejected.

Just then both the gates to G-wing swung open. The radios went completely quiet and the sound of keys jangling stopped dead. There were 20 or more officers lining the corridor, 3 Governors that I could see, and a few psychologists, who all went silent as the ferno gurney slowly came out with what could only be a dead body, as the blue blanket covered the face, obscuring my view. Everyone stood to attention like a Guard of Honour, as the 4 ambulance guys pushed the trolley with the help of the helicopter crew. All the medics carried their kits on their shoulders, leaving one hand free to push the trolley. All seven passed me and the respect every member of staff and medics showed was admirable and something I will never forget.

It was another 10 minutes until Dean came to collect me. He looked subdued but I asked him what happened anyway, but all he would say was there had been an incident. Jackie met us at the gates to F-wing and told me to bang up. She also informed me that a sandwich and a drink had been left out for me in my cell. All the other guys on the wing had been fed and were all now banged up.

I then asked Jackie if the visits were still on, as my kids were coming. She said yes as she shut the door behind me.

My door was opened at 2 sharp by Dean who asked me to go straight to the visits hall, as everyone on the wing was still banged up. And, as I left the wing I could see that Jackie was still visibly shocked, but I had to put this morning's events behind me as I didn't want to worry my kids.

When I eventually get over to the visits hall I was given the normal pat down, then allocated a table, which today was table number 9 which was a good seat as it was near the window. So, I quickly took my place and waited for my beautiful girls to come through the door.

But just as I looked up I suddenly noticed bible basher Andy making a beeline towards me, as he too had a visit and because he was now my new best friend now that Mac had left the wing, he sat down next to me, asking me if I enjoyed the book he gave me. So, I said it's a page turner and gave him a smile and with that he gave me the thumbs up, then I asked him who was visiting him, the normal bollocks chit-chat. He said his visitor was a Christian do-gooder, associated with the prison church that operates in most prisons.

Living amongst the beasts: The rise and fall of the Grendon experiment

He then asked how the no smoking was going, again I gave him the thumbs up and another big smile hoping he would just fuck off. But on seeing me smile he stood up then reached out and placed his hand on my head, then started praying. I could have died with embarrassment, but all I could think about was what if the kids walked in now, they would definitely think I'd lost the plot and gone completely round the fucking bend. But what could I say.

Just then the girls walked around the corner. Chloe first, then Charlene and Terri. It's funny what a hug does. It takes all the pain away just seeing them smiling. We sat there for just over an hour and a half on a visit. We had tea, coffee, cokes, chocolates and talked about Grendon. They talked about their home life, telling me what they were doing at school. It's a great visit, for the first time in a long time it was nice to see that they were all nice and relaxed. But I think they could see in me that I was in a bad place as Grendon had calmed me down a bit over the last few weeks, but I didn't know how long that was going to last especially after what had happened this morning. Anyway, I didn't say anything to them about what had happened, I just enjoyed their visit and then it was time to say goodbye.

When I returned to the wing I could hear and see that everyone was still milling around the dining room and office, so I asked Mick what was going on and with a broad smile across his face he said the proverbial shit had hit the fan. One of the paedophiles on G-wing had been killed, adding one less paedophile off the streets, then he walked off towards the dining room, so I followed him as now most of the guys seemed to be assembling there. Everyone looked shocked and were huddled together in little groups. Bird hand Alan and Sam looked frightened. Chris, Phil, fat Mark and x2 Steve, all rapists were sitting near the window. Steve looked like he had the horrors. Fat Mark looked all pasty and Phil and Chris were white as ghosts.

Bible basher Andy and Nick were holding court, as Howard, gay Mark, Clacton Andy, Mick, Nigel, Lewis and the Hobbit looked on. All looked flustered. Dennis and Norman sat by themselves in the corner like two frightened little school girls, which was quite amusing considering Norman had killed his girlfriend, and Dennis had killed a school girl. All these bastards would learn a lesson in here today, as they would feel a little of what their innocent victims went through.

The only person in the dining room I could see that looked indifferent was Craig, because as soon as he saw me, he smiled and gave me the thumbs up. Which made me laugh, as I gave him the thumbs back hoping no-one would see.

Terry Ellis

That evening after tea Jock and a guy called Taffy were brought over from G-wing as they had been witnesses to the murder of the paedophile. So, it was felt for their own safety and, for the foreseeable future, they would be placed into the witness protection scheme on F-wing as it, and us, were insulated from the rest of the prison. Also, as most of us on F-wing were fairly new to Grendon, it was thought our loyalties to the accused and his friends were neutral as far as taking sides was concerned. So, we ended up with the pair of them, who were now sitting in front of us in the dining room, preparing themselves to tell us all about the gory details of the mornings events.

Jock said that two days before the murder it had kicked off on the paedophiles group as he and a guy called Lee had gotten into an argument, which finished with Lee threatening to kill the guy. A threat that on any other wing would have resulted in Lee being removed from the wing and placed on a commitment. But for some reason his threats were disregarded as just one of those things, even though Lee was built like a brick shit house and the other guy 6 stone ringing wet.

Jock said even Lee's group has requested that Lee be spoken to. Even after it was heard he was going around the wing collecting all his belongings, while at the same time telling anyone that would listen that he was going to kill the guy. But once again the staff and wing psychologist believed Lee was just talking out of his arse.

Jock said that he was talking with the guy outside Taff's cell when Lee calmly approached them, and as calm as you like he asked the guy if he could have a quiet word with him. So, to appease Lee the guy agreed. So, both of them went into the peodo's room for a chat, while Jock and Taffy waited outside listening intently as Lee started remonstrating with the guy before knocking him to the ground with a flurry of punches.

Once the guy was down on the floor Lee straddled his chest, then started raining down blows, pummelling the guys face until the guy passed out comatose. He then stood up and looked at his unconscious victim, he then started stamping on the blokes face before jumping up and down with all his might and all his 17 stone of weight, until all that was left of the guys face was a mass of blood and pulp.

Lee then calmly went back to his cell, as Jock and Taffy shouted for help, as they could now see the whole horrific scene. There was blood everywhere and the aroma was sickening as the smell engulfed his senses. He said he could also smell sick, and that mixed with the smell of blood made him and Taffy recoil out of the room. As they left the

Living amongst the beasts: The rise and fall of the Grendon experiment

room the screws turned up and sounded the general alarm, at the same time the screws locked Jock and Taffy in the opposite cell.

He also said that the ambulance crew and staff worked tirelessly to save him, but it was pain to see from the state of the guy's face and his limp body that he wouldn't survive.

Jock then started to cry as he said the noise of the bones splintering and cracking were so loud it would stay with him for the rest of his life. Also, the smell and the sight of the blood-soaked walls would haunt him, but most of all he said he would never forget the cold blank look on Lee's face. A look he said that wasn't human.

When Jock had finished regaling us, the room went deadly silent, until fat Mark asked angrily where were all the screws, Jock replied it happened so fast. This seemed to shock the guys as they couldn't believe something like this could happen here at Grendon. And the way Jock explained the circumstances surrounding he murder, I couldn't blame the deviants' for being scared, as he hadn't left anything to the imagination. He gave them everything, both barrels.

As soon as Jock had finished talking the screws came into the room and asked Jock not to say anything about the incident, as the police wanted to talk to him and Taffy about making a statement. Jock just nodded to the screw and gave him a wry smile. As for me I thought it was a bit late to ask him not to say anything as Jock had been on the wing now for the last 20 minutes or more.

If this was Grendons' policy of containment of the situation, then I'm afraid their contingency plans were definitely flawed. Taff and Jock were then informed that they had to go over to the Healthcare Department as both had been promised anti-depressants for helping the prison and the police with their enquiries. Plus, both had claimed they had been through a harrowing experience. But it was plain to see that their co-operation to help convict Lee had been brought by a monthly supply of pills, as it was well known that both of them were addicts.

Just as they were leaving Andy the bible basher came bounding into the room posturing as he informed us that there would be an emergency community meeting in the morning to discuss todays' harrowing events, and its ramifications on the prison. Also, news had filtered through to the wing that Lee had been rushed through the induction process in only 6 weeks, all because G-wing was a new wing at the time. So, the Governors' wanted it occupied as quickly as was possible.

Terry Ellis

Once the guys on the wing found out about this, a clearer picture was starting to emerge that normal procedures had been circumnavigated in favour of bums on seats, as a fully occupied wing meant more money for Grendon. But, as in this case it had come at the cost of someone's life. It was only through good fortune that it was a paedophiles and not a woman prison officer, as Lee had form for killing women, as he was doing a life sentence for killing the mother of his child.

I wondered if Mr Bean would bring all these little indiscretions up in the meeting, or even the Governors for that matter, or would they hold on to it until the trial was over.

At 9 o'clock sharp I made my way to the community room. The place was packed with Governors, screws and prisoners. As I took my seat next to Craig I looked over to Mr Bean, looking for any sign of nerves or anxiety. But like the true professional he was he started off by saying we should all take time to think of the peodo's family and if anyone needed to see the Chaplin, then he would arrange it. He also informed us that an investigation was underway, and as soon as he knew anything, he and the Governor would let us know. You lying bastard I thought, we already knew, and so do you, as Jock had told us all the day before. So much for honesty and a really good start to therapy. However, I refrained from saying anything. Then the Governor said his penny's' worth. Then it was time for the community to have their say. Most said they were shocked, and how could this happen here, blah, blah, blah. Some even threatened to leave. The whole community was up in arms and went into automatic meltdown. The establishment went on the defence and nothing got sorted.

No-one even mentioned the 6 weeks it took for Lee to get on the wing. All I thought, was what did this lot expect? The truth or a fucking miracle? But, at least now they all knew Grendon wasn't infallible, especially when it came to admitting their mistakes. I pondered on the thought of asking Mr Bean if he could guarantee the safety of my fellow Grendonites, but wondered if I could keep a straight face (so thought better of it). Plus, he had already fobbed everyone off with the party line.

Later that day I spoke to John, the wing cook, who told me he knew Lee when he was on the wing. He said his own observations of Lee was of someone who was a little off key, and not suitable for therapy. He even said at the time that 6 weeks was just not enough time to be evaluated, especially as far as interactivity with other inmates in therapy was concerned. Even the obligatory 3 months was just enough time and had been the norm for the best part of 50 years or more. And, if that wasn't broken then why try and fix it? Then he said it wasn't the psychologists' fault or the Governors, it was the prison authorities that wanted Grendon running at full capacity, and that nothing else mattered.

It took poor old Jock and Taffy a few weeks to get over their harrowing experience and feelings of guilt that they could have done more to help their fellow Grendonite out. This was due partly to the fact they were still getting bundles of anti-depressants by the good old Healthcare Department. Which got me thinking about prescribed drugs at Grendon, as I was led to believe when I applied to come here that Grendon's policy on drugs was a 'no no', as you couldn't do therapy on them, as therapy was about managing your emotions and behaviours, not suppressing them by taking anti-depressants. Over the last 6 weeks I had seen on many occasions, my fellow Grendonites taking all manner of concoctions and medications, such as Prozac and psychotropic substitutes that affect a person's mental state. Which made a mockery of the psychiatric treatment undertaken at Grendon, but once again I kept it to myself, hoping that things would change once I got over to one of the main wings.

CHAPTER NINE

It took a few days for things to get back to normal, but in a strange way it seemed to unite the wing as we could see that the wing staff were still pretty upset. Which made me take a step back as it meant they actually cared. This new -fangled approach renewed my faith in them and what they were trying to do here. So, with this new optimism I started to mix and try harder.

I even started talking to Phil the rapist, who I had fallen out with the first day I met him, as he was from West Hampstead, just up the road from where I lived. I fell out with him because the first thing out of his mouth when I asked him what he was in for was the usual shit. He said no-one could punish him more than he had already punished himself, it's funny all rapists say this, as they believe it will stop you from asking any probing questions. As I'd heard it a million times over the last few weeks, I told him to grow up and stop feeling sorry for his rapist-self. Which didn't go down too well at the time, as he brought it up on one of his small group meetings and then again on the community meeting. But, I kept to my guns and told him and the rest of the rapists to own their deviant shit, instead of trying to manipulate me by playing the victim by saying I was being insensitive towards them. But as I said that was weeks ago.

We were now talking like old buddies. He was telling me about his life and the lead up to the rape, and again he started the usual bollocks. He met a girl in a pub, took her home, they were both pissed and he still can't remember anything as he was so drunk, blah, blah, blah. But, all that aside what really surprised me was when I asked him what his family thought about him being a rapist. He said they didn't know as he hadn't told them that he was in prison yet, even though the lying bastard had been away for 2 years. He had kept up the pretence by telling them he was living and working abroad. This new information didn't help me form a better opinion of him. In fact, it only reinforced in me that all rapists never really change, as they are manipulative and deceptive by nature.

Living amongst the beasts: The rise and fall of the Grendon experiment

It also told me that Phil would go to any lengths to hide, deny and even minimise his part in the rape. Because his ego and shame wouldn't allow himself to do any significant therapy while he was at Grendon, because if he couldn't be honest with himself or his family then how could the guys on the group trust him. When I asked him this, he just shrugged his shoulders and smiled. I felt like smashing his fucking face in, but instead I just smiled back as I kept telling myself that if anything came out of my stay here, it would definitely be tolerance of scumbags like Phil and his deviant mates. It was something I wasn't renowned for but I was getting better. If I am honest I never thought for one minute, or even imagined myself being in a fucking place like this, with my tolerance levels being tested in this way on a daily basis but in a macabre way I was starting to understand the ideology behind us mixing together, and as much as I hated the rapists, it was working.

There was also parts of his conversation and his life experiences that in some small part was helping me to humanise him and the other deviants who I had taken the time to talk with. These little glimpses helped you separate the deviants from their crimes, which I'm sorry to say was happening faster than I ever imagined.

Today I also spoke to another lying bastard called Dennis. Dennis was about 35, a bit simple, about 20 stone, 6' 2". He was a big bloke but had a really small head for the size of his body and the biggest ears I'd ever seen on another human being. Dennis was doing a life sentence for killing a young school girl, who he tried to convince me was his girlfriend. But one of the guys who knew him had told me the real story.

You see, Dennis was standing outside his Mum's flat when a young girl came past and apparently, he had got talking to her, and after a few minutes he asked her in. But when it was time for her to go home, he tried to kiss her but she wasn't interested and rebuffed his pathetic advances. She also started shouting at him to let her out, so he grabbed her round the throat and choked her to death. But the girl's friend had seen her enter the flat, so when she didn't arrive home she and the girls family called the police, who found her dead under Dennis' bed. A waste of a young girls life at the hands of another deviant beast.

I was starting to realise that all the guys here would quite freely tell you what they were in for, but at the same time they would minimise the parts they played in it.

Phil was a perfect example of this as he had tried to convince me that he had met his victim in a pub, as this was his way of showing me that they'd had some sort of relationship, which had then turned into a rape. And, just like Dennis who too had said

Terry Ellis

the young girl was his girlfriend, and that her murder was an accident. Both had lied to me.

I believe it was because it was important for both of them to believe their own lies as it detracted from the fact that they were predators of the worst kind, and that by lying it would somehow ease their consciences. I saw these behaviours played out daily by most of the deviants, which was teaching me a valuable lesson. Never to trust anyone at Grendon, especially at face value as everyone here was definitely playing a game, as they were all looking for some sort of salvation from their deviant crimes. And, what better validation could they get than some prison psychologist saying they had been cured of their deviant nature all because they had spent time at Hotel Grendon. It was a win- win situation for everyone as it meant years of employment for the psychologists, and years of prison utopia for its' perverted population.

Andy the bible basher was another one looking for salvation, but he had gone for the tried and tested route. The one that most of the deviants go on, the God conveyor belt. They get jobs in the church, then find Christianity, professing to anyone who will listen that they've found God and have changed. They then start showing all the qualities associated with the Christian movement, like having visits from the local Christian Society, hoping the Vicar will notice this, thus bringing them into the fold. So, when it came to their lifer review boards, the Vicar's recommendation would not only be backed by him, but by God himself, hoping it would sway the Board of Governors. I know it sounds delusional, but it's true, as I've seen this scene played out so many times over the years. The funny thing is though, the prison Chaplaincy encourages this sort of behaviour, because they need bums on seats, just like the psychologists, as no bums means no bleeding hearts congregation and no job.

There was one thing that I could rely on at Grendon and that was the weather as it brought out the best in me as I'd started running every day. And I was also doing circuits on the wing, which wasn't too bad apart from the fact that Grendon was built on a landfill site, so the place was always swarming with wasps and millions of flies and the odd honeybee, that were the size of a golf ball. But thanks to the night-san system, I was able to get out of my cell rather quickly. The night-san system worked like this – you press your bell, and as long as no-one else was out of their cell, your door would open automatically for about 10 minutes so you could use the toilets. None of the cells on the 2s landing had toilets in them. If you didn't get back to your cell within the allocated time, the night screw would get on your intercom and give you a bollocking. Once you got back in your cell a red light would come on with a 5-digit number, which you had to punch into your door keypad which was on the wall, which would then allow your door to be

Living amongst the beasts: The rise and fall of the Grendon experiment

locked. You were only allowed to use the night-san twice in any one hour, and God forbid if you took a liberty such as taking a shower, as some mug would grass you up under the guise of bringing your selfish behaviour to the attention of the community. You would then be winged, which meant you had to explain why you thought you were exempt from the rules and regulations set out by the Grendons' Health and Safety. Which soon made you realise that breaking any of the rules wasn't conducive to you making it through to one of the main wings. So once again, it was lesson learned.

This afternoon I was asked to go to one of the classrooms where I was met by Sue, another wing psychologist. Sue was about 40. She asked me my name, then told me to take a seat before we were joined by 3 of the deviants, who like me were told we would be taking a psychometric test. We had to read the questions, then tick our answers in a box. It took the best part of an hour and was really boring, but I carried on in the name of science. When I finished I was informed by Sue that my answers would be sent over to America, so that they could be put in a computer and examined methodically for the purpose of explanation regarding my mental health. Also, it would give me a label such as 'psychopath' or 'sociopath' or any other fucking name they could come up with. Sue then told me that it would probably take a couple of months for my results to come back, and if I was lucky enough to get through, she would come and find me so we could discuss the computers findings.

Andy asked me today if I wanted to go over to the church as a few of the guys were being baptised. He also said tea and cake would be up for grabs, so of course I said yes.

But first I had to see Faz, one of my group members. Also, I had promised Martin I'd pop in to see him. Faz was an Iranian guy who spoke really good English, who told me he had kidnapped 2 of his friends who he had lent some drugs to and because they had been late paying him back, he had got his henchmen to strip them naked and made the 2 guys perform sex acts on each other, it was a perverse act. He then let them go under pain of death and if they grassed he would bring them back. Unfortunately for Faz they both went to the police. However, afterwards one of them was so ashamed about what he'd been made to do, he killed himself, which got Faz an 8-year IPP sentence.

After speaking to Faz, I then called in on Martin. Martin was an ex-army guy who was doing a sentence for robbery. He was about 5' 8", 45 years old and ginger haired. He did not have a lot going for him especially in the looks department. He had told me that he and his accomplice had been drinking all night in their local snooker hall, the one they had actually robbed. He said they left the hall and picked up 2 balaclavas and a shotgun

Terry Ellis

but he and his pal were so drunk they had forgotten to change their clothes, which the CCTV and the police had picked up on. Which brought an end to Martin's criminal career. He had fired a dozen shots into the ceiling for good effect, which secured him a lengthy 15-year sentence. Martin wasn't too bright, he never smiled and the guys on the wing were scared of him as he had a broken nose and missing front teeth. He really did look a scary character, but I liked him, as I could see he was very insecure and not smiling was a trick he'd learnt over the years to keep people away from him and also to keep himself safe.

When Andy came back to fetch me, I was in the middle of finishing my cigarette. So, once again he'd caught me bang to rights, smoking. But, for once he never said anything. He just asked me to hurry up as we were running late. When we entered the gym where the Baptism was being held, I noticed a guy from Pentonville I knew called Cookie as I'd lent him my phone a few times to phone his girlfriend so they could sort out their visits. The last time I'd seen him he was skinny and looked like a junkie, but seeing him now he looked like a million dollars. He'd put on weight, was more muscular and looked healthy. We chatted for a bit about old times, then the subject turned to Grendon and how much it had changed his life. He'd become a born-again Christian, he also informed me that it was him who was getting baptised today. He then introduced me to his uncle and girlfriend who'd both been allowed into Grendon for the ceremony. Cookie acted and looked as if he'd turned a corner, but a part of me doubted him, and I wondered if he like the rest of them was blagging it just to see his bird or get some drugs off his uncle, I really wasn't convinced . Cookie then introduced me to one of the other guys who was also taking his baptism today a guy called Norman, a black guy who I also knew as we had worked on the prison paper the 'Voice of the Ville'.

Norman was a funny guy and a good writer, we used to make up stories for the paper together. When I first met him, he'd told me he was doing a 6-year IPP for GBH as he'd had a fight in a night club. But it was all lies, as Cookie was now telling me the real story. He said Normal had beaten his girlfriend up one night and raped her, then he used a hot soldering iron by inserting it in her fanny, the bastard.

Every day in this place brought me new lows, as the honestly aspect at Grendon meant everyone knew everyone's offences. But this truth at any cost was more than I could handle, especially when it came to old friends who'd lied to me. I was learning fast not to trust anyone just because they spoke like me or came from the same area, or knew people I knew. Once again, the word had just changed.

Living amongst the beasts: The rise and fall of the Grendon experiment

As I looked around the hall I couldn't help but notice that everyone looked so content. Everyone was smiling and talking, it looked like any other Sunday church gathering. Everyone was drinking tea, and biscuits were being handed out, and the table was laid out with sandwiches and cakes. A surreal moment in the devils waiting room, I'd never seen anything like this before in prison.

There were 60 or more people in the hall, mostly made up of staff, prisoners and their families. Also, the vicar was there and the normal gathering of Christian visitors, which I was glad to be part of as I'd spent years surrounded by hate and fear and all the other shit that went with that life. So, to feel normal again felt good, even though I was in Grendon and admittedly it was packed to the rafters with deviants. I could see what Grendon was trying to achieve by giving the men here a little slice of heaven, as I now wanted it myself. So, I had to ignore what Cookie had said about Norman and his perverted crimes. I had to act as if I too really understood what Grendon was really all about, hoping I would eventually understand it myself. It was so confusing my head was spinning with all these new atrocities, but I had to grin and bear it.

I was now seated and waiting for the baptism to start. But first Cookie had to say a few words. He spoke about the joy of having Jesus in his life. He thanked God, the vicar and his family and friends for standing by him on his march towards redemption. He then started crying, which started his girlfriend and uncle off, then everyone started crying. The tears were flowing, what was it about this place that made grown men cry and brought about this change in so many men, because I'd never seen this before. I just couldn't work it out, was it real change or was there some sort of subliminal brainwashing going on, even Cookie's family seemed taken in by it all.

Then out of the blue Andy stood up and put his hand on my head, praying for Jesus to save my soul, at the same time he asked me to pray with him for forgiveness, which I did only because I was embarrassed now as everyone was now looking at me. So, this is how they did their brainwashing, incrementally through embarrassment. Before Dopey Bollocks finished, he demanded the devil leave me, I felt so embarrassed I could have killed the cunt, but at the same time I wanted what he had, I wanted faith. But most of all I wanted it to be real because I really couldn't feel it, I couldn't feel anything. So, once again I blagged it, hoping like everyone else here, that eventually I'd find it.

After Cookie and Norman had finished their testimonials it was time for them both to be drowned in a large tank of water. Cookie went first followed by the Vicar, who too was fully clothed, he then immersed poor old Cookie until he was spitting water and fighting

Terry Ellis

for his breath. His purification to the dark side was now complete, he was now a paid- up member of Grendons God brigade.

I was still hyped-up from the night before, when Jackie came on the intercom asking for me to join her in the office. She also wanted me to bring my dairy. When I got there, Jackie asked me to take a seat, as her sidekick Mr Bean took notes. She started off by asking me how I was feeling, the normal bollocks, before she opened up on me.

She said "Terry, you've been here 8 weeks and in all that time, you've called me a racist, broken all the rules, called Mark a rapist, Phil a deviant, cursed everyone on the community and generally been a pain in the neck. Have you got anything to say for yourself?" "No, not really" I said "Apart from it's been a hard few weeks, and it's also taken a while for me to adjust". She was silent for a few minutes then she then said "Terry you have also shown us that you are capable of change, as we have seen a marked improvement in your behaviour. You seem to be getting on well within the community, however, you still need to up your game. So, we have decided to put your name forward for the wing Foreman's job and Storeman's' job. It is a big responsibility as it will test you and your ability to mix. It will also prove to us you are capable of working within a team. Also, your diary seems up to date, so keep up the good work". They then both thanked me for coming, as for me, I was made up as this was a good sign that I was moving in the right direction as far as change was concerned.

The next morning whilst on the community meeting, I was voted in as the new Wing Storeman and following in second place was rapist x2 Steve. The guys showed their approval by giving us a round of applause, which I took graciously.

Andy then asked me how I was feeling. I couldn't say I didn't want the job as it had been forced on me by Jackie and Mr Bean, so I just said I was honoured to get the job and that I would also work hard for them and the community, as I've been a dick-head over the last 8 weeks. So, by getting this job I hoped to gain back their respect, adding I would also like to thank my Mum, Dad and family, as without them I wouldn't be here today. While I was saying this Jackie was eyeing me up, so I gave her a little wink which reminded me I still had to work on my sarcasm, as I could see it still annoyed her. I could also see that my behaviour was my way of fighting back, as I used my sarcasm as some sort of defence mechanism when I'm up against it. A behaviour problem that I needed to work on if I wanted to continue in therapy, otherwise I'd be out on my arse again.

The meeting went on for just over an hour as Lewis, a little mixed- race guy and Jason the sumo wrestler had had an altercation, and as Lewis was only 5' nothing and Jason the sumo was 6' and built like a brick shit-house, it was taken seriously especially after what had happened to the paedophile on G-wing who'd been killed. So, both guys had been winged, which meant being put through the therapeutic mill. You could say a mini inquisition by their deviant peers to establish what had brought about this escalation of violence between two best mates, which eventually we as a community got to the bottom of after banging their heads together for 40 minutes. Apparently, it was over 2 slices of bread that Jason had taken out of Lewis's cell.

Over those 40 minutes, we talked about what was going on in their heads. Was it the same thoughts and feelings that Lewis had before he shot his last victim? Was it the same for Jason, did they both see the red mist.? If they thought they could pull the wool over the guy's eyes, they were wrong. This was why Grendon was so effective, because the guys here had real experience they knew about violence and knew all the answers, as most were old hands at knowing their real thoughts and feeling behind their assaults. This was what Grendon and therapy was all about, making people own their shit and admitting it to themselves that their thoughts and behaviours were inter-linked. It was good to finally see it working in this way.

Terry Ellis

CHAPTER TEN

We spent 12 weeks on the induction wing as it was believed that this was the length of time or period it would take for someone's real personality to rear it head. This period was important for the staff and psychologists alike to make a proper evaluation of our traits or our behaviours. However, most of the guys were on their best behaviour 24/7 which was detrimental in as far as making a proper assessment of their real dispositions. Because, as far as I could see only the guys who were self-opinionated or confrontational were getting through as they were being themselves, as they were argumentative but never crossed the line to enforce their beliefs. This showed self-control, they were also able to take criticism on the wing meetings, and learn from them. This was exactly what the staff were looking for, and as therapy on the wings were run by the inmates, it was important for me not to use their offences against them or as an excuse for my own bad behaviour, as the psychologist could see straight through that move. I was taking everything on board and I tried my best not to disregard the deviants opinions in front of the staff, which I hoped would be my passport to the main wing.

The use of a diary to me at first seemed strange but over the last few months it became a release, a way for me to vent my anger and inner rage, also to express by emotions without the repercussions. I quickly saw the logic of writing my feelings down, because as men we find it hard to express ourselves. When I used to read my diary back after a visit from the kids, I could almost feel the years of pent up emotions just ebbing away. These feelings of regret and shame of not being there for them were immense as I'd let them down as a father. I saw their suffering and it brought back bad memories of me being put in a children's home, how I felt about being away from my family, how alone I was as a kid and now I was doing the same to my own kids. I'd never expressed these feelings before as I'd bottled them up for years, they were the reason I was always angry and seeing my thoughts and feelings on paper upset me at times. It even made me shed tears. This self-pity, it was hoped, would open up the flood gates of my emotions, which

Living amongst the beasts: The rise and fall of the Grendon experiment

I'd denied myself for years. Also, self-pity would help me empathize with others, which in turn would help me feel empathy, a feeling, an emotion I'd turned off over the years.

Reading papers in the screws office, using the dining room and turning our telly's off, were all tried and tested methods designed to make us bored so we would socialize more, which in turn broke down social barriers as our need for human contact and conversation would eventually bring us together as a cohesive community. Which would allow us in our own good time to integrate more, thus humanizing each other in our minds eye, even though we had been forced together by the constraints of our incarceration. The actual choices we were making were of own fruition which brought us together in a way that made it more acceptable to us. Once this imaginary line was crossed there was no turning back as it was too late as we were now on the therapeutic train heading towards Shangri-La, a route that we had assumed was of our own free will.

I was learning to interpret certain behaviours by the weaker members of the community who complained relentlessly about the smallest of things, such as noise on the landing or shit marks down the toilets. But their anger and complaints were disproportionate to what was actually happening but it soon became apparent that this was their way of spilling out and venting their frustrations. This was who they really were, angry men. They had been hiding their true natures for 8 weeks but they couldn't contain themselves anymore so, they pissed in the bins, shit up the toilets, broke plants, hid the pool balls, you name it, they did it. It was the only way they could act out their predatory behaviour and get away with it. They wanted to cause as much drama as they could, anything to deflect attention away from who they really were. They just hid in the shadows, enjoying the chaos they'd created. All because they couldn't articulate their thoughts or feelings into words. That is why so many self-harmed, it was their way to express themselves, a form of self-expression that one day would lead to them offending again. All because they couldn't change their behaviours as they were too busy manipulating the psychologist.

The wife killers also had certain moralistic behaviours. I think it was because they thought of themselves as straight guys. They had a tendency to look down their noses at everyone, as if their shit didn't smell. The stupid fuckers actually believed their offences were acts of revenge for their wife's infidelities, which made their acts of murder morally right in their eyes, or they would normally lie by saying they couldn't remember doing it or they were drunk or on drugs. The most common excuse from the wife killers was that it was an accident, as if this would somehow give them atonement for their sins. They lied to themselves, their families and anyone else who would listen to their pathetic excuses.

Terry Ellis

So, once again there were valuable lessons I was learning here at Grendon about human behaviours, even though I was already consciously aware of them. Seeing them played out day after day helped me better understand the behaviour of the beast and also my own behaviours.

Before Chris the rapist left the wing, he volunteered to show me how to do my new job, which duties now included ordering all the wings supplies. I also had to clean all the empty cells, then re-stock them with toiletries, pillows and water jugs. Once a week on a Friday, I had to hand out fresh bedding and take the old bedding back, which I had to sort out by hand before it went back to the laundry. The storeroom also held all the paint tubs, floor waxes and polishes, the wing buffer and also disinfectants all had to be ordered out of the miserly £50 budget I was given each week. The storeroom when I found it was a mess, so I asked rapist x2 to help me reorganise it as he had OCD (Obsessive Compulsive Disorder), which came in handy for me as left to his own devices Steve would clean for hours, which meant the place looked immaculate, especially after he'd spent the best part of the day cleaning up. This left the day free for me to sort out the wings jobs rota. I gave new jobs to all the guys I thought were slackers. I put sumo Jason and his best friend Lewis together cleaning the screws offices as it had to be done every morning and afternoon. While they were in it, they also had to clean the windows and water the plants. I gave Sam the child beater the job of cleaning the toilets as he was a stroppy little fucker. I kept the rest of the guys in their old jobs as they all seemed to be knuckling down.

Every week we had a voluntary drug test where I had to pee into a little pot, which used to drive me crazy. But here at Grendon it was different as the screws were a bit more relaxed as they turned away while you relieved yourself instead of just standing there, which made it so much easier for me to urinate and not the usual chore like in most prisons, where they strategically place the mirrors at angles with some irritating panjandrum standing there with a smug smile on his ugly mug, watching you.

And talking about ugly mugs, this evening fat Mark tried to bond with me. He came into my cell and showed me some pictures of his new girlfriend, who wasn't a bad looker but a bit chunky for my liking, who he said had asked him to marry her. What a fucking joke, I couldn't believe it, this guy is a serial rapist and here he was bragging about getting married. The only thing I could say or do was tell him how lucky he was as I sat there in disbelief, wondering how a grown woman could be such a fucking imbecile. It just didn't make sense.

Living amongst the beasts: The rise and fall of the Grendon experiment

This morning when I went down for breakfast, there was a new guy sitting in the dining room who gave me a funny look. I said good morning, but there was no acknowledgement just a blank expression on his face so I asked Andy who he was. Apparently, the guy had come over in the middle of the night from Spring Hill open prison he had been found drunk in his room and was now being held at Grendon until he sobered up, before going in front of the Governor for an adjudication. I was told this was a common occurrence at Grendon and these guys even had their own names, they were called Lodgers and like most Lodgers they had their own ideas about Grendon and the people in it, as they believed all the guys here were either child killers, rapists or nonces. So, knowing this I couldn't really blame him for blanking me, even though it did make me feel uncomfortable with him believing I was one of them. For a moment I felt like enlightening him about my situation, but thought better of it as the last thing I needed was to try and explain myself to some ignorant piss-head who couldn't even keep out of trouble in an open prison. But, it didn't feel good at all, but at least now I knew how all the other guys here felt, especially with me around as I didn't make it easy for them. So, I thought I'd bring it up at the next community meeting to let them know how it made me feel, believing it would help them understand how I felt about them and what I was going through by me just being here. My words just seemed to open up an avalanche of honestly as Howard said I made him feel nervous as I was always being sarcastic to him and on a few occasions, I had called him a fat cunt and once asked him, on our small group, how long had it taken for him to strangle his wife.

Then Sam the baby beater said I also made him feel uncomfortable as I had said to him one morning at breakfast that I understood the reason he beat his little girl up, as I have 5 kids myself and I can remember how spiteful they could be at that age which drew a few gasps from the watching community. Alan said I had mocked him and the way he walked, also every time I passed him I put him on edge. I could almost feel myself getting smaller in my seat as fat Mark put his hand up and said he'd overheard me talking to Craig in the shower saying all rapists should be put down at birth. Then Phil said the same thing, before Mark the guy on my group who'd killed his boyfriend said I had said his boyfriend had probably committed suicide after waking up next to him as he was an ugly bastard, so had stabbed himself 10 times in the heart so it would never happen again, which sounded so bad now in front of all the community. So much for honesty as it had well and truly backfired, but at least now everyone had said their piece and gotten all the shit off their chests. I apologised to all of them for my behaviour and promised to change, which showed that I could take their criticism and at the same time I had proved to all and sundry that I'd come in here to change today. This was my way of setting out my table and making a clean breast of things so I could move forward.

Terry Ellis

Even though this morning had been hard for me, I actually felt as if I'd turned a corner, as normally I would have gone on the attack regarding their slanderous comments. But, today I had grown up and admitted my faults and apologised. I also told them that it had taken me a few weeks to adjust to my new environment, which in part was true as I'd found coming here harder than I ever imagined. I also said I'd learnt a lot in the short space of time I'd been here and hoped from this day forward I would do my best to stop being sarcastic. I would also make myself more approachable as I hated the thought of being perceived as a bully, adding it was important for me that all the members of the community pull me if I ever said anything out of order again. And, just like in here today I would take it on the chin and learn from my mistakes.

When we all left the community meeting Andy and most of the guys made a bee-line towards me. Andy said that he had been praying for me and had always known I was one of the good guys as he could see the good in me. Sam, Howard, Mark, Phil and Alan also patted me on the back and said their doors were always open for me if I ever needed a chat. There were lots of pats on backs and shouts of 'well done mate', everyone was smiling and seemed relieved that I had finally come on side, even Jackie smiled as she walked past me also Mr Bean nodded. So, it looked as if I'd come through it in their eyes whiter than white, but inside I felt like shit as it didn't feel good having had to listen to all of them talking and slagging me off about my behaviour. If I was back in the system I would be a hero for what I had said to them, but here I was in their world, which meant my attitude was deemed inappropriate and demeaning to everyone. The whole episode seemed to humble me as I could see how intolerant of them I was, as they were now prepared to forgive me and my past deeds.

So, I had to keep my opinions to myself. I also had to be mindful of them, which meant no more sarcasm in the future as I had been using it as a weapon to get my point across, which made me look like a bully, which I didn't like as I don't like hurting people, even if they are deviants.

I spent the afternoon in my cell going over the events. This self-introspection and what I had written in my diary over those last few months was helping me see and understand my behaviour. I was also thinking more and more about my family and all the people I'd loved and let down over the years, as I had blamed everyone for my problems, I blamed being in care, my upbringing and my lack of education. I justified all my life's actions in this way as I believed the world owed me a living. But really, I was a selfish fucker who didn't like himself but at the same time I thought I was better than everyone else and it didn't matter to me who I hurt in the process, as long as I got my own way because that's all that mattered to me.

Living amongst the beasts: The rise and fall of the Grendon experiment

I hadn't even started therapy yet but already I was thinking differently, so maybe Grendon was having a positive effect on me. Before I came to Grendon I always saw myself as one of the good guys, but all I could see now was a trail of misery caused by me as my life really wasn't how I imagined it to be. In fact, it was a disaster.

Over the next few days I saw an induction bloodbath as Cockney Nick, Jackie's blue-eyed boy, was informed that he would be returning to his previous establishment as he had failed to shine. I felt sorry for poor old Nick as he was the wings Vice Chairman, which in most cases would have guaranteed his advancement through to the main wing. To say he was upset was an under-statement as he took his rejection rather badly by slagging off Grendon and all it represented, even though he had championed it for the last 11 weeks.

Next to go was Jim, but he was different as he had resigned as he couldn't cope with being around all the deviants any longer. Unlike Sam the baby beater, who was told this morning that due to his immaturity he too would be 'returned to sender'. This upset the spiteful little fucker as he started on bird hand Alan, his best mate, as they'd had an argument after the community meeting which had turned a bit nasty. So, Alan was winged and the outcome was that he too would be 'returned to sender'.

The irony of the whole situation made me laugh as most of the guys here thought they would be going through on the merits of their despicable crimes, but that wasn't the case now. I tried my best to look sympathetic but my attempts failed miserably because I was glad they were all going, as I'd seen them all manipulate their way through, which had now backfired on all of them. So, to see them all crying gave me some pleasure as their suffering was overwhelming, which made the last few weeks more bearable for me.

This constant battle between the good and bad side of my personality was something I was coming to terms with as I was fighting it every day. I kept telling myself I was here to change but the dark side of my personality would say fuck the deviants, they're all mugs, scum, they don't matter. Which normally remedied the situation as my criminal beliefs and behaviour would tell me that as long as I conducted myself properly, then that would be OK. It was perplexing but I knew I had to work through it.

We were soon into the middle of the next week when I met Martin and Musa. I spent about 20 minutes talking to both of them over in the gym. I picked their brains regarding therapy. They both told me that they were doing life sentences. Martin had killed his girlfriend and Musa his mate. They both came across as laid back and very knowledgeable but at the same time I thought they were both strange, but again I put that down to all the years they'd been away. Both had come to prison in their early teens but were now in their late 20s. They championed Grendon and all its therapy. Everyone I spoke to also said the same thing, which made me start to worry that I might not get through as now I really wanted what they all had. The experience of doing Grendon as I believed I'd earnt it as I'd gone against all my so-called criminal values by associating with rapists, child killers, wife killers and all the other deviant crimes I'd heard over the last few months in my pursuit of find the Holy Grail of Rehabilitation that would change my life forever. From bad boy criminal to born again patron saint of reformed recidivists.

My job as Storeman was having an effect on me as the wing looked unrecognisable, but with the help of x2 Steve and his OCD, he had worked wonders. The plants were flourishing. The landings had been painted, thanks to gay Mark as he had painted non-stop for the last 2 weeks. He was like the Forest Gump of painters.

The cleaners were also doing a great job as I was praised by the staff at the weekly meeting, which I took graciously by thanking everyone, even my family, which once again didn't go down too well with Jackie, but I could see she was now softening toward me as she gave me a little smile before quickly giving me a look of disapproval.

After the meeting I went on exercise with Craig, but Howard joined us and straight away he started telling us jokes, but again they were racist. So, I told him to drop me out as my ex-wife was Indian but he just carried on, so I told him to fuck off. It was the third time I'd had to warn him and enough was enough. I was going to wing him in front of the whole community and for the first time in my life I was going to use words instead of my fists to take this fucking mug down.

CHAPTER ELEVEN

Monday morning started as normal, I had my shower then breakfast but today I was going to wing Howard for his racist jokes, which meant grassing him up in front of the whole community, something I wasn't looking forward to doing, but what could I do. I couldn't bang him out like I would have done back in the system as there was a no violence rule here. So, my only redress would be to do what he had done to me on the last community meeting, which was to bring his behaviour in the room, if it was good enough for him to do to me, then I would return the favour, which was to use the therapeutic process against him to correct his behaviour. Be it right or wrong I had to do it.

As soon as the community meeting was called to order, I raised my hand to take a minute. The room went deadly quiet, my heart was beating like a drum, my mouth was dry but I had to do it. I started off by saying I'd like Howard to know that my wife is Indian, and that's why I'm sick of his racist jokes and if we were in any other prison than Grendon, I would have ironed him out days ago, but I can't do that. So, I have decided to bring this matter to the wing for his own good and for the sake of changing his behaviour, also to help him reflect over the vile content of his morally unpleasant jokes, as it was about time he started looking at his own humour and the way he used it to make friend because it really isn't acceptable in this day and age. I then sat back and waited for Howard to say something but the poor fucker looked mortified and for once he had nothing to say. I enjoyed his embarrassment as I wanted to eradicate the prick. I also wanted pay back for what he had said about me being sarcastic So, today I had killed 2 birds with 1 stone. I knew it wasn't a good start to therapy, but that's life.

Howard started saying he was sorry and that he never realised his jokes could be perceived as racist, but then he added he wasn't a racist. So, I asked him if he didn't think his jokes were racist, then why he hadn't he told Lewis and Julian, or was it because they were black.

Terry Ellis

Julian asked Howard to repeat the joke for the benefit of the community to see if the joke was racist or not. Julian's question seemed to be the knock-out punch I was looking for as Howard had now started to cry, the normal defence of someone who doesn't want to answer any more questions, so I backed off. The whole wing could see Howard for what he really was, a racist and me in the eyes of the community I was now seen as the upholder of all that was just.

The staff believed I had turned a corner even though it was partially motivated by revenge, but even so it felt good getting it off my chest this way without banging him out. Howard quit the next morning.

That same afternoon Jackie said she wanted to see me in Mr Bean's office in the morning at 9 o'clock sharp. I wondered if I'd over-stepped the mark by bringing the racist card into the community room. There were so many thoughts going through my mind. I tried to convince myself that I hadn't done anything wrong, but I had attacked Howard verbally and I wondered if they thought my attack was an act of revenge. Then I blamed Howard for spoiling my chance of getting through. This self-validation that I didn't do anything wrong was my way of reinforcing my bad behaviour. I did it all the time and the normal outcome regarding my thinking was always the same because I go into defensive mode, which normally gets me through these situations.

It was now the next morning and I was outside Mr Bean's office for my X-factor moment. I knocked on the door and took a deep breath and walked in. Mr Bean wasn't there, so immediately I thought something was up as Jackie was sitting behind his desk. She asked me to take a seat then asked me how I thought I was doing, but I was nervous so I just rambled on. I said I believed I was doing alright. I believed I had turned a corner as far as bringing my issues into my small groups and the meetings instead of me bottling them up all the time, even though it was still hard for me. I told her I still find it hard to talk about other people in there as I still saw it as grassing people up. I said I was learning all the time I'd learnt a lot about my sense of humour and the way I use my sarcasm and I also admitted I was self-opinionated and argumentative to the point of coming across as aggressive, which I'm more aware of and am working on changing it. I also see things clearer I said, like both sides of an argument instead of just my own, which has brought about a better understanding within me of certain situations. Jackie just sat there is silence with a stony look on her face before Mr Bean entered the room and took a seat opposite me. He said "Terry you seem to be willing to learn and you have definitely shown us you have the ability to challenge yourself and others. You have many behaviours we can work with, so we have decided to give you a chance to change your life. You will be moving over to C-wing. Congratulations you will be going over to C-wing tomorrow for tea, then on Saturday morning you will be moving over for good. Will you be OK with that Terry?" "Yes" I said. Then Jackie congratulated me, telling me at the same time "don't let me down Terry". "I won't" I said, then I took my leave thanking them both as I shut the door behind me. As I walked back to my cell the pressure of the last 12 weeks just lifted off my shoulders as I was now one of the favoured few to make it into Grendon, which I took great delight in telling everyone who I passed on the way.

Well, it looked like from day one I had shown them all my flaws, which had given the staff and psychologists something to work with, unlike Nick, Alan, Paul, Sam and even Howard and Dennis who had all tried and failed because they had all tried to manipulate their way through. I could see their mistakes as I was better placed to see both sides of their behaviours. The ones' they used in front of the staff and the real behaviours they hid, as I could see and hear all the racist and misogynistic jokes and behaviours. Most of them tried to portray themselves as victims but it hadn't worked. I was glad to see that their deceptions were transparent. I had learnt valuable lessons on F-wing. I was lucky to have spent 12 weeks seeing the true nature of the beasts I would be working with, as it gave me the opportunity to see behind their masks. I only hoped Grendon was a real place for change and not the den of iniquity I had been told about, where deviants come to pass away a few years in relative comfort. But only time would tell.

As I entered the dining room for breakfast the next morning with my new air of superiority, that I Terry Ellis, had made it through and was now one of only a few selected members of men who would be able to experience this unique opportunity to see if this intensive psychological exploration into my psyche would unravel the mysteries of my life. I felt like a criminal astronaut who was taking one small step for me, and one giant step away from the criminality kind. As I surveyed my new kingdom, looking back and forth across the room, I noticed bird hand Alan and cruelty to little baby's Sam looking in my direction, so I said good morning and gave them one of my best smiles, but they didn't react. But, who cared now, I'd made it through and was now a paid- up member of the Grendon elite, and in a couple of days, F-wing and it's deviant community would be but a distant memory.

After breakfast I was informed I had to see one of C-wings facilitators Alan, who I will call Monkey Boots as he had cropped hair, a beard and a pair of high length monkey boots. He came across as an OK guy. We both spoke for about 20 minutes about what was expected of me, we also talked about the therapy I would be doing. Monkey Boots said he was the head of psychodrama, a form of psycho- therapy, in which an inmate acts out events from their past so as to better understand the psychological elements of their actions and behaviours around their crimes. Once Monkey Boots finished, he invited me over for tea. The tea would start a 4:30 which would give me the opportunity to meet my fellow graduates and also get a look around. After Alan monkey boots went I went back to my cell and spent the rest of the afternoon wondering what it would be like on my new wing. Would it be everything I wanted it to be, a therapeutic utopia where I would find the answers to my criminality? Would I be able to handle the intellectual rigours of therapy and have the diligence to work through my behavioural problems? There were so many questions that had to be answered.

At 4:30 I was summoned to the office as it was now time for me to go over for tea. Jackie did the honours and let me off the wing and for the first time since I'd come to Grendon I was actually on my own. It felt surreal walking along the empty corridors as it was eerily quiet, especially as I walked past the chapel. Then I turned the corner onto the M1 corridor and started walking down it's incline slope, I noticed that the walls were covered with prison artwork which looked rather impressive. After 20 yards or so I came to G-wing where the paedophile had been killed then another 20 yards I came to B and A wings. A-wing was for all the kiddie fiddlers, I was told it was packed to the rafters with them. So, I aptly named A-wing the Jimmy Saville wing. After another 100 yards or so I came to C and D-wings. The 2 doors were separated by an enormous mosaic of the London underground system. I knocked on the door and as quick as a flash the door was opened by a smiling screw called John, who asked for my ID card as I had to hand it in, as I was still only considered a visitor to the wing. He then asked me to follow him into the dining room where I was met by Mac who invited me to sit down at his table. At the same time, he introduced me to all the other guys, who all seemed pleasant enough as they all came over to shake my hand and welcome me to the wing. The whole atmosphere felt different, the dining room was much bigger as it sat about 40 people, everyone seemed happier and content with their lot, a far cry from F-wing which now seemed a dull and manky place.

Once we finished tea, Mac took me on a tour of the place. The first thing I noticed as we left the dining room was a giant fish tank, I also heard soft music coming from the TV room which reminded me of the film One Flew Over the Cuckoo's Nest. I just hoped I wouldn't wake up in the middle of the night with a pillow over my head.

Mac then took me up to my new cell on the 2s landing. It was identical to F-wings apart from it too had a fish tank and the view was out of this world. It looked like a picture post card, it had an unbroken view complete with farm house and woodland, a spectacle that took my breath away. I was now in therapeutic heaven. My landing also had a separate shower room, pool room, TV room and a therapy room. There were 2 phones on the wing and even a suicidal cell for inmates with mental health problems. All in all, it looked alright as I took a brief look around before I made my way back to F-wing.

Friday morning, I had to stand up and tell everyone on F-wing about my visit to C-wing, I must admit I added a few embellishments for those who wanted to go through and a few highlights for those who had been rejected. I told them about the music, the fish tanks on every landing, the giant rubber plants, the yuca trees, the pool room, the therapy room, the farm house and the woodlands, and I also mentioned sky television and also how clean it was compared to F-wing. I than thanked the staff, Jackie and Mr Bean for their help and support over the last 12 weeks, adding I wouldn't let them down before giving everyone the thumbs up as I burst out laughing before the end of the meeting. I then spent the rest of the day with Martin and Craig who both kept wishing me well, and they even promised to help me down in the morning with my gear. We laughed off the rest of the day taking the piss out of everyone's faces when I told them about how good it was on C-wing.

That night I was handed C-wings Constitution and told to read it, as it would explain C-wings social code, it's rules and regulations and fundamental principles it's members lived by if they wanted to remain on its community. I read it from page to page. Then I understood why everyone seemed so docile and submissive as the Constitution was being swung like a therapeutic sledge hammer, as any infringement of the laws laid down would result in you being put on a wing commitment and then voted out by your fellow Grendonites. If I'm honest I disagreed with this sort of democracy as it was open to abuse from staff and inmates, which I had seen first- hand on F-wing over the weeks, as the deviants were quite manipulative. So, if you had a strong deviant community the chances where they would come out on top.

Well, at least I knew the possible dangers, and forewarned is forearmed. However, I wasn't going to worry about this tonight as I needed some sleep before my big day tomorrow.

Saturday morning, I was up bright and early. My stuff was packed and I was ready to go, but first I had to have my breakfast as it's an old tradition inside that you have to eat your last breakfast otherwise you eventuality come back to finish it off. I know this didn't apply to me this morning as I wasn't leaving prison. But I was leaving F-wing plus I'd seen Julian come back, so I ate my porridge and 2 toasts, then Martin and Craig helped me down with my gear. We talked for about 10 minutes before Terry P, a GBH merchant and a rapist called Esca picked me up. So, I took one last look at F-wing and said my goodbyes before we set off to my new home C-wing and away from the induction wing.

Terry Ellis

Once we arrived on C-wing I was told to wait in the office so I could collect my key and sign the wing compact. When I left the office, I noticed Terry P and Esca had taken by stuff up, which I thought was quite civilised. I then spent the next hour sorting my cell, which now had been freshly painted and there were also new carpet tiles laid and nets and curtains. The place looked pretty slick.

It was now 10:30 and time for exercise so I made my way down stairs where I met Mac who greeted me like an old lost friend. He told me not to say anything until we were outside, as walls have ears, blah, blah, blah. So, I just stood there in silence with him until the gate opened. When we got outside I could see the yard had a large football pitch and there were guys sprinting up and down. There was also about a 100 guys in small groups walking around anti-clockwise. There were also benches. Mac then pulled me to one side and said I should never talk off the wing about anything that had been discussed in my small groups or the community meetings, otherwise I would be put up on a commitment, and then voted out of Grendon. He also said the wing was full of deviants who were spiteful fuckers who hated anyone who wasn't one of them. So, I'd better be on my guard, as the bastards would smile to your face but at the same time would be plotting to get rid of you as fast as they could. This was their world and we were the enemy, adding that I should never forget that. Mac also said he was doing some good work on his group. It was now the end of exercise, the hour seemed to fly by.

When we got back to the wing they had just started serving dinner. Mac sat on his table and I sat on my own on an empty table by the window but after a few minutes Mac joined me. He brought with him a big bowl of fruit, ketchup, spicy sauces and salt and pepper pots. He then said this was going to be our table and he named it 'the good guys table'. Mac's old table mates didn't take it too well as they looked a bit put out that Mac had deserted them at the first opportunity of someone new coming on the wing, as the look of abandonment was etched on their faces. If they'd come to Grendon with any abandonment issues then this act of betrayal by Mack would only reinforce it in them all. But what did they expect, we were different from them, plus we were only doing what they were doing, sitting with our own kind. Why should Mac or I feel guilty as long as we didn't say anything openly or show any open hostility then whatever they imagined of us was down to their own paranoia and no concern of mine as I wasn't the one who had moved.

All I wanted was to do some therapy to see if it actually worked, I wasn't concerned about the deviants on the wing as their feelings meant nothing to me because as far as I was concerned they were all scum, and no amount of therapy was ever going to change them. I wasn't being elitist, I was just being pragmatic as paedophiles, rapists and child killers never change and life should mean life for these people. Anyway, they aren't my concern so fuck them.

When I woke up on Sunday morning I was surprised at how quiet it was. Apparently, we were not allowed to make any noise, i.e. hoover, play music, bang doors or even talk until after 10:30. They called this time the quiet time, if you broke this rule you could be winged by your small group or the whole community and have to explain your actions. I was told no excuses would be tolerated as there was no such thing as mitigating circumstances because all the wing was concerned about was you owning your mistakes and that you were a self-absorbed prick who cared about himself and no-one else. This I was told was the only way you could placate your peers. This sort of confrontational therapy was supposed to embarrass you into changing your behaviours.

Mac said the only problem with this therapy was it led to resentment and getting your own back on the person or the group that winged you. This led to a culture of one-upmanship, which I was told was endemic on all the wings. It was like an infectious disease and regardless of your intelligence if you were winged it was hard not to let it go, and probably why the paedophile on G-wing was killed. Even the screws and psychologists were susceptible to this sort of one-upmanship behaviour as I'd seen it on F-wing with Jackie and Patrick. It was pathetic to watch and one of the reasons I was worried about this sort of therapy, especially when you considered the nature of the crimes most of the guys were in for. They were spiteful and vindictive by nature and evil was ingrained in them as I could see it in their eyes. They were crafty within the rules, bullies and cowards who wouldn't think twice about stabbing you in the back. So, the thought of antagonising them wasn't something I was looking forward to as they were dangerous guys.

I only saw a handful of people that weekend so by the Monday I was chomping at the bit to see my fellow compadres and what would be my first community meeting. I felt like a little boy going to a new school half way though term. I just hoped I wouldn't stand out like a sore thumb, so I got up, showered, shaved then went down for breakfast. Everyone I met smiled and said good morning which still felt a bit surreal but refreshing at the same time as the civility was such a contrast to F-wing, or any other prison I'd ever been in. I found it easy to reciprocate as I've always been a social person believing good manners cost nothing, even if the person I was responding to was a deviant scum bag.

It was now 5 to 9, everyone was making their way to the community room so I followed them and took a seat by the window. The room was bigger than F-wings as it sat about

Terry Ellis

50 people, it had the same soft blue chairs around the edges of the room. The only difference was that there was a small coffee table placed in front of 2 red high-backed chairs, which seemed to be the focal point of the room as this was where the Chairman and Vice Chairman sat. On the coffee table sat 3 large books, one was for writing in the minutes, a jobs book and the dreaded commitments book. Everyone took their places before the screws and the psychologist Smitty came in. When he did he seemed to have an effect on the whole room from the moment he walked in as everyone sat upright in their chairs as he smiled and nodded to them.

The wing Chairman then said good morning as the guy nearest the door closed it. The door was pushed shut at 9 o'clock and anyone who came late was turned away. If you were late 3 times you were winged by your small group then put in the commitment book for dereliction of the therapeutic process. Terry P was the wing Chairman. He called the wing to order and then said we have a new member to our community, so could you all please welcome Terry Ellis and introduce yourselves.

Terry P then started off by saying he was doing a 6-year IPP sentence for GBH on his girlfriend. He had poured petrol over her head, then had set her alight. Terry was about 55 years old, 5' 9",12 stone with a country accent and was a shifty looking fucker. Next was Chris who was also about 5' 9", 12 stone about 40 years old. Chris had killed his wife and 18-month-old baby girl with a golf club. Brian was next. He was about 30 years old, again about 12 stone, 5' 10" and bald head. He, like Chris, was doing a life sentence for killing his Mum and Dad with a cricket bat. Each guy went through their introductions all ending with 'welcome Terry' with me just smiling back and saying "thank you". It was like being at the mad hatters tea party but this was real.

Once everyone had finished, it was time for the head psychologist to welcome me. Smitty was about 55, 15 stone, 6' 2" and was immaculately dressed. He came across as the Darwin of the Deviants and he knew the power of the pen and used it from what I had heard. He smiled and then welcomed me to the wing.

Terry then brought the meeting to order again. He then did the minutes which gave anyone on the wing a chance to air any grievances they might have regarding anyone's behaviour on the wing that might have taken place over the weekend. The first hand up was Mac, who said could people be more mindful when using the toilets in the evening as he goes to bed early most nights at 10 o'clock so he could rise at 4 am to do his studies before going to his therapy group. He said people were banging doors and leaving their doors open with loud music on. He could also hear people laughing and joking through the doors which he said was taking the piss as the wing Constitution forbids this behaviour. Terry P then asked if anyone had anything to say or add regarding this matter. A few of the guys started to agree with Mac saying the wing had got louder at night over the last few weeks. Terry P then asked for names but no-one said anything. Then Smitty interjected by asking if anybody was prepared to name names or would anyone like to own up to their behaviour. Be it through fear or being exposed, Lewis a young guy about 21 years old, 11 stone, 5' 8" who was doing a life sentence for killing an old man who he'd had a gay encounter with, said it might have been him as he had been talking to his mate Ian. Ian was doing a life sentence for killing his wife. It was the second time he'd been at Grendon, the first time was for rape of a young girl, which was funny as Ian was as bent as a ten-bob note, he was about 45 years old 6' 2", 17 stone. Lewis said he had knocked on his door over the weekend and also had left his door open. He then apologised to the rest of the community but Smitty wasn't finished. He then asked Ian why he had kept quiet about Lewis knocking on his door and with an embarrassed look on his face he said he was sorry and that it wouldn't happen again.

Smitty then asked if anyone else had anything to say. Then a hand went slowly up by a guy called Westley, who had impaired hearing and talked as if he was deaf. He was about 25 years old, 6', skinny about 12 stone, he said Ricky was also taking through the door the night before to golf club Chris.   Ricky had ginger hair and came from South London , and on hearing what Westley had to say, he started calling him all the cunts under the sun, calling him a grass and a liar. This went on for a couple of minutes before Ricky calmed down and said he might have been talking but he couldn't remember. But, we could all see he was lying which was what Smitty wanted us all to see, that there was no hiding place here at Grendon if you were lying because sooner or later someone would grass you up to save their own skin.

This sort of grassing was looked upon as helping others to look at their own behaviour and a gauge by the psychologist to see how far you had come in your therapy, as the more you grassed the more changes you were making. It was hoped through this period of sweet grassing that the person being grassed on and the guy doing the grassing up would both start to change their criminal behaviour. The guy who had been grassed up would remember that everything he said on the wing was being monitored, so he had to think twice before he did anything wrong. He would also go through feelings of resentment toward his accuser, which would normally be one of his neighbours or even a friend. If he thought his friend had done it for the right reasons, he would take it on the chin and possibly change his ways. But, if it was someone he didn't like he would then bide his time and return the favour. Smitty then asked Ricky if anyone else was involved. Ricky then turned to his mate Jamie and grassed him up. So now Ricky was seen as a grass by his mate Jamie who now held Westly and Ricky responsible for grassing him up. This created a bad atmosphere on the wing that they, and the whole wing, had to deal with. It was believed that working through these feelings without using violence would bring about new coping strategies, hence stopping the guys returning to prison in the future. So, you had to act accordingly, which meant speak no evil, do no evil and don't participate in any evil because if you wanted to be part of the community you had to be whiter than white. You had to play your part as this was the nature of therapy.

I was told that in our small groups we could be more confrontational with each other so we could better understand the consequences of our actions. The logic behind this was very simplistic. However, the implementation was another story and could get very volatile but Smitty thrived on these interactions as it brought out the worst in our behaviours, giving Smitty all the information he needed to write our wing assessments. If you reacted verbally and were aggressive you were then written up as confrontational, argumentative and that you had anger management issues. The list I was told could be endless and normally by the time you learnt this it was too late as the damage had already been done, which meant months if not years in therapy for you, which in turn taught you never to show any anger or emotion when arguing with one of your fellow Grendonites.

You learnt from these altercations to read your body because when the adrenaline kicked in you read that feeling as being under attack. But as the weeks of therapy went by you learnt to articulate your responses to any confrontation which in turn made your body act accordingly. So, instead of fight or flight you became a more controlled person and by doing this in front of the whole community you learnt very quickly that owning your own behaviour at the first opportunity saved you from a period of prolonged and intrusive questioning from your peers.

After all the minutes were done Terry P asked if anybody had any backings. All wing backing had to go through your small group first. Also, the whole group had to back you before you could bring it to the wing, which meant you had to convince them your backing was worthwhile. Today Derek was taking a backing. Del was an old guy of about 65 who was doing 12 years for killing his wife. He killed her then drove her body to France. His case was in all the national papers. Del said his backing was for some hair dye which brought about a cacophony of laughter and a few smiles but not from Smitty who asked Del what he was hiding from. Del said he wasn't hiding from anything. Then someone asked if it had anything to do with his ego, then another said he shouldn't be worried about what he looked like he should be concentrating on this therapy. Del then said he had a new girlfriend and just wanted to look good on his visit. Someone then asked if his new girlfriend knew about his past, Del said yes she did and said he just wanted to look a bit younger. Smitty then said, "so it is about your ego". "No" said Del "I just want some fucking hair dye, does everything we ask for have to have a reason?" The questioning went on for about 20 minutes before it was put to a vote but not before Smitty said he wouldn't be backing Del. One by one everyone voted by raising the hands, unfortunately Del lost the vote by a small majority which left him red in the face as he looked infuriated.

It was now coming to the end of the meeting so Terry P asked if anyone had anything to say. The first hand up was Del's. He said he was very disappointed with his group as he had seen a few of them vote against him, which he couldn't understand as they had backed him on the group, so he wanted to know why. Then he said he believed they voted against him because they wanted to take favour with Smitty as he couldn't see why they had changed their minds and for that reason he had lost trust in all of them. The meeting was then called to an end. It was now 10:30, Del was still fuming but there was nothing he could do as everyone just got up and walked out.

The whole experience was intense. The 1 hour 30 minutes seemed to fly by but I could see from today's meeting that this was going to be a fucking drama and a lot harder than I ever imagined. The politics of therapy and the actions of Del's group by siding with Smitty brought into question was this real democracy or Smitty's kangaroo court for whatever he deemed right or wrong. The complexities were vast but once again only time would tell how things would play out.

Terry Ellis

CHAPTER TWELVE

That afternoon I was told I was going into Group 2 so I went to see Mac and told him. He said I'd had a touch as Group 2 was a strong group. By the morning I was well rested as I'd gone to bed early.

I made my way up to Group 2 as it was on the 3s landing, it was now about 5 to 9. As I entered the group room Terry P tapped me on the shoulder and said "welcome to my group mate". Terry P came from a little village near Bristol. He also had a set of false teeth that gave him a slight lisp so when he smiled all you could see was white teeth. It was a little off putting as he looked like the Joker from the Batman movies. He was a strange little man and as shifty as fuck as I've already said.

We both walked into the room together and took our places. There were 9 chairs laid out in a circle. I sat down next to the window which I hoped would give me a better vantage point to see everyone as they walked into the room. As we waited I made small talk with Terry P until the other guys started to come through the door.

The first to come into the room was a black guy called Jabbi. He was about 30 years old, 5" 5", well- built and had a big smile. After him came Daryl and Martin. Daryl was about 6' 1", in his 40s, a well- built guy, just like Martin who was 6' 2" and about 30 years old. I'd already met Martin over at the gym with his mate Musa. The next 2 through the door was Dan and Bilal. Dan was about 6' 2" and 18 stone. You could see that him and Bilal had never used a gym before. Bilal was a black guy of about 5' 6", an odd- looking guy. Rob was next through the door followed by Monkey Boots our facilitator which made 9 of us.

Monkey Boots was the first to speak. He welcomed me to the group then said once you get to know everybody Terry you will see we are here for you. Trusting each other is paramount as we will be discussing some deep personal issues and being able to discuss such deep and disturbing painful events about our lives will take us all on a journey of discovery, which at times can get emotionally upsetting. Being able to trust your fellow group members will be the first step on your personal journey, so Terry it's important you take it slowly, give yourself time to get to know each of us and us you. Is that OK?

One by one they all told me what they were in for. First to speak was Bilal or B as he wanted to be called. B said he was doing 16 years for killing and torturing his girlfriend's little boy. He said his girlfriend went out every weekend leaving him with the kids, so to get his own back he started taking his resentment out on the kids. At first, he said it started as a joke and that the boys liked it as they thought he was playing with them. He used to lock them in the cupboard then made them stand on one leg, he made them do press ups. As time went on he started to burn them with cigarettes, always making it look like an accident and to cover his tracks in front of the neighbours he used to take the boys over to the park on the swings every day and on the way home he used to buy them fish and chips. But as their weeks went by the torture sessions turned into months, he started to punch them and kick them , even started giving them the belt but he said they got used to it. So, one night he punched the little six -year old so hard that he busted his spleen. He said he was sorry, he also said that the look that passed between them as the boy was just about to die would stay with him for the rest of his life, adding that as the little kid was dying he said "Daddy what have you done?" B said he then took the boy in his arms but he died as he and his brother looked on.

B was now crying and as I looked at him I could see those little boys being tortured. I put my head in my hands, I had to keep it together. So, I wiped my eyes and looked up at the little degenerate fucker as the scenes of depravity played over in my head, I wondered what sort of man could do that and then come in here and blame their mum for going out. He disgusted me. This poor excuse for a human being just sat there like a cartoon character with his thick bifocal glasses on and his mole shaped face. The resentment I felt for this disgusting little man was more than I could take. I made a mental note to torture him with my words over the next few months. There was so much I wanted to say but I had to keep it to myself. The others just sat there and one even patted him on the shoulder and thanked him for sharing his experience and being so honest.

I then wondered what deviant new holocaustic depravities the other monsters were hiding behind their smiles and could I handle or stomach anymore of their sick and depraved imagery invading my subconscious, and would I be able to sleep tonight.

I still had to listen to the rest of them before this fucking morning was over.

Terry Ellis

The next person to off load more misery was Rob the little Scottish guy who I had spoken to over the weekend as he was my next-door neighbour and, as luck would have it, so was Bilal. So, whatever I thought of them both after today they would still be my neighbours. A lovely thought.

Rob said he was doing a life sentence for murder. He had been working away from home which gave him the chance to explore his bisexuality as none of his family knew. However, this made him angry as his family looked at homosexuality and it's behaviours as depraved. Rob said every time he had sex with a man he used to beat them up afterwards as this behaviour somehow made it right in his own head that he wasn't really gay. Which in turn made him feel even more bitter. This bitterness manifested into anger and resentment which he took out on an American tourist one evening. He said he met a girl in a pub and befriended her, he then asked her back to his place for a drink. Once through the door he smashed her over the head with a hammer then throttled her until she died. He then said she had reminded him of his Mum who he hated as she had sexually abused him as a kid. It was a cold premeditated murder of an innocent woman. The way he described the sordid affair came across as cold and as black as his eyes. There wasn't an ounce of empathy or regret for what he had done and just like Bilal he had blamed everyone for his deviant behaviour. He blamed his Mum, the poor woman tourist for being so trusting and looking like his Mum. He blamed them for not understanding his sexuality and blamed the world for everything else. The funny thing was though he came across as unassuming. He was well spoken and you would never have thought he was capable such atrocities. Like most of the women killers I'd come across over the years they were always very polite and shy and came across as insecure. I can only assume it is a method they used to snare their unsuspecting victims.

There was something I was starting to notice about most of the guys I'd met over the last 12 weeks. None of them ever said they got any pleasure out of their sadistic behaviour. No matter how many times I asked, they always blamed their upbringing or said it was an accident brought on by drink or drugs. No-one in all the time I was there admitted they enjoyed it. It seemed to be taboo. Not one rapist said he enjoyed it, even though a few of the cowardly misfits had been in prison more than once. If they never enjoyed it why then did they repeat their crimes? To admit to me or themselves that they were predators was like pulling teeth and no matter how much I tried, the psychologist always asked me to back off. I really couldn't understand why the psychologist never tried to push them for the benefit of all the women and children who had been raped by these bastards. It was mind boggling.

Living amongst the beasts: The rise and fall of the Grendon experiment

Terry P was next to speak. He had been really friendly to me all morning and he had the biggest smile though I had a feeling he was in for something grim, as the real bad deviants hid behind their smiles. It was the one thing I was starting to see, especially in a place like this because if someone was over-friendly there was definitely something up with them, as they like Terry P could all be sneaky bastards.

Terry P welcomed me to the group. He said he was doing a sentence for Grievous Bodily Harm, GBH. He had been drinking in his local boozer and had drunk too much so didn't know what he had done until the next day, so he said. He said he was told he'd had an argument with his girlfriend and a guy who lived in the same street as him so had gone home to get a tool to fight the fella. His girlfriend had stopped him so he poured some petrol over her and lit a match and set her coat on fire. He said she wasn't burnt, just upset. He then said it wasn't until 3 months later that he was arrested over a domestic incident at their home that she reported him. He said he was then charged with GBH and subsequently given a 6-year IPP sentence. I could tell he was minimising his offence because you don't get a 6- year IPP sentence for burning someone's coat.

Martin was next. He was 6' 3" and had been away since he was 18 years old. He came across as a bit of a Mummy's boy as he didn't stop talking about her. He had a posh accent and a mop of hair that Kojak would have been proud of. He was also very naive. He was also someone you prayed your daughter would never bring home. His story was short and lacked any real emotion as he had just been given his D-Cat so would be moving to an open prison any time soon. He really didn't want to talk about his crime but after hearing what he did say in these few moments I believed he was a proper nut job. He said he had killed his girlfriend because he'd met someone else. The nut then said that he had killed her because he didn't want to upset her. He then tried to give a reason for his deviant behaviour by saying his own Dad had cheated on his Mummy which had caused the family lots of stress and suffering. And, because of that he thought it would be better to kill his girlfriend than put her through the same misery. Martin was a fucked -up individual and his thinking was so off key. I couldn't believe they were letting him out, because with thinking like that he would definitely be back. I could see as Martin was speaking how his Dad's affair had affected him. You could see how disgusted it made him feel. In his own eyes what his Dad had done was more heinous than what he had done to his poor girlfriend, whose only crime was to love a psychopath. I really did worry for Martin's Dad as I could see him killing him one day for what he had done to his Mummy.

Jabbi was next, but he too had just gotten his D-Cat. He said he was leaving in a few weeks. He told me he had learnt a lot whilst at Grendon. He told me to trust in my group

Terry Ellis

members, then wished me well. Jabbi was in for robbery this time, his last sentence was for rape. He portrayed himself as a model prisoner but I never got the chance to know him.

Dan was supposed to talk next but he was in a bad mood. He just welcomed me to the group and said he was doing a sentence for robbery and carrying a firearm. Dan was a big guy and I could see he was psychopath material.

Daryl was next. He was another big guy 15 stone, 6' and in his 40s. He came across as a bit of a geezer. He was white but talked like a black man and wore his trousers round his arse and even walked with a spring in his step. He looked like a proper mug especially with his cap on back to front. I just hoped he wasn't another deviant. He was now my last hope of finding someone half normal in this group. I crossed my fingers and waited for him to start.

Daryl went a bit round the houses before I found out what he was in for. He said he was a robber who used to rob drug dealers. Just before he was due to go into rehab he'd decided to have one last fix ,so he phoned a dealer who he arranged to meet behind some shops. By the time the dealer got to him Daryl had started 'clucking', which meant the only thing on his mind was getting the drugs at any cost. When the dealer asked him for the money for the drugs, Daryl panicked and pulled a knife on the guy and demanded that the guy give him the drugs. The guy just laughed it off as he thought Daryl was joking so to prove his point Daryl punched the guy in the face forgetting he still had the knife in his hand, which meant the guy had now been stabbed in the face. He started fighting back so Daryl stabbed him in the chest straight through the heart. The guy then slumped forward bleeding in his seat. Daryl went through the guys pockets and retrieved a small amount of drugs, then scarpered not realising the guy was dying in a pool of blood. Daryl said he never intended to kill the fella. Daryl constantly mentioned the guy's name and seemed to be deeply troubled by what he had done. Out of all the guys I had met in here this morning he came across as the most genuine. I could also see that Daryl was the alpha male of the group.

It was now my turn. I said I was doing a sentence for robbery where we used to pull up in police cars and vans. There were normally 5 of us all wearing police uniforms complete with flashing lights and Alsatian dogs. We would enter buildings or factories and ask to see the Manager or the Head of Security who we would show a search warrant to so we could search the premises for drugs or guns. Once we were inside we would handcuff everyone and secure the premises, then we would radio one of our guys who was waiting outside in the lorry so he could drive in and then we would have a load up. I was then asked by Monkey Boots to explain about the robbery that had brought me to prison. The place was called Verizon Business in St Pancras Way , Kings Cross. It's a large Telecommunications company that holds computer chips and motherboards. The place had 8 security guards on duty , 4-night cleaners and technicians. It had a biometric swipe card system but our biggest problem was the main entrance as it was on a main road and there were 3 police stations in the area which meant there were police cars driving past every five minutes.

We needed about an hour to get the motherboards out which meant we couldn't afford getting seen going in. We pulled up on the pavement outside the place with blue flashing lights on, a dog on lead and us in police uniforms so the security guards inside could see us on their cameras, also they could see us from the lobby. I could see 5 security guards when we pulled up, the rest were patrolling the building, so I got their attention by showing then my warrant card and my mate was beside me with the dog. We looked the part so I pressed the buzzer and said we were a fast response team and that we had reports that there was a robbery at this address adding someone had been seen on the roof so could they open up so we could search the building.

The first security guard came over and I showed him my ID card again, then he opened the door. All the guards were wearing biometric cards around their necks so we had to get them off fast as the cards opened every door in the place. If we couldn't get them we would be fucked. But, as usual our ruse worked as all the guards believed we were real police officers which once again went in our favour as we never use weapons on any of our jobs. Once the doors were opened I told the Head Security Guard to follow me into one of the stairwells. Once inside I told him that for my protection and my officer's protection all the guards had to be handcuffed until we found out who everyone was, with that he put his hands behind his back and then told the others to do likewise. We then rounded all the guards up, 10 in all plus 4 cleaners and two technicians. We then left one of our guys on the reception to man the phones and monitor the security cameras. We then went to work for the next hour, even letting the night workers in. We put all the guards in the stairwell and left one of our guys to look after them with the dog.

Once we found what we were looking for we called over the radio for the 5 carriers to come in so they could take all the motherboards out. There were 10 of us, 5 in police uniforms and 5 plain clothes. After we finished I thanked the guards for their co-operation, then we were gone. It had taken just over an hour but it was worth it as we had £5,000,000 worth of computer chips. I was nicked a year later. After I finished they all looked a bit gobsmacked but what did they expect, I wasn't like them, I was proper.

Terry Ellis

After our Small Groups we had to go downstairs to the community room for what was called 'feedback', which meant all the Group came together after each therapy session to explain what was going on in each Group in detail. One person from each Group had to speak for about 10 minutes about everything that had been said. This was to let the whole community know what was going on with certain people, so that everyone would be aware at the same time that a Group member was going through some difficulty. These feedbacks lasted for about 30 minutes on Monday, Tuesday and Wednesdays.

When we finished I went straight back to my cell and had a cuppa as I was emotionally spent, especially after listening to Bilal and all the others and for a moment I wondered what the fuck I was doing here as I was only a robber and would be out regardless of doing any therapy. Why was I putting myself through all this bollocks? I was nothing like this fucking mob who were all off key. I had come here for answers as to why I was a criminal, but after being here for 3 months I was starting to think that being a criminal wasn't such a bad thing compared to this lot. I had principles. I never fucked over old people or messed with women or kids. I was a clean-living person who never once physically hurt anybody on any of the jobs I did. I looked after my family, I carried no shame unlike these guys who destroyed lives and compared to them I was practically an angel. So why was I here? Did I really want to change or was I just going through the motions of change? The only thing I really knew was that if I ever got nicked again I would be a very old man before I got out of prison so to run now would be a shame. If I wanted to stay I had to stop focusing on the deviants and using their crimes as an excuse for me to quit because I was also a scumbag who had robbed and humiliated people. I'd even hurt my kids by me being here so if I left now without completing therapy I would be letting them down. For that reason, I had to stay.

I had a pretty restless night and I wasn't in the best of moods in the morning for going to my Group, so I took it easy and went downstairs for breakfast. I also had a chat with Mac. I explained to him how I felt about the guys in my Group but Mac just smiled and said he went through the same thing when he started his Group. He said that I shouldn't take it to heart as it would take me a few weeks to get used to my Group members, for the time being I should just sit back and listen to them and see what was going on around the wing. Mac said it was a mad place to live but if I wanted to survive Grendon and all the lunacy then I'd better concentrate on what I really wanted out of Grendon. It was good advice so I thanked him and then went to my Group.

I was the last one to enter the room so I just said "good morning" and took my seat, everyone replied likewise except Bilal who had a face like a smacked arse.

Living amongst the beasts: The rise and fall of the Grendon experiment

The Group was called to order, Monkey Boots asked if anyone had a minute, Daryl and Bilal put their hands up. Daryl took his minute first. He talked about his daughter and girlfriend. Bilal then asked to use the group. He said he had received a letter from the courts and he reckoned they'd made a mistake when they worked out the amount of time he had to serve as their new calculations had just put 3-years on his sentence. He said he wasn't happy about it then started effing and blinding. Monkey Boots tried to calm him down but he just went on and on then he started crying and saying that he had just got used to the fact he had to do 15 years but now with the added 3, he now had to do 18 years. He then said he'd already had a heart attack brought on by all the stress and even his kidneys had packed up and he was now on dialysis which he had to do every 3 days and the reason he had tried to commit suicide only 2 months before.

The whole Group looked concerned about him, Jabbi in particular as it was him who had cut Bilal down. They were now all trying to calm Bilal down. Terry P gave him a tissue, Martin was saying "it's going to be alright Bilal", Rob was patting him on the shoulders, even Dan the group psychopath was giving him words of comfort. Daryl added his 2 pence worth. As for me I had to contain myself from laughing. After a few minutes I'd really had enough so I raised my hand and asked Monkey Boots if I could say something. The room went quiet as everyone looked at me. I took a deep breath and said "see you, you little prick, you have killed a little kid and ruined his brothers' and Mums' life and probably the whole fucking families life for that matter and you now have the audacity to sit there and complain about doing an extra 3-years. Are you for fucking real you fucking parasite? If I had my way you would never get out of prison you little prick". With that I sat back in my seat. Bilal's face looked a picture and the rest of them looked somewhat perplexed. What surprised me the most was Daryl's reaction as he went into one, by ripping Bilal a new arsehole. He called him all the cunts under the sun adding "what you did to that little kid was disgusting, you little bastard". With that Bilal ran out of the group followed by Jabbi who said we were out of order and that he wouldn't be coming back to the Group. After they'd gone I looked over at Daryl who said he had been waiting a long time to say that but had bottled out of it because he feared upsetting Bilal and Jabbi. I looked over to Monkey Boots and said I thought that went well mate, he said that sometimes the truth hurts people but next time try and say it without all the swearing Terry. When I thought about what he said I realised he was right as I could have said the same thing without all the profanity as now I had alienated myself from most of the group. At least Daryl was OK but I could see from Terry P, Dan and Martin they were a bit upset as they could see things were going to change on this Group. No more fucking about patting each other on the back but I had learnt a lesson, I needed to take all the swearing out of my arguments if I wanted to move forward. So, good advice from Monkey Boots, I would take it on board. I had enjoyed this morning.

Terry Ellis

CHAPTER THIRTEEN

That afternoon Kevin, one of the Officers, popped his head into my cell to ask me how I was doing which then gave him an invitation to come in and sit down on my bed, a situation I still felt very uncomfortable with. But, there was nothing I could do or say about it as I was still on my best behaviour. He talked for about 20 minutes about the wrongs and rights of Grendon which I found rewarding as Kevin was quite passionate about the benefits that therapy had to offer. However, that all changed the moment he started talking about religion as the stupid git tried to convert me into becoming a Mormon, which I found somewhat disconcerting as his whole demeanour changed as he talked about the Mormons ideology. The whole situation felt surreal and for a moment I just switched off and asked myself what was it about me that attracted all the religious nutters towards me. First there was bible basher Andy and now Mormon Kevin, was God trying to tell me something or did I need to be more assertive when dealing with the bedlam brigade.

No sooner had Kevin left than Derek walked in and parked his arse on my bed, folded his arms then introduced himself to me. The moment Derek opened his mouth I knew we would get on as he had a good way about him even though he was a bit of a snob and looked down his nose when he spoke, I liked him. After a few minutes of being in his company he started to open up to me. He told me that Kevin, the Officer who had just left my cell, had just come back to the wing after taking a few months off as he'd had a breakdown whilst working on the wing. Apparently, Kevin had been found up on the 3s landing in one of the cells rocking back and forth and talking to himself. He'd had a proper melt down. Since he'd come back to the wing his whole personality had changed. He was constantly smiling and talking about God. It was a classic case of the nutters running the asylum as Kevin was now a Facilitator on one of the Groups. I believe this was due to the lack of funding and not Kevin's experience as a Therapist. I was just lucky not be on his group. As Derek told me this he couldn't stop laughing, his facial expressions made me nearly wet myself.

Living amongst the beasts: The rise and fall of the Grendon experiment

It felt good to finally be able to laugh especially after what I'd been through over the last 3 months. Derek was like a breath of fresh air. After a few minutes he asked if I wanted a coffee and biscuits in his cell which I thought was quite civilized of him, so I agreed and off we went to his cell.

A few minutes after being in Derek's cell he pointed out a photo of a pretty woman who he said was his late wife. He said she died about 6 years ago and it was him who had killed her. For some reason I said I was sorry for his loss, then I asked how she died. Derek said they had been together for 36 years He had a £1,000,000 house, a gardener and even a cleaner came in every day. She was the love of his life, she kept herself in good condition by going to the gym most days. Derek said he had worked away from home most of their married life as he worked on the oil rigs, which meant for 6 months of the year his wife was left on her own. Compared to Derek his wife looked about 20 years younger, as poor Derek hadn't aged well as he had the looks of someone much older than his years. Also, while the cats away the mice will play. Apparently, she had been going to swinger's parties on her own which Derek said he never had a clue about until he retired.

One night she said they were both going to a dinner party but once they got there she got him a drink and put her keys in a bowl on the bar. A minute later a fella picked her keys up and came over to her, they both then went upstairs without so much as a word to poor old Derek. He said it took him a couple of minutes to figure out what was going on but once the penny dropped he was out of there like a shot. Derek was a passive sort of guy and didn't like any sort of confrontation so he just went home.

When his wife arrived home a few hours later he never said a word to her he just carried on as if nothing had happened. A few weeks later she said she was going on holiday with her mates and like an idiot Derek agreed. On her return she showed Derek loads of photos of her and her mates dancing with different blokes but once again Derek kept quiet as he didn't want to lose her. This carried on for months as Derek thought it would all blow over but it didn't. One night she came home from one of her parties and dropped a bombshell on him by asking for a divorce. Not content with half of everything she also wanted an extra 300 grand or she would grass him up to the tax man regarding all the private work he had done over the years, as he had put all the cheques through her account and she could prove it all. She also told him that she had met someone else, someone younger. Derek pleaded with her to stay but she wouldn't listen, all she wanted was a divorce. The more he pleaded the more spiteful she became, she mocked his prowess by telling him stories about her new young lover which Derek said was the catalyst that sent him into a rage, which brought about her tragic demise. He said he

Terry Ellis

pushed her to the floor then straddled her whilst at the same time putting his hands around her neck and strangled her until she was dead. He then put her dead body in the boot of his car and booked a ticket on Eurostar as he had decided to take her body to France. In happier times they had enjoyed stays there in their favourite hotel, which he thought, should be her last resting place.

He booked into the hotel but after a few days her body started to smell which in turn alerted the staff so Derek went to the police and tried to confess. Due to the language barrier they couldn't understand him and as he was still in a right old state after killing her they thought he was just another English nut job so they flung him out of the police station. Derek went back to the hotel, grabbed hold of the Manager and showed him the body which prompted the Manager into phoning the police. Derek spent a year in a French prison before he was deported back to Blighty where he received a life sentence with a minimum 14- year tariff and at the age of 68 Derek still had 6 years to serve. As Derek finished telling me this I told him that I remembered reading about his case some years ago and to think I was now in the presence of deviant royalty so to speak.

Derek also showed me another photo of a woman on his picture board who he called his little treacle. She was a school teacher and had been visiting him for a number of years. He also showed me a few photos of his children and grandson who he said he doted over. I asked Derek what his kids felt about him killing their Mum. He said it had been hard on them and for a number of years they returned all his letters and when they did write they would address the letter to 'dear murderer', but that all stopped the day the kids went through their Mum's belongings. Amongst the boxes they found their Mum's diaries which detailed all of her affairs and even mentioned the night Derek went to the swingers party with her and how she humiliated him. Once the kids found these diaries they asked Derek why he hadn't told them of her infidelities. He said he loved her and didn't want to blacken their Mums name so with this new information they forgave him. Now they send him photos of the grandkids and letters but he said it was still early days and he and the kids were taking it one day at a time.

I then asked him about the hair dye situation and what he really wanted it for. He said he just wanted to look his best when his school teacher girlfriend came up, adding that he still couldn't understand why his group had backed him for the hair dye and then voted against him the moment Smitty opposed it. He said it was always the same at Grendon. Whenever Smitty objected to something the whole wing would side with him, adding that he believed Smitty only objected to most things to get a reaction as part of therapy was to see if people could let go of things rather than holding onto them as it's a behaviour that got most of them into trouble in the first place. I suppose there was some logic in it as I too was one of those people who couldn't let go if I thought I was right. Unfortunately for Derek he also couldn't let go because as soon as he came out of the wing meeting he had asked to see the prison Governor. He had also written a letter of complaint against Smitty. He also reinforced his behaviour by telling everyone who would listen that in all the women's prisons hair dye could be bought. If that was the case then why did he have to ask for permission? He felt it was wrong as we were all supposed to be treated as equals in prison.

After I left Derek's cell I bumped into my other next-door neighbour a young guy called Andy. Andy's nickname was Stutter because when he spoke he talked so fast that he tripped over his own words which made him stutter. Andy was about 25, a friendly sort of guy who had been in prison for 11 years out of his life sentence. He was 6' 1" and had shoulders the width of a barn door but unfortunately the brain of a peanut. He asked me in for a cup of tea and a chat. We talked about Grendon for about 20 minutes but like most of the guys here what he really wanted to do was unburden himself of his crimes. He said he was in for murder. He and his best mate had been watching the news and the news item was about the killing of James Bulger, a case where a little kid had been taken from a shopping centre and then stoned to death by two little pricks on a railway line. On hearing this on the news Andy and his mate thought it would be a good idea to try and emulate the crime by going out and killing a kid. When I asked him "why?" he said that he and his mate were just bored as there was nothing to do where they lived. "Surely it wasn't purely out of boredom " I asked but he said yes honest mate it was. "What happened next?" I asked. He said he wanted to kidnap and kill a young kid just like the Bulger kid so he and his mate could be famous. They went looking around their town but it started raining so the town was deserted and because it was raining he and his mate had ducked under a bridge to shield themselves from the rain. As they were waiting they saw someone sleeping under some boxes so they took a peep under it and saw it was an old tramp so decided to kill the old man.

Andy said he picked up a large concrete slab then stood over the old guy, raised the slab over his head at the same time looking at his mate who was encouraging him on so he couldn't back out. He smashed the concrete down on the old man's face. He said the old man opened his eyes just before his face was smashed in. He even put his hands up but it was too late as Andy kept smashing it down on the guys' head until it was flattened. He said once it was over he panicked as there was blood everywhere all over him and his mate. But he said his mate just stood there laughing. They covered the guy with boxes and went home as if nothing had happened. A few days later they were arrested as they had been seen on CCTV walking across town, also their DNA had been found on the old guy.

Terry Ellis

I stayed in Andy's cell for a few minutes after he told me this, then I made an excuse to get out of there and prayed to God that Andy didn't ever get bored again as poor old Derek lived opposite him.

The day before, I had arranged to meet Craig on exercise as he had passed his induction and was now on B-wing. I was pleased to see him as he was one of the good guys and someone I could talk to as he was the only guy I knew who wasn't a fucking deviant or a nut job. As I walked out onto the exercise yard I could see Craig sitting there with a guy called Bradley. We both greeted each other like long lost friends even though it had only been a week since I last saw him. Mac also joined us so I left him to talk to Craig whilst I started talking to Craig's mate Bradley. Bradley was about 6' 2" and in his 40s, he had a little scar over his eye which gave him a sinister look. He also had a cockney accent like mine which made me warm to him. He said he had been in therapy for 8 months. He was also finding it difficult as he hated having to mix with all the deviants on his wing, but because he was a lifer he had no choice but to put up with it. I had heard Bradley's name before so I asked him if it was true that he was Reggie Kray's boyfriend. He looked a bit put out by my question but answered me anyway.

He said he had met Reggie in Parkhurst but he himself wasn't gay as he was groomed by Reggie over a long period. He said Reggie had bought him presents and even took him on visits to meet some of Reggie's celebrity friends.

As Bradley was naive and vulnerable he succumbed to temptation as Reggie was a master manipulator who he now believed took advantage of him. For many years he believed they were good friends with benefits so to speak. He said he actually liked Reggie's company as they played chess together and talked a lot about boxing as it was his and Reggie's passion. Brad said that since he had come to Grendon he hadn't really thought of Reggie as a predator but now believed he had been taken advantage of and to finally be able to talk about it had helped him immensely and now he has accepted that Reggie had used him like a piece of meat and not the friend he thought he was. However, Brad intimated to me that he was writing a book about his time with Reggie which he hoped would show their relationship in a different light. He also said he had photos of them playing chess and other board games in their cell and drinking etc, a side of Reggie that only he knew and understood which he hoped would humanise Reggie in the eyes of the world.

Bradley also liked to name drop as he had met a lot of old villains over the years through his association with Reggie. He told me stories about one particular guy called

Living amongst the beasts: The rise and fall of the Grendon experiment

Dave Courtney, he said Dave had persuaded Bradley to do Reggie's funeral and he wanted to been seen as the enforcer of the underworld and doing the security would give him that kudos as he wanted to be a celebrity villain. As Dave ran a few doors up and down the country he would also be able to showcase his business, a win-win situation for him.

But being seen as a top geezer in the criminal underworld back-fired spectacularly on Dave as he boasted at the funeral that he had 500 doormen at his disposal that he could call on at a moment's notice. However, the old bill didn't take too kindly to what they saw as a threat, so overnight the constabulary joined forces up and down the country and gave every pub and club owner an ultimatum to get rid of Dave and his goons otherwise their licences would be revoked overnight.

Bradley was also a fitness fanatic like me so after our first meeting we would meet up regularly over the gym. We also talked most days about therapy and what was happening on our small Groups and to be honest I found him interesting and a pleasure to talk with. After I finished talking with him I spent the remainder of the exercise period talking with Craig and Mac but it was plain to see by the look on Mac's face that he felt nothing but disdain for Bradley regarding his past liaison with Reggie Kray and as the weeks passed I found it harder and harder to keep them apart. Mac would always mock or cast aspersions on Bradly's sexual orientation which became rather tedious at times but it was the price I had to pay for having them both as friends.

CHAPTER FOURTEEN

On Monday morning I made my way down to the community meeting as usual. We started off by doing the usual minutes, then it was time for the whole wing to take their backings for family day. As I was new to the wing the criteria dictated I would miss this opportunity as I had to be on the wing for 3 months before I could go for any backings. I sat back and listened as everyone went through the motions. Anyone who asked for a backing had to run the gauntlet of questions from their peers. Questions like 'who was coming up?' and 'what was their relationship with the person or persons?'. The questions were endless but it was the normal third degree from all the amateur psychologists on the wing. If you were lucky and actually received your backing from the wing it then had to go in front of the staff but most importantly it had to go in front of Lord Smitty who had the last word on everything that happened on the community. If you were successful after all that palaver your family and friends would be officially notified that they would be allowed onto the wing for dinner and even get a chance to look into your cell. There would also be a raffle and tea and cakes laid on, it would be a merry day for all the family. A family day meant that you could spend 6 or 7 hours with your family which to me was a good enough incentive for me to keep my nose clean.

After all the backings were done we were all given jobs to do for the big day. I was also given a permanent job of cleaning the toilets and showers every day. The Chairman then asked for volunteers to repaint the wing, repot plants, buff the floors and clean all the windows. My voluntary job was to serve tea and cakes on family day with Mac. It was hoped that by me doing these jobs we would feel part of the community. It was also something I was looking forward to as it would make a refreshing change from the normal mundane rigors of prison life and plus, it would be nice to see a few smiling faces around the wing.

Once all the jobs were allocated it was then time for a member of the community to do his assessment. An assessment meant you had to read aloud a comprehensive dossier

Living amongst the beasts: The rise and fall of the Grendon experiment

on yourself and your crimes which would give the whole community the opportunity to see you for what you really were and not the sugar-coated version you have been giving them for the last 6 months in your small therapy Groups and also to your friends. This is what Lord Smitty had been preparing on you for months, so God forbid you missed any of the gory details out as he would take you through it bit by bit, asking you at the same time to read it out loud and once he was satisfied he would then back track and ask you why you had negated the negative parts, adding you were trying to deny yourself and the existence of your deviant past or for that matter your part in it. Most on the wing had seen the consequences of this behaviour so came clean on the day, which in turn meant said deviant walked around with his head down for a few days as his true nature had been exposed to his new deviant friends who now saw him as more deviant than they were. Today's lucky recipient was Chris.

Chris was an unassuming quiet guy of about 5' 6", 11 stone wringing wet with an old style 60s mullet. He came across as a gormless looking twit but cross him at your peril as he had a reputation for chucking piss under your door if you upset him. Chris I was told was also a good artist and had lots of his work up on the walls and around the prison. Chris lived opposite Mac on the 2s landing and most days when I popped in to see Mac I always saw Chris in his cell with gay Ian playing on their PlayStations. Their game of choice was always golf which I found quite amusing considering what he had done with a gold club.

You see Chris used to be the landlord of a pub-come-restaurant and one night when he had finished late he decided that he'd had enough of the restaurant game and life in general and the only way out for him was to make a fresh start which meant no ties. He made his way upstairs to his flat where he was met by his wife who was preparing his dinner while their 2 year-old baby daughter was asleep in her bed. He said he ran a bath then had dinner with his wife. After they'd finished he called her into the front room where he produced a nine-iron golf club and as she entered the room he crept up behind her and smashed her head in until it was pulp. He said all he could remember of the murder was her shouting "what are you doing Chris?" and "why Chris?" but he said he couldn't stop, he just kept whacking her until she was dead.

His baby girl was 2 years old and upon hearing her Mum crying she climbed out of bed to investigate. She walked in to the front room calling out for her Mummy and on seeing her Mum lying there the baby went straight to her side and started cuddling her at the same time she got covered in blood. On seeing this Chris walked over to her but he said something strange came over him. He said the baby was smiling and putting her arms out for him to hold her but before he knew it he was smashing her head in. He said the

Terry Ellis

blood was everywhere and he just lost it and went completely mad. He said he sat there looking at them for hours before moving their bodies to the cellar believing once he got rid of their corpses all his troubles would be over and that he could begin his new life. A few days later her parents came around and saw all the blood over the walls and ceiling and immediately called the police which meant the game was up for Chris.

The whole community sat there completely shocked by his crime but mostly by his lack of remorse or any emotional response for what he had done. He didn't even say sorry for what he had done, he just sat there and answered everyone's questions as cool as a cucumber. He was one very cold cunt who stayed in control of his emotions at all times. He really was a nasty piece of work and over all the months I knew him he was always polite. Every now and again his mask would slip as he would give you a look but that was all as like most women and child killers he was a fucking coward. Chris was also a people pleaser because no matter what happened on the wing he would always support both sides. It was his way of manipulating everyone as it kept him off the revenge radar.

Apart from this assessment I never heard Chris speak in any of the community meetings. In fact, the only time I heard anything about him was from feedbacks from his Group. On one occasion he accused his Group Facilitator Jamie of treating him differently when he came back from leave after his wife had a baby. The accusation was a load of drivel as Chris would do anything to detract from doing any real work on his Group. Even his own Group had tried on a number of occasions to put him in the book for not using the therapeutic process, but Smitty had always overturned them so nothing ever came of it. Unfortunately, being submissive to the point of being subservient was the acceptable face on C-wing as this was enough to keep you safe if you were a deviant because having an opinion was deemed a behavioural problem. So, Chris and most of the others kept out of the spotlight which meant they learnt early on in therapy that out of sight meant out of mind. The staff perpetuated this kind of behaviour. I believe they thought that if everyone on C-wing portrayed some sort of harmony when it came to opposing factions the whole world would believe real change was happening at Grendon. Unfortunately, that was not the case as a lot of the guys abused the chance they had been given at Grendon.

After the meeting I was again believing that nothing could ever shock me but then I met Shaun. He was a peculiar sort of chap and probably one of the most dangerous serial rapists I met at Grendon. He was about 6' 2", ginger haired, had a long beard and kept himself to himself. He was a keep fit fanatic who was always running. On the outside he used to work as a sports Psychologist. He also lectured at a university, a job that afforded him the opportunity to meet young girls who he would eventually go on to rape. I was told by one of the Group members that when the net was finally closing in on him he went to the beach, drank 2 bottles of whisky then tried to commit suicide by cutting his wrists, but his deviant luck was in as a young woman chanced upon him and quickly bandaged his wrists before he died. When he came to he thanked her in the only way he knew by raping her and leaving her for dead. By all accounts he was a proper piece of work but like most rapists he was a coward because as soon as Mac and myself came on the wing he told his group he felt uncomfortable being around so many dominant personalities so he just pulled out of therapy. Even being near him at first made my skin crawl. He also had a bad hygiene problem as he stank to high heaven and his cell was like a cesspit. Every time he came near me I couldn't help but imagine what those poor women had gone through.

One day when I was over the gym he asked if he could jump in with me as I was doing some bench presses, I said yes to be polite as I was still on my best behaviour. No sooner had we started I imagined myself dropping the bar across his neck but somehow, I kept myself in check. However, he took my act of kindness as a sign of friendship and over the next couple of months we spoke about therapy. He would give me advice on how to approach therapy. I found him quite knowledgeable and extremely intelligent even though his thoughts on therapy were quite extreme at times as even he himself thought that a rapist could never change which he said was the reason he had really pulled out of therapy. He also said he disliked confrontational therapy as the lines of mutual respect at best became blurred.

Even though he was self-opinionated I learnt a lot from him over those first 4 months. However, I wasn't sorry to see him go as he, like most of the rapists on the wing, displayed similar traits to each other like when a woman came onto the wing they would never look at her for fear of being seen as a rapist. I noticed this behaviour on many occasions. I think they believed that if they never showed any interest in a woman then the Psychologist would believe they had changed. It was so pathetic at times it was laughable but they all carried on with the pretence. The best one was that they never purchased any porn magazines for it would be noted and put in a future report, instead they would borrow them secretly from each other. This sort of manipulating was characteristic amongst the deviants and something I found disconcerting as all the rapists I met at Grendon would tell me that rape wasn't about sex and just like Shaun they all portrayed themselves as the real victims. They would use every excuse in the book to justify their actions and God forbid that you ever asked one of them a question in one of the community meetings as they would always say they didn't feel safe talking about their crimes as it was too painful. When that excuse didn't work they went back to the tried and tested one, that they felt bullied, which gave them a free pass by Smitty to hide in

Terry Ellis

their cells. This was due partly because of their shame, a common trait in all of them and when that didn't work they would all self-harm. One guy actually put bleach in his eyes just to get out of therapy and for him it worked.

My own experience of rapists on the wing was that they only last a few months as they became angry at being asked questions regarding their index offences, especially if the question came from someone with no understanding of their crimes, which told me that they should never have been placed on the wing in the first place as their crimes should have dictated what wing they should have been placed on. At least then with like-minded rapists they would have felt more at ease working with each other as who better to link in with than their own kind. I looked at Shaun and the others and felt that they had been given a wasted opportunity, all because of the amateurish induction process here at Grendon.

CHAPTER FIFTEEN

Today the wing was a hive of activity. Geordie Gary who was in his 40s, 6' 1", well-built and about 15 stone was in charge of buffing all the ground floor and delegating the cleaning for the forthcoming family day. I had known Gary for about 4 months. He told me he was in for armed robbery. He portrayed himself as some sort of hard man. He was always talking about all the gangsters he knew up in Newcastle but unfortunately it all turned out to be hot air to detract from the fact that he was just another 2-bob cunt which came as a surprise to me as I liked his company and enjoyed talking with him on the exercise yard, but all that changed the day he read out his assessment.

Geordie Gary had broken into an old man's house beaten the old geezer until he was unconscious and, in the process, broke the guys arm and nose, a despicable act from a low-life scum bag. It was also freezing cold and the middle of winter so for good measure Gary turned off the electricity as he left the house. It took the old man 3 days before he froze to death. The funny thing about Gary was he always slagged off the deviants, especially anyone who had killed old people.

But today he had to read out his own assessment and come clean about his past deviant behaviour. It was really a wake-up call for me because over the years I had trusted people for no other reason than they lived or came from the same area as me or because they acted the part. So, Gary's betrayal actually taught me a valuable lesson, not to trust anybody ever again period. As I looked over at Gary his face was a picture, another wanker who went from hero to zero. He couldn't look me or Mac in the face after that day, so to make up for his shame he took it out on the rest of the community as he was always arguing with his small Group and all the staff. He even threatened to kill poor old Henry the wing hoover after someone turned it on early one morning and Grendon being Grendon the whole situation was blown out of proportion as Gary was winged by his small Group for threats to kill. The whole thing looked farcical as he was put up on a commitment and nearly voted out of Grendon. However, it was easy to see the logic

Terry Ellis

behind the commitment and the reason for it so I held back from asking him any silly questions. He spent about an hour in the hot seat answering questions like "what did Henry ever do to you?" and "where did your head go mate?", "what were you feeling/thinking at the time or was it misplaced anger left over from your assessment?" The questioning went on for about an hour before Gary broke down begging for forgiveness and pleading not be thrown out of Grendon.

That happened a week ago and now he was in charge of getting the place ship-shape for family day and just to prove that he had turned a corner as far as his behaviour was concerned. This was Grendon working at its best, as they would break you down before building you back up and to see Gary working his bollocks off was justification enough that therapy was working in his case.

On the morning of the family day everyone had their best clothes on and all hostilities between the Groups had been suspended for the day, everyone acted as if they were the best of friends. The change in everyone wasn't motivated by compassion for each other, it was out of necessity, as we were aware that if there was any trouble family days would be lost forever. So, it was big smiles all round as we waited for the visitors to enter the wing. I took my place behind the tea urn with Mac serving the teas, while Mac gave out cakes and biscuits. We probably had the best job as it gave us the chance to meet everyone's family, which would make a refreshing change as they treated us as equals instead of patients in a nut ward.

That morning before we came down I could feel the buzz of excitement coming from my fellow Grendonites as the anticipation of weeks of preparation was finally upon us. We were all up bright and early this morning ironing our clothes. I had to come down earlier and turn on the tea urn which had 20 or so gallons of water hoping I had turned it on in time as the visitors were now coming onto the wing. So, when the red light came on indicating that the water was ready my relief was palpable. Also, the feeling of accomplishment that my work station was now ready to greet our honoured guests gave me a sense of pleasure which must have been seen etched across my smiling face.

The dining room soon come alive with all my fellow Grendonites families. Also, the community and therapy rooms would be used as dining areas, so individual family groups could eat together making it a proper family experience. There were even tables in the hall way for the over-spill of visitors. Even the garden was open to the visitors today so they could walk off their dinners. Also, if they were lucky enough they could get their photos done.

Living amongst the beasts: The rise and fall of the Grendon experiment

The thinking behind this charade of normality was to put our visitors minds at rest that we were living the therapeutic dream, especially when they saw the fish tanks and manicured gardens and lawns. But what they didn't know was that the gardens were out of bounds to us and only used 3 times a year on family days but still we all pretended to play along with the masquerade for the benefit of the watching Psychologists and our families. It was a small price to pay to see them all happy believing we were all living the dream in our very own therapeutic utopia.

The first visitors to enter the wing were Bilal's, his 3 sisters were all done up to the nines, all wearing their Sunday best. They were all smiles as they greeted their infanticidal killing brother as if he was an upstanding pillar of society and he standing there smiling back like a well-groomed peacock. It was a sight to behold.

Next through the door were Chris Golf Clubs family, which bemused me because if my son had killed his wife and daughter like that bastard did, I would disown the little prick. But I suppose it takes all sorts to make a world.

Dan's adopted husbands parents were next through the door. Dan's husband was doing a life sentence for killing two gypsies. I was told it was a fairy tale meeting by 2 psychopaths who met and then married in prison. Dan was a particularly strange chap because one minute he would be shouting from the rafters that he was gay, then the next minute in our small Groups he would turn into a 6', 17 stone gay hater. The guy was so fucked up and I found it hard at times to talk to him or even to take him seriously.

Next person to come through the door was Daryl's Mum who was all dressed up as if she was still 21, which used to drive Daryl insane as his Mum was in her 60s but to be honest she wasn't a bad looking woman, if you liked 50 Shades of Grey. Daryl was very protective of his Mum as she visited him every week and doted on him and it was very endearing. God only knows what the Psychologists made of it.

By now the families were flooding in. Eugene, a big black guy with arms the size of my head, was talking with his family. Eugene was doing 10 years for robbery. He was a likeable guy who the staff and Psychologists were terrified of, but I found him polite and always respectful. However most of the deviants on the wing were petrified of him as he spoke his mind when it came to them. He had only been on the wing for a few months but it was plain to see he wouldn't last long as Smitty wanted him off the wing from the start.

Terry Ellis

I went upstairs to use the toilet, on my way back I met Alex who was another rapist. Alex had refused to partake in any of the family days. He was an angry guy who had recently pulled out of therapy because he couldn't take it as his shame and ego wouldn't allow him to work. I had read about Alex in one of the newspapers. He was a sick puppy who should have been put down at birth as he thought he had a God given right to rape old women. He was a real sicko. After talking to him I bumped into Peter, a mixed-race guy of about 6' and 12 stone, who was another mixed-up individual who had been adopted at birth. Peter was an arsonist who had come to Grendon from a mental home. He was also gay and had an unhealthy infatuation regarding a young kid called Lewis who was on his Group. Lewis was in for killing an old man who he had been having a relationship with but had killed him after having sex. Another classic case of gay panic which was quite common amongst some of the young guys who had killed to hide their sexuality. Unfortunately, today Lewis wouldn't be having a visit from his Dad as he had been stopped at the gate drunk and in possession of cocaine, so now Lewis was crying and Peter was trying to calm him down. Things were hotting up and it wasn't even half past nine yet.

All the palaver at the gate had brought out all the screws in force. Kat a good-looking polish Officer and Pauline were now patrolling the wing gates. John, Dave, Jamie and Simon were on full alert marching up and down the corridors. It was turning into a right old pantomime.

I still hadn't made my mind up about all the screws on the wing yet because it was still early days, but they were growing on me as I could see they really cared about the guys on the wing.

There were still people coming in, Ricky had 2 good looking girls come up. Ricky was in for GBH. He couldn't read or write which made him angry at times. He was 6', 13 stone, ginger haired and came from Bermondsey. Even though he couldn't read he was good at expressing himself and I liked him.

Shaun the serial rapist was in the laundry on wash up duty today because nobody wanted him mixing with their families, especially after what had happened on G-wing. Apparently one of the rapists had rubbed himself off against one of the women who was visiting her husband on the pretence of trying to get by but she cottoned on to him after the fourth attempt and told her husband who subsequently knocked the guy out breaking the perverts jaw. Instant justice, the deviant was taken out of the prison the same day as the whole wing wanted to string him up.

Living amongst the beasts: The rise and fall of the Grendon experiment

After everybody had finished their meals it was then time to take a trip around the garden before having their photos taken. Then it was back inside as it was time for the finale, the raffle, which today consisted of hundreds of little items such as teddy bears, books and CDs. Everything was donated by various charities for the rehabilitation of the favoured few. Once the raffle was over it was time for the speeches.

Dan was the first one up. He thanked his parents for coming up and the staff for their contribution in keeping everyone safe over the last few months. He thanked the Psychologist whose understanding and professionalism had brought him to this point in his life. Then someone else got up and started saying how much Grendon had changed his life, blah, blah, blah. This went on for about 20 minutes and at the end I felt a bit sick of all the drivel. However, the staff, Psychologists, families and friends couldn't get enough of all the sycophantic bollocks as they all listened with open mouths, clapping and nodding their approval that their deviant sons had all turned the therapeutic corner. This out-pouring of benevolent good will was contagious as even I was clapping and joining in with the applause. It was akin to Stockholm Syndrome where the kidnapped started siding with their captors, which was worrying to say the least.

At 4 o'clock sharp all the visitors were asked to leave and after a few tears and tribulations all the tables and chairs were put away. Staff and inmates patted each other on the back before all getting ready for tea and early bang up, which we were all looking forward to. The whole day had flown by and after writing letters to all the charities for weeks and collecting money for all the food, it now felt like an anti-climax but, at the same time a surreal experience that I actually enjoyed. Even though I found the whole situation farcical at times and manipulatively deceiving on so many levels, it felt quite rewarding serving teas all day and being part of the whole process and even seeing some of the guys families and how much they all appreciated it. It made me more determined to one day having my own family day as I would love to see my girls faces and show them my cell with all my mod cons like TV, CD player and even my play station and don't forget the DAB radio. It would go a long way in putting their minds at rest that I was OK and that prison was nothing like it is portrayed on the TV. So, with that in mind, I was prepared to do whatever it took for me to get through to the next family day, for their sakes.

Terry Ellis

CHAPTER SIXTEEN

It was now only 4 weeks until Christmas and Anne, who worked over the Chaplaincy, had seconded me into joining the Christmas choir, playing a tambourine and singing Christmas carols, which wasn't that bad until she informed me that I was the only one out of the whole of C-wing that she had been able to persuade to sing this year. But, then to add insult to injury the only other singers she had been able to persuade were from the Jimmy Saville wing. Four of the wankers to be exact, I never asked their names but I was told by Craig that the guy I was standing there practising with was doing a life sentence for what I can only describe as a grotesque crime. He was about 65 years old, 5' 9", 11 stone and looked like any old grandad but he was a fucking monster who had killed his sister's baby. He had placed the baby in a pillow case before smashing her against the wall until every bone in her little body was broken. He then picked up a kitchen knife and crept into his sisters bedroom and stabbed her repeatedly until she too was dead.

A reprehensible crime by anyone's standards. I really couldn't understand why he was at Grendon. He was too old and set in his ways to ever change or be rehabilitated and to be honest I hated being around him but I had given my word to Anne that I would sing in her choir so basically, I couldn't pull out now. So, every Friday for the next 4 weeks I had to sing with the beasts on A-wing over at the church and my reward for all my efforts was that I was asked to sing a solo hymn by the Vicar as he said I had the voice for his favourite hymn. I couldn't really refuse him as I had asked him the week before to pray for my son, who was in the army. I prayed for his safe return as he was still in Afghanistan and, for this and Gods help I had promised to go to church every Sunday. Also, once a week I had promised to pop into the drop-in centre for coffee and biscuits and a little chat. As I've always been a man of my word I had to go, but what I had to endure for Gods help was really taking the piss but what could I do?

I was looking forward to Christmas as I had been told we would be having 2 weeks off from therapy, thank God. And, as I had volunteered for the choir I was given a free pass over Christmas, which meant I didn't have to volunteer myself or my services for any mundane jobs like running the wing cafe. The cafe was called the Chillax Cafe and was the brainchild of Adam, a lovely guy of about 35, 6', 12 stone but as nutty as a mad hatter on speed. Adam like a lot guys I'd met at Grendon was a good artist. His work had been shown in a number of prison magazines over the years.

His story was quite a sad one.

He used to be an alcoholic. He said he drank just to fit in. He would do anything for anyone and this I'm afraid was his downfall. He said one night he was in his flat drinking with 2 guys who started arguing with each other, which he said soon got out of hand as a fight broke out and the stronger one of the 2 guys ended up overpowering the weaker one and tying him up. He then started torturing the guy with a hot iron and a knife. Adam said he was so scared that he couldn't even move. He also believed the guy would turn on him if he said anything, so when the guy asked Adam to help him out he did as he was told. First, he helped to retie the fella as the bonds had worked themselves free, and for the next 8 hours he watched as the guy butchered his friend to death. He obeyed his every word and, in the morning, when they had both sobered up the enormity of what they had done hit home but, they still had a dead body on the floor with a kitchen knife sticking out of its chest. So, the sicko asked Adam to pull the knife out and put it in the bin. He also ordered Adam to clean the place from top to bottom while he went to fetch a wheelie bin for the body.

So, Adam cleaned the flat for what he said seemed like hours as there was blood everywhere, and when he had finished he realised his so-called mate still hadn't come back. Adam panicked and popped outside and retrieved his own wheelie bin, put the body in it and then dumped it about a mile away from the flat, job done he thought. However, the body was found 2 days later with Adam's door number on the wheelie bin. It didn't take long before the police were at his door with their forensic teams as both men were known to each other, so his flat was searched with a fine-tooth comb and the only DNA found on the body, knife, bin and iron was Adam's. His so-called mate, the real murderers DNA and prints had been wiped clean by Adam making him the number one suspect. He protested his innocence but to no avail. Adam said the police believed him but the evidence told another story. His mate denied everything and got off scot free and Adam got a life sentence. Adam said the only good thing that came out of it was he had found a real home in Grendon and didn't want to leave.

He also had a new best friend, a budgie called Sproggit who he loved more than life itself. He told me on more than one occasion that he didn't want to get out of prison, but

Terry Ellis

if and when he ever did he wanted to open his own cafe. He said that was the reason he volunteered every year to run the Chillax Cafe over Christmas, so he could get some experience. Adam was so naive, but as I said I liked him.

Up until now I hadn't done any real therapy, I'd only skipped over bits and pieces of my childhood and criminality. I'd also spoken about my childhood and the relationship I'd had with my Mum, but nothing too deep as I was still getting used to my Group as it was still the honeymoon period. But, I knew sooner or later I had to start doing some real work as I was getting bored of listening to my Group talking about the same old shit every day. They were always crying about their sentences and complaining at how hard their lives were, but to be honest I really didn't care or have any sympathy for them or their crimes. However, I was starting to understand that before I started any therapy I had to put my own house in order because I still had 3 girlfriends visiting me, which in the eyes of my Group and community was seen as a criminal behaviour. So, I had to do the right thing and let them all go so they could carry on with their lives. Years of cheating had left me with some pretty fucked up principles regarding relationships and juggling 3 women wasn't a problem for me as I'd done it all my adult life.

But, one day after a visit I was pulled into the office by Monkey Boots who tried to explain it to me and the reason why I cheated, which in turn made me realise why I had been unfaithful throughout all my adult life and for most of my relationships. It was due partly to my childhood. You see as a young kid I was put into a care home. My Mum was the one who dropped me off there, the person I loved more than anything in the word and would do anything for. I was only about 10 or 11, I thought she was only dropping me off for a couple of days, but the days turned into weeks. I still remember that first day because as it got dark outside my window, the staff showed me to my new room and informed me that this would be my new home for the foreseeable future. I never believed them so I sat up all night waiting for my Mum to come back but she never did. All I can remember was her smiling and walking away, waving and telling me she loved me. That one act of betrayal left an indelible mark on me and my subconscious, and I never trusted anyone again especially if they said they loved me and smiled at the same time, so I made sure I would never go through that pain again. That's why I always have someone to fall back on, which in my case were lots of women because if one left me in the morning then by the afternoon I would be in the arms of another as sex was the only thing I believed could make me feel loved and wanted again. So, after that visit I wrote to all of them pretending I had found someone new. I posted all the letters after Christmas as I didn't want to ruin their day and that was that I'm afraid to say.

Living amongst the beasts: The rise and fall of the Grendon experiment

I knew the Psychologist and staff would read my letters and inform Monkey Boots, who was now my Group Facilitator, so when I actually used my group there would be no ambiguity regarding my relationship status. With this in mind I carried on with renewed enthusiasm that I would be making a fresh start in the New Year, but first I had to get Christmas out of the way.

Christmas in prison is usually a time for reflection and contemplation but most of all it's a time for self-recrimination regarding family and friends as they come to the forefront, accompanied by feelings of guilt and sorrow caused by the suffering you have brought on them and others over the years from your incarceration. This self-flagellation is normally the catalyst for you to put pen to paper for the first time that year, so you put a few poignant words in a Christmas card hoping for clemency from the people you love the most. This outpouring of sadness and regret regarding your failings was normally enough to evoke or elicit a response from your most ardent proponents of your family such as the ex-wife or girlfriend. Through this gentle coercion you were likely to get a disproportionate amount of Christmas cards delivered to your cell doormat that year making you feel loved and appreciated by your ex-concubines. The most precious cards of all came from your nearest and dearest, but the most treasured of all came from your kids, and in my case my 3 girls and sons. So, as I looked upon my picture board this year at the 38 cards I'd received, it gave me the strength to carry on in my quest for enlightenment. As I walked the landing on C-wing looking at the empty picture boards in my fellow Grendonites cells it was easy to see why so many of them felt dejected at this time of the year. So, to cheer them all up I left my cell door open so they could bask in the warmth and sunlight of my overflowing picturesque grotto, with my new DAB radio playing Christmas carols in the background.

It was about this time I started to feel empathy for my fellow Grendonites which gave me a warm glow inside. I even asked Brian into my cell so as to remind him what it felt like to have a family, especially after he had killed all of his. I even mentioned to Golf Club Chris how good it felt to receive cards from my kids forgetting he too had killed his. After I wondered if I should apologise to both of them for my insensitivity but thought better of it as it wasn't me who had killed their families. However, I did remind myself to work on my sarcasm in the New Year. But for now, it was time to enjoy my Christmas.

I had brought £80 of goodies for the 2 weeks over Christmas. Chocolates, cakes, crisps you name it I had it. I would comfort eat my way through the holiday period watching films into the early hours, then sleep all day. I would only get up Christmas day to phone the kids, well that was the plan anyway. The rest of the wing had other ideas

Terry Ellis

as the newly appointed game's reps had organised pool and darts competitions, even a quiz night.

I walked into the community room and saw that Adam had already transformed it into the Chillax Cafe. He had also set up the karaoke machine for the days entertainment. There were all the old favourites such as Frank Sinatra 'That's Life', Tom Jones' 'Green Green Grass of Home' and of course 'White Christmas'. So, I had a go and sang 'Please Release Me, let me go', well it was Christmas. I also played chess with Brian and cards with Ian and Golf Club Chris. I was still dreading Friday as I still had to sing and play the tambourine over at the church, which was now being held at the old visitors hall next to the exercise yard. It was a one storey building with its' own stage and seating for about 200 people or more which I had been told would be packed to the rafters with inmates, staff and hundreds of do-gooders like ex-magistrates, voluntary organisations and charitable institutions such as the Grendon Trust whose actions are motivated by giving to the disenfranchised through handouts of musical instruments like keyboards, drums, guitars and even the tambourine I would be using. There would also be a brass band playing compliments of the Salvation Army, who too would be out in force dressed in their normal flamboyant regalia pumping out the tunes. And, as I pondered the thought of singing with them I started to practice my doh, ray, me in my best baritone voice, at the same time I prayed to God that I wouldn't fuck up on the night.

Friday morning, I was having breakfast with Mac, Scouse Mick and Daryl who were all teasing me about tonight's extravaganza which seemed to ease the anxiety I was feeling. The more they joked the more determined I was to hold up my end and the honour of the wing as they and the rest of the prison would all be there.

By 5 o'clock I was ready to go over to the hall for a sound check. Once there I helped out by putting out the chairs and tables and even helped the old Salvation men and women with their instruments and by 6 o'clock we were ready and waiting as they started coming through the doors. The first to be allowed in were the outside visitors, there were loads of old birds and geezers, Probation Officers and Psychologists from all over the prisons. Once they were all seated it was time for the inmates. A-wing and the Jimmy Saville merchants were first through the door followed by B, C, D and G-wing, all beaming with smiles from ear to ear. I tried my best not to make eye contact with Mac or Mick so as not to distract me as the last thing I needed was to break out into a fit of laughter watching them pull silly faces.

The Vicar then got up on stage and started off the nights proceedings with a few well-chosen jokes to get the audience going before he settled into a long speech about donkeys and the baby Jesus and the three wise men. After him the Governor got up and said a few words, the brass band played, the whole atmosphere was cordial, an escapism from the reality of prison life which we as prisoners grasp with both hands on the odd occasions we are lucky enough to get them, just like tonight. To the outside world it must have looked like a night of decadent moral decline seeing so many weirdos and deviants in one place singing along at the top of their voices with the Salvation Army, but that was Grendon for you, unconventional. I suppose it was designed that way to bring about change in its' morally corrupt graduates.

It was now time for me to go up on stage to sing my Christmas carol, but as I looked out at the audience I couldn't help but wonder what my kids would make of all this. Would they see it as me turning a corner or would they be laughing their socks off? I prayed that they too were having a good time on this special night. I took a deep breath and sang my heart out with my backing band of DJ Saville's and by the time we were finished the guys on our wing were up on their feet clapping and giving it large. The rapturous applause seemed to last an age. Scouse Mick and Mac were standing on their seats and from the look on their faces it was plain to see that the night had been a success. All that was left to do now was eat all the Christmas pies that had so kindly been laid on by the prison Chaplaincy then it was back to the wing. Before we left we spent a little time talking and mixing with all the old dears', Probation Officers, staff and Psychologists, congratulating ourselves on what was a night of opulent indulgence before heading back to the wing, patting each other on the back for a good night out. Once on the wing we were informed it was bang up, so lights out, time for bed.

I woke up Christmas morning with Cliff Richard on the radio singing 'how I miss you'. So, I jumped out of bed and made my way down to the phones with my phone book in hand hoping that all my kids would be up. After 40 minutes I'd spoken to all of them, also my Mum and Dad and my guilty pleasure Melanie, who I'd met in Pentonville, who was partly responsible for me being here in the first place. She still gave me therapeutic advice so with her, Kelly and the kids in my life things were looking up. As I made my way to the Chillax Cafe I said good morning to everyone I passed as I was in good spirits after talking with my babies. Even though I was still surrounded by this lot who were mostly schizophrenics or manic depressives doing life sentences I felt pretty good. Adam was sat behind the counter with his bird Sproggit sitting on his shoulder feeding it biscuits , while smiling as he offered me a cup of coffee. Bipolar Dave was sitting in the corner on his own as usual as he suffered from bad mood swings brought on by his bipolar which sometimes lasted for weeks. His moods could vary from deep depression to very elated, but most people with bipolar get very depressed. It normally runs in the family, about 1 in every 100 adults I'm told develops bipolar, it usually starts during their teens and gets progressively worse without treatment. Stress can trigger severe symptoms. There are 2 types of bipolar called 1 and 2, these days both can be treated with drugs. Dave had just been diagnosed and was a week into his treatment. He was still very volatile and paranoid and that's why everyone was still giving him a wide berth.

Dave was doing a life sentence for kicking some geezer to death after the guy had asked him to stop pissing up the wall on his house. Another pointless killing by a senseless killer who happened to be the size of a barn door. In the other corner of the room sat x2 Steve eating his breakfast while reading a magazine. Lewis and Chris were playing cards while Pete was talking to Wanda, one of the screws. Mick and Mac were evenly matched playing chess. Jamie was on his play station on the wide screen TV watched by Billy and Andy. Old boy Derek and Daryl were reading the papers, and me, I sat there looking at all of them whilst I drank my coffee, before I went back upstairs so I could have a shower and a shave before dinner. After I did all that I watched TV wondering whether or not I should go back downstairs to the Chillax Cafe, but decided not to as the atmosphere down there felt like a funeral parlour and to be honest that was the last thing I needed on Christmas day, plus dinner would be being served any minute now. So, I would err on the side of caution and give it a miss.

At 12 sharp the shout went out that it was time for dinner, turkey roast, pudding and all the usual trimmings, so I made my way down with these culinary delights titillating my taste buds. On the way down , I picked up a bottle of coke and 2 chocolate bars that I had wrapped up the night before for Christmas presents for Mick and Mac along with a few Christmas cards as we would all be eating at the Good Guys table this year. So, once I'd put the presents and cards down I queued up with Mick and Mac like all the other recipients, eager for some Christmas cheer the likes of which I had not seen before. But once again my mind turned to Kelly and the kids as the smell of sprouts engulfed my senses and took me back to happier times from yester years when I would wake up on Christmas morning before the kids woke up so I could arrange all their presents under the tree as Kelly prepared the dinner. Kelly like myself used to love watching the kids open their presents so we could see the magic of this time of year through their eyes as they played with their new bikes before we took them over to Hampstead Heath riding around the pond with all the other families, making snowmen and throwing snowballs at each other, then back home to watch the Christmas films until they all fell asleep.

I was now at the front of the queue with my plate in hand watching it being filled to the brim with turkey and all the bollocks. It felt civilized especially when I compared it to what the rest of the prison population would be having today. In most prisons the guys would be banged up in their cells like Pentonville or Wandsworth who had got Christmas day

Living amongst the beasts: The rise and fall of the Grendon experiment

down to a fine art, banged up all day, no exercise normally down to staff shortages, the normal bollocks which could be hard on some inmates at this time of the year. The hypocrisy of a duty of care to all prisoners was laughable especially when you considered how many men in prison commit suicide this time of year. A normal prisoner gets nothing compared to all the deviants in Grendon and places like Broadmoor who live rather well compared to normal prisoners who are demonised and given nothing. So, you can see why most prisoners feel a sense of injustice.

However, I had to put that thinking to one side now as I was at Grendon being treated like a king, exchanging presents and cards like normal people, eating dinner and toasting my friends with the finest bottles of coke that had been chilled the night before in our fridge. As I looked around the room on this day- of-goodwill to all men, I couldn't help but wonder what the families of all their victims would make of all this nonsense.

The rest of the Christmas break seemed to go past without any incidents apart from Eugene hitting the roof after Kat the Polish Officer told him he looked smaller than she remembered him before the Christmas break. Which to someone like him who has body dysmorphia it was like a psychological slap in the face and to say he never saw the funny side of it was an understatement and when you considered that he was already at breaking point due to the fact that the gym had been cancelled all over Christmas, it would only be a matter of time before something gave.

The other thing that happened was that Mick had decided he wanted to pull out of therapy as his Dad was really ill and he also missed his family as the distance they had to travel was out of the question. Mac and myself tried our best to talk him round, purely for selfish reasons as we didn't want him to leave our table as the shortage of tables meant we might get an undesirable at ours which we said was reason enough for him to stay. We all had a good laugh about his situation and by the end of the day he said he would consider staying. He said Christmas always made him miss his family but hopefully the New Year would change his mind.

Also, Bilal had threatened to smash up the office and for that little indiscretion he was put in the book for a possible commitment by the staff but first, he had to come to the Group where we would all question him about his behaviour and why he did it, because at the moment he had refused to talk to anyone about it.

I had also had a little argument with Terry P, one of my Group members. I had gone into the office and he was reading the papers and talking to the Screw, so I went into the filing cabinet to get an application form. But Terry P being the prick he was made a joke

Terry Ellis

about me wearing shorts and flip flops in the office as they were forbidden. I pretended not to hear him so the prick said it louder and in front of the Screw but the Screw never said a word, maybe because it was Christmas. But, Fuck Face wouldn't let it go and started getting all serious with me. He even got out of his chair saying rules were rules and who did I think I was, adding that I should put the application form back in the cabinet and change before I came back. So, I looked at him and told him to fuck off and mind his own business and, in the future if he wanted to say anything to me he shouldn't start off with a fucking joke to test the waters. He should be upfront like a real man because only a slimy prick would pretend to chastise someone under the guise of a joke before turning it into a serious antagonistic question like he had just done. But, I expected nothing else from someone who beat up women as he was a low life deviant scum bag and a spineless piece of shit. I turned around and went back upstairs wishing I had kept my mouth shut and kept my cool, All I had to do was change my shorts and flip-flops but that wasn't me. I never could keep my gob shut, it was something I really needed to work on. I had also used his offence against him as an excuse for my outburst and bad behaviour, even though I felt he had acted underhanded. He was only doing what he was supposed to do and that was to point out the rules, which he did. I was the one to blame as I'd known about the flip-flops. I should have articulated my response, instead I acted like a spoilt little brat throwing my dummy out of the pram. This self-analysing wasn't new to me as I'd always known that I could be very volatile at times but this behaviour in my world made me someone you wouldn't fuck with and even respected. But, here at Grendon it made me look an idiot, especially now I was older as this behaviour only pushed people away from me as they were scared to say anything to me. What I had always saw and thought of as one of my strengths was now looked upon as one of my biggest weakness and the only way I was ever going to remedy this was to make myself more agreeable or amenable.

So, I went back downstairs and apologised to Terry P, who at the same time was being apologetic to me. He also tried to explain how I made him feel. He said he felt intimidated by my size and the way I came across and the reason he joked about me wearing my shorts first was he was trying to build up the courage to make the first step towards letting me know that what I was doing was wrong and to approach someone like me would be the first step for him in gaining the confidence that he needed as he was very insecure in himself. Even though I still felt he had gone round it in the wrong way I had to appreciate what he had actually done, which in turn made me feel like a bit of a bully, something I'd always hated in other people. This realisation that I too had been seen as one of those bullies humbled me to the point that I decided to take it to my small Group at the first opportunity as this self-introspection was limited unless I put myself in the firing line and the only way I could do that was to talk about the quarrel and how it made me feel. Maybe then I might be able to evaluate what I had done and then act upon it in a more constructive way. In the meantime I told Terry P that if he saw me in the future breaking any rules then he shouldn't hesitate to mark my card. I also told him I would take anything he said to me on the chin as it would help me too and at the same time it would help him with his confidence. We then shook hands and patted each other on the back, he believing we had made a breakthrough and me believing I had turned a corner as that really was all that mattered. Conflict resolution, step one.

That was the beauty about living on a wing at Grendon because if I was living anywhere else in the system I would never have given myself the chance to see the after effects of my aggressive retorts on the people I had berated, as it was easier on me just to character assassinate the person in my minds-eye as it dehumanised them, making it easier for me to accept my behaviour as normal which was a far cry from the reality of the situation. But, here at Grendon and because of the restraints of our living conditions, we were forced to resolve any conflict we might have with each other by sitting down and discussing them. This in turn helped us to see the consequences of our actions, normally from both sides of the coin, giving both sides the opportunity to empathise with each other and move on with our therapy, thus re-humanising. So now I had to re-programme my thinking and accept the rules regardless of whoever tried to implement them. This small insight through self-introspection would help me get through this and it would also help me put safeguards in place to prevent me from making the same mistakes again.

These realisations would be paramount if I was ever going to make it through Grendon but at the same time I had to ask myself was this real change or was it just self-preservation? Whatever the case it still made me look at my behaviour. I was making changes incrementally so I could fit in with my fellow Grendonites but was it real or were the rest of them acting like me and masking their true behaviours just to fit in with their new environment as their behaviour like mine is characteristic of your everyday run of the mill sociopath. So, was I really being realistic when interpreting what I was thinking or was this self- psychoanalysis really just another double- edged sword of realisation and manipulation? Only time would tell.

CHAPTER SEVENTEEN

The New Year started off rather badly as we were on lock down but we were informed there would be a wing special at 2 o'clock sharp. When we were finally opened I was still none the wiser as to what was going on. However, the prison grapevine had exploded with the usual speculation and supposition, of course none were true, but what we did know was it definitely had something to do with Eugene. He wasn't in his cell or on the wing but his belongings were still there. It could be a million things so I just ignored the bollocks and went downstairs to collect my dinner. I could see by some of the faces on the wing that they were pleased it had something to do with Eugene as he was their nemesis and with him out of the equation they were now in their deviant element. But the whole situation was still a quandary which I could only assume would be resolved at 2 o'clock.

We all filed into the community room still bemused by all the fuss. Smitty was surrounded by all this subordinates, Emma sat to his right. Emma was a young woman of about 26, slim and not bad looking, she was Smitty's' prodigy. The guys on the wing called her cry-baby as she used to cry the moment she came up against anyone who was confrontational, it was her defence mechanism. She had mastered it to elicit sympathy from the inmates which actually worked as I'd seen her cry on many occasions. To Smitty's left sat the Security Governor, a tall women of about 40 who too was a pretty woman who the guys called Miss Hitler. Next to her sat the wing Senior Officer Miss Piggy a well- rounded woman who wore glasses. Sporadically placed around the wing were a disproportionate number of staff some I knew but quite a few I didn't. So, with this new intellectual firepower on the wing so soon after Christmas some shit must have hit the proverbial fan. We had all taken our places and were just waiting for the room to settle down before Smitty made his opening speech and any optimism I may have had that Eugene might be coming back diminished up the therapeutic chimney. Quiet had descended over the wing like a blanket of doom as the Darwin of the deviants Smitty said "with regret I have to inform you all that Eugene's therapy has been terminated due to information received by the Security department that Eugene had intended to flood the prison with 120 steroid tablets".

The whole wing sat back in their seats appalled and astonished that anyone had the audacity to perpetrate such a heinous crime that would bring about the moral decline of C-wing which most of us knew was a load of bollocks. Jamie even asked Smitty if he knew anything about steroids. Smitty look bemused by the question as the guy said 120 tablets were actually one man's course, a 3 months' supply with no surplus left over to sell. If they had given Eugene a chance to defend himself against these allegations he would have explained that to them. Also, we as a community should have been given the chance to question him regarding said matter as it is a behavioural problem and the reason Eugene had come to Grendon in the first place. Mac then said he too felt let down as there should have been a community commitment vote, not a kangaroo court by the staff and it's Psychologist. Mac also said it was underhanded and manipulative to suggest in the first place that the steroids were for sale as it implied he was a drug dealer, which he wasn't. Plus, the idea was outrageous as it would now be written in all further reports jeopardising any chance that Eugene might have had in the future of getting a productive move because they had blackened his name throughout the prison system as a drug dealer instead of just a steroid user who had a problem with his body.

The whole situation had been triggered by an Officer called Kat in the first place as she had told him he looked smaller since she had been away for a break. Rightly or wrongly Smitty had gotten his way as he wanted Eugene out of Grendon, because we all knew that lots of guys over the years had been caught taking drugs but they had all been put through the therapeutic process and not ceremoniously kicked out like Eugene. It must have been because of his size as Smitty couldn't control him, so lying was the only way he could get him out and a trumped-up charge of bringing steroids into the prison was the smokescreen he needed as he knew a commitment vote wouldn't stand up to scrutiny, especially as it was hearsay brought over by Miss Hitler from the Security department. For the benefit of the whole community and the greater good, which was laughable, but to be expected from a totalitarian regime run by a dictatorial despot like Smitty under the guise of democracy. which was a shame as most of the guys that came here had trust issues, and to see this abuse of power only reinforced in them that the patriarch of the wing Smitty couldn't be trusted which was setting a bad precedent. All the guys felt the same apart from the deviants who wanted Eugene gone anyway. The Hierarchy has gotten their way and the beasts of depravity were over the moon as they had their trophy scalp, but that was the nature of the beast. Happy New Year.

Terry Ellis

CHAPTER EIGHTEEN

Over the next few weeks we were tasked with using our Group on our thoughts and feeling regarding Eugene's departure. Also, Jabbi and Martin from our Group would be leaving at the end of the week so we were asked to lay on a leaving party.

Martin was going to an open prison and Jabbi was off to Huntercombe, a Cat C prison. Also, Musa and Sean the serial rapist would be leaving for pastures new along with little Jeff another rapist who had been out of therapy for over a year due to the fact no other prison would take him as he was high maintenance. He was the guy who had poured bleach in his eyes. I didn't get to see him much as he never came out of his cell.

One of his Group members told me that Jeff used to break into old people's houses so he could rape and molest them. He was as white as a ghost and always wore dark sun glasses as he had become photosensitive from his many attempts of bleaching out his eyes. He was about 5' 3" and looked like Mr Magoo. He like the rest of the rapists wouldn't be missed. It felt like C-wing was having a deviant cull which somehow seemed to remedy the fact that Eugene had gone, but it still didn't elevate the thoughts I was having that Grendon had a two-tier system which seemed to favour the grotesque element of our society, as their shame made them more manageable. This demeaned the whole ethos of Grendon as they tried to control people's attitudes through humiliation instead of trying to understand their deviant true nature and behaviours. Eugene may have stood out because of his size but he was being true to himself and his normal behaviours which were plain to see. But, for being real he was put in a therapeutic box and labelled a prisoner with control issues.

A text book generalisation from a Psychologist who hadn't done his homework because if he had, he would have seen the good work Eugene had been doing on the wing because, like me, he had to fight an internal struggle daily just to be around all of these degenerates and deviants on the wing, but none of the Psychologists seemed to take that into account. Even though we were criminals we had different values and there are lines that should never be crossed, but we were asked to cross those lines every day, which meant treating these deviants as human beings, also equals. It took a monumental amount of self-control and tolerance on our part which we were never credited for as it was easier for the Psychologists to pigeon hole us, which again meant we were put under more scrutiny leaving the deviants looking malleable in the eyes of the staff, which was a false economy as they were the real evil. But, because they cried foul at every opportunity the moment they felt threatened by Eugene whose only crime was that he wasn't a deviant. Eugene told me that he felt as though he was not only up against the staff but the whole deviant mafia who out-numbered us 20 to 1. This is what we were up against on a daily basis, but I wasn't going to let the deviant mafia beat me, so it was chin up and chest out. I would play them at their own game, letting them all believe they were my equals because I had to stay the course if I wanted to see if Grendon actually worked, which meant I had to keep out of trouble because the last thing I needed was to get myself thrown out as I hadn't even started therapy yet.

When I was sitting in my cell that evening, a news flash came on the radio, apparently 2 inmates at Long Lartin prison had killed Subhan Anwar, a deviant who had killed his girlfriend's 2-year old daughter. Now, I could feel sorry for him as he was a fellow human being, but actually I want you to make up your own minds, especially after hearing what he actually did to that little girl.

Anwar was jailed for life in 2009 after being convicted of murdering the toddler. She suffered 107 injuries during a month of unbelievable cruelty in which she was battered with a metal pole breaking 4 of her limbs. The kid was also afraid of the dark so Anwar disciplined her by repeatedly locking her in an unlit cupboard. She was put in a tumble drier then dumped in a bin for amusement, he also splashed aftershave on her nappy rash and open sores and left her fractures untreated. In her final days she was suffering so much from her injuries that she could not walk and died when the fat deposits from her broken bones entered her blood stream. A post mortem examination revealed that along with her broken arms and legs there were 36 bruises to her head and neck, 26 to her arms and 10 to her abdomen. After she was dead he put her body in the bath and said she had drowned. The Q.C. at the trial said it was a truly terrible case, adding it must have been unbelievably painful, the pain she must have gone through, not just once or twice but repeatedly over the weeks at the hands of this cruel selfish individual.

Was I glad that he was dead? Yes. If he was alive could I ever see him as my equal? Definitely not. These are the sort of people I had to live with on a daily basis and every day I had to mask my thoughts and feelings, an act that is beyond comprehension especially for someone like me. But, it has taught me restraint from my tolerance of these deviants and it's only because of my daily incursion to the dark side through therapy that I'm able to control my anger instead of my anger controlling me. It takes a great deal of effort on my part as I could easily snap like Lee who killed the paedophile on G-wing or the 2 guys who killed Anwar, but where would that get me, a few decades behind bars. I had to keep telling myself we live in a fucked-up world where people go to considerable lengths to hide their true nature and acts of depravity. You only have to look at Jimmy Saville's 54- year reign of sexual abuse, whose name is now synonymous with nothing more than kids nightmares. Yet his litany of depraved acts remained one of Britain's darkest secrets until his death. He like most deviants covered his tracks with charity works and made thousands of kids dreams came true on Jim'll Fix It. He even raised £30,000,000. So, going up against people like him at Grendon on a daily basis knowing the lengths they would go to hide their true behaviour was a daily battle. But, by living with them I soon learnt to see the games they played with the Psychologists. Unfortunately, the shrinks couldn't see their charades as their only concern was treating the deviants as victims. But, I lived on the wing and I saw their behaviours before they stepped out into the therapeutic spotlight. It was over these months that I noticed their performances for what they were, contrived.

The deviants played this game just so they could appease their Facilitators, who were not trained Psychologists in some cases, but merely Officers with a basic understanding of psychoanalysis who could be easily fooled by a few crocodile tears from these criminally corrupt individuals who ran rings around them on a daily basis which to me was irremissible but common practice at Grendon. All because they couldn't procure professional Facilitators due to a lack of money here, which we found out on our next therapy group as Monkey Boots was being laid off, again due to funding, he was being replaced by an Officer called Pauline and when she was off, Andy an old Officer in his late 50s would take over. This all came as a shock to our Group as Pauline wasn't that bright and Andy suffered daily from narcolepsy. Leaving the only 2 trained Psychologists on the wing Smitty and Cry-baby, to write wing assessments. So now every group was being run by Officers also, Liz on Group 5 was retiring and Jo from art therapy was going on maternity leave for 5 months as she had gotten herself pregnant, which I found hard to believe as the tide wouldn't even take her out she was so fucking ugly. I only hoped it wouldn't debase the work we had to do here over the next year or so, but again only time would tell.

It had only been a few weeks since Eugene had been dispatched but the place already felt different somehow. The atmosphere seemed lighter and not so oppressive, maybe Smitty was right that one person like Eugene could change the whole dynamics of the wing by their presence, which took me back to a conversation that I had with Eugene after he shut everybody down on a community meeting all because someone had disagreed with what he had said. Even Smitty had jumped in to call Eugene a bully telling him at the same time he needed to look at the way he treated people as they were scared of him. However, in his indignation Eugene said he shouldn't be judged on his size as he was just as amenable to everyone else on the wing, adding it was their problem not his that they felt the way they did, but the damage had already been done.

After the meeting I made a point of going to see him but, like most people in denial about their behaviour, he just went on about Smitty and how the whole community was against him. So, I said they had a point mate and with that he gave me one of his looks, but I carried on and said what did you expect, you have spent your whole life making yourself and your body look big and mean and to the outside world because of your job as a doorman and bodyguard, to most people you scare the shit out of them and no matter how much you profess to being a normal Joe Blogs, your actual persona contradicts that. I then said he needed to go on a charm offensive and act like a victim like the rest of them otherwise Smitty would find an excuse to get rid of him, because the deviants would carry on pretending they were scared of him and he Smitty, would have no option but to act on their behalf. Eugene seemed to acknowledge what I was trying to tell him but I think we both already knew that the damage had already been done which was a shame as I believed he could have done well at Grendon.

However, Grendon being the revolving door it was, we had to say our goodbye's that morning to Martin, Jabbi and our Group Facilitator Monkey Boots. Also, the rapists Sean and Jeff would be leaving which meant we would now be getting new people over from F-wing for tea on Thursday. Three new graduates to be exact which would now make me a senior member of C-Wing's community. It would also give me the chance to re-invent myself, especially after what had happened to Eugene. So now I could officially say I was a fully paid up member of Grendons doctrine which meant I now had to show a willingness to change.

Even though I understood now why Smitty had to get rid of Eugene, I still felt he favoured the deviants over the recidivists, purely because they were presumed to be more manageable in his eyes, which I believed was wrong, and still do, but I had to look past that now and get on with what I had come here to do and that was therapy.

The next day felt strange without Monkey Boots. It also felt empty without Martin and Jabbi but I hoped Pauline would change all that as she would make a refreshing change with her smiling face and big personality. As she walked through the door I wondered if I could open up in front of a woman especially regarding my failed relationships as I wanted to use the Group today. But, Bilal scuppered my plans as he needed to use the Group as he had been put up for a commitment vote by the staff for threatening to smash up the office. Also, Daryl wanted Bilal to use the Group as he had seen the incident at first hand, but they had spoken to each other all weekend which was noticeable by their body language and their eagerness to get the commitment thrown out. It really did look contrived and not organic like it was supposed to be, so if they thought it was going to be easy they were mistaken. Not because he was guilty, it was purely because he was a child killer, which was the reason I didn't believe in commitments as people tended to put you up for no other reason than they didn't like you. Which in this case was true, but I would let Bilal have his say first.

He started off the Group by saying that what he had done didn't warrant him being put on a commitment and added that Daryl would corroborate his interpretation of the events. So, I said shouldn't we as a group be the judge of that? Because if not, why the fuck were we here in the first place if they had already decided that our opinions as a Group were not worth anything or for that matter valid. Pauline then interjected and said the incident in the office was deemed as very serious by the staff and that the decision had already been taken by Smitty and was now out of the Groups hands as Bilal was going in the book regardless of what was said in here today. I asked Pauline why we hadn't been informed of their decision straight away instead of letting us go through this farce this morning, but she just shrugged her shoulders. Dan then said that in all the time he had been at Grendon this had never happened, as the normal procedure was to bring the commitment to the Group to be discussed as Grendons ethos is dependent on democracy. But again, Pauline said the staff and Smitty believed Bilal had stepped over the line and it wasn't the first time that he'd done it, in fact she said it is the third time. With that Bilal hit the roof. He started effing and blinding and shouting the odds that they were out to get him and it was unfair the way they were treating him. Even though I didn't like him, it was plain to see that they were using the same exit strategy as they had on Eugene, again orchestrated by the staff because if they wanted you out then you were gone and there was literally nothing you could do about it.

I then turned to Bilal and said surely, he should have known the consequences of threatening to smash the office up, especially as he had been at Grendon 2 years as the whole idea of coming here was to learn from your mistakes, but he just looked down at the floor. So, I told him it was inexcusable of him and Daryl to come in here today and try to fuck us all over by saying the incident didn't warrant a commitment. It was taking the piss, not only out of us, but out of Pauline as it was her first day and as I was a Group member I felt let down by both of you for trying to pull the wool over our eyes. They both knew they had been caught out as they never said a word and I loved it, taking the moral high ground felt good.

However, after I came out of the Group I couldn't help but wonder how many Group members on all the other Groups acted like Bilal and Daryl, who had tried to deliberately minimise their bad behaviour in secret deals between themselves, making the whole therapeutic process fallible. Because, if this sort of manipulation was the norm, I could only imagine what sort of sub culture was operating here at Grendon if today's example was anything to go by then I could only assume it was rife. Which was worrying especially considering the wing was meant to be run as a democracy, as it would give the more senior members of the Community who were smarter than the rest, the opportunity to pick and choose who they wanted on the wings through a flawed commitment process.

Even though the real power was held by Smitty I felt that if one person was denied the chance to lose his place at Grendon through this underhanded coercion, it would be one too many. The reason this situation worried me was because the deviant element on the wing was very strong but with luck that would change on Thursday as I had found out that ginger Martin and mixed-race Sean would be coming over, also a rapist killer called Richard who I used to call the Hobbit as he had a long beard and walked with a shuffle. He was about 5' 6" with long hair and was a peculiar looking chap from what I could remember of him on F-wing. He was also an attention seeker of the highest order as he was always complaining about the food, going on hunger strike and refusing to eat for days. To be honest I was surprised he'd made it through the selection process. The only good thing about him was that he hated rapists and was doing a life sentence for killing one.

The Hobbit's story was that he had been drinking round at a friend's flat when a guy joined their company but after a few bottles of wine the Hobbit remembered that an old girlfriend had mentioned that the guy had raped her. So, with a skin full of booze inside him he decided to confront the guy and subsequently a fight broke out and they ended up rolling about on the floor. The Hobbit grabbed a knife from the kitchen and stabbed the guy through the neck, then twice in the chest before leaving the knife sticking out of the guy's stomach and, as the guy slumped to the ground the Hobbit kicked in his front teeth and 5 minutes later the guy bled out. The police were called, the Hobbit was nicked and then given a life sentence, all because he was an angry little man who couldn't hold his drink. I once asked him if he had used the fact the guy he killed had raped his girlfriend as a mitigating factor. His reply was 'no' which I found rather strange, but something I would get used to at Grendon as they all had a valid excuse for why they killed their victims. They were either rapists or. paedophiles but strangely none of them had mentioned this in court, it was a common phenomenon amongst the gay panic killers.

Lewis a young guy from Southampton had killed an old man who he said had raped his niece, but that all turned out to be fabrication, all because he couldn't admit that he was gay to himself or his family. He was later arrested on a gay cruising beach a few minutes' walk from where he murdered the old man. Also, a young guy named James had a similar story to tell. James was about 21, well built, 5' 9", 12 stone he was an angry mixed up kid. He said he had been out drinking with an old guy that he met in a pub. They ended up at the old geezer's house as James had acquired a taste of hide the saveloy even though he tried to portray himself as a bit of a ladies man, behind closed doors he liked men. However, a few weeks after their encounter he bumped into the guy with his brother and thinking he was about to be exposed as a homosexual and a sausage muncher, he panicked and told his brother the guy had raped him while he was drunk and asleep. Of course, it was a lie but his ego and reputation meant more to him than the guys life. So, he and his brother went around to the blokes house that night knocked on the door and thinking James and his brother had come around for a bit of how's your father, he opened up and asked them in. They were both carrying iron bars and when the old guy turned his back they set about him. The guy was 70 years old, they smashed his skull in and broke his neck. The attack was so monstrous and outrageously disproportionate to what the guy had supposedly done that James and his brother were given life sentences, that was of course after they both grassed each other up. Also, it came out at the trial that James and his brother were both gay, which was a real tragedy as their secret double life's had cost an old man his life and also theirs. Which only goes to show people will go to any lengths to hide their shame, embarrassment and to save their egos.

Ginger Martin was also coming over. Martin was ex-army and seemed to be one of the good guys, I hoped. He was the guy who had robbed the snooker hall however, what Martin hadn't told me was he had given the money he'd stolen to his mate so he could go back to Ireland, an act of generosity that cost him an 8- year IPP. Martin wasn't the brightest guy I had ever met, in fact he was somewhat obtuse, but if you were his friend he would do anything for you. Martin's problem was easy to see, he just wanted to be accepted by his peers and that was one of the reasons he had come to Grendon as he had been thieving and giving all the money away to his so- called friends who used and abused him. All his life he wanted to have friends and that's why he joined the army, to be part of something. But, that didn't work out either as he kept getting into fights after drinking and taking drugs, which was another one of his demons. This was to mask the shame and pain that he went through as a kid at the hands of his abuser. Martin had been sexually abused by one of his friends so to block out those experiences he became a boxer in the army to prove to himself he was still a man. Unfortunately, it never solved his problems or helped with the issues that he had as all it did was mess up his face as it looked like a smacked arse now as he had lost all his front teeth. Also, his nose was spread out like a bucket of water which made him look really mean, a look he now used at Grendon to push people away so he could isolate himself. Martin was only a small guy with ginger hair which meant he was always trying to prove himself. He would make a good addition to our table.

However, Shaun a mixed-race guy, was a different kettle of fish. He was an experienced robber who'd already done a life sentence for murder. He was about 38, 6' and 15 stone. He like the rest of them also said he had a good reason for murdering his victim. He, like ginger Martin also wanted to fit in so he had joined a gang called the Twenty- Eights who he said spent most of their time doing robberies. His initiation into the gang meant he had to go on the pavement plundering the local area and giving all the proceeds to the gang believing like Martin he had found his family through his brotherhood of crime. As I said he was a mixed-race guy who had been adopted by a white family. He had a white stepbrother who he believed his parents favoured over him. This left Shaun feeling very bitter, so he joined a gang of just black guys thinking this would change his life, which it did in some respect. He also told us that one of the gang members girlfriends had been raped so Shaun was dispatched to give the guy a beating but ended up killing him, hence a life sentence.

When Shaun was released this time, he tried to go straight. He met a nice girl with whom he had a baby. Two months after the baby was born one of his old gang members came back and asked him if he wanted to do a jewellery shop and Shaun being a fucking idiot went back to work. His mate sat in the car while Shaun robbed the place but the owner gave chase so Shaun turned around and let one off hitting the geezer in the chest but luckily for Shaun the bullet hit a metal glasses case in the guy's shirt pocket saving the poor fuckers life. Shaun was caught on CCTV and subsequently arrested and given 20 years. His mate was never identified.

This is a common story as it's happened to all of us over the years. We believe our friends have our best interests at heart especially when we get out. But the first thing they offer us is easy money through a bit of work they can't do themselves due to the fact the intended target is known to them. So, to do you a favour they offer to drive and you being skint accept believing they have your best interests at heart, as they are true friends, but nothing could be further from the truth.

Terry Ellis

I remembered a guy I met called John. He said he knew a mate of mine who had helped him out the last time he was released from prison. He said my mate was a gentleman and a diamond geezer as he had only been out of prison 2 days when my mate had offered him a bit of work with the same excuse that he couldn't do the job himself as he knew the intended target but instead he would drive him. John did the work and got £20,000 for a nights graft giving my mate half the cut before disappearing into the night. On hearing this I said to John "how can you call him a friend when you have only been out of prison a day or so away from your family for years and this parasite friend had asked you to do a job he couldn't do himself all because he hasn't got the fucking bottle and you actually thanked him? Can't you see he used you because he's a shit cunt?" We have all made the same mistakes but this realisation that I never really had any real friends, because if I had they wouldn't have offered me a nights work before I'd even seen my kids. They would have helped me out with a bit of money but because they are all selfish cunts like most criminals they only think of themselves and not the likes of me and John who, on his first night out should have been spending some quality time with his family before any work. Another lesson learnt by a chance encounter with John, another Grendonite who too was starting to see the light.

This is what made Grendon so unique because you would always meet new guys coming in who were still raw with their system heads on whose only form of communication when trying to ingratiate themselves with you was to drop a few names and talk about their past crime hoping you would make a conceptual connection between each other which would help you to bond together. This bonding through criminality or criminal associates is common amongst the criminal fraternity, like an invisible passport which we accept at face value turning your new acquaintance into a long-lost friend, and before you know it you are introducing your new friend to all your buddies as someone who can be trusted, all because he intimated he knew a few acquaintances of mine and my intuition agreed with him. This absurd behaviour is quite common amongst most criminals. It was only by talking to John and others of the same ilk that I was able through our shared experiences to better understand my own thinking processes which helped me see how fundamentally flawed my thinking was. This realisation was instrumental in changing the way I now accept people into my life, as I too in the past have been guilty of letting mugs into my circle for no other reason than they said they knew an ally of mine. I have paid the price over the years for this insane thinking to my detriment as I've had to walk around many an exercise yard with a few numpties all because I never took the time to get to know them properly as I made snap decisions that they were OK. This awareness that I too had been making the same mistakes as my peers for years would now save me from any more headaches as I would now make more informed decisions, which hopefully would free me up, so I could have intellectual conversations with more like-minded people.

I also made the decision to get to know more people on the wing as my Group were worried that I'd started to isolate myself from the rest of the Community. So, I decided to make a conscious effort to introduce myself to someone new every day. The first one on my list was Mark, a big guy who lived on the 3s landing, who would definitely make it as a Broadmoor finalist as he was a paranoid schizophrenic who was always pulling people for talking about him. But ,he'd recently been given new medication to make him more manageable, but he was still prone to outbursts for no apparent reason than he wanted to let off steam which everybody accepted but if you were on the receiving end it could be a bit nervy, but today I found him in a good mood. Mark was about 40, 6' 2", 20 odd stone and a major league fat bastard when it came to food. He would always go up for seconds and even thirds if he could get it. I think this was due to the drugs he was on. The drugs also gave him a God complex because no matter what you said to him, he always knew better which brought him into conflict on more than on occasion with Smitty. Mark was also another one who threatened to put his papers in most days to leave but never did as he was just playing the system as he knew all the moves and manipulated Smitty and the staff like a fiddler. He had been in and out of prison all his life. He was a petty thief and a life-long drunk and druggy but now he was serving a life sentence for murder. He told me he had gone around to a mates flat to have a drink and a fix of crack and heroin. After a couple of hours, he decided to go home and sleep it off but just happened to bump into a couple of his drinking buddies so decided to sit with them and have a drink. As the hours passed he and his friends had an argument. Fists were thrown and knifes were pulled and one of his mates ended up dead on the pavement. Mark's interpretation of the events was like most lying deviant low-life's, it was lacking any real substance because all he wanted to do was manipulate me by minimising the actual events of the murder so as to fit in with his bad boy persona as a drug dealer and hard drinker. He even intimated that he was an enforcer for a local crime family in the area, which again was all bollocks. This level of manipulation suggested he was in control of everything he said and did even down to pretending the medication he was taking to manage his behaviour wasn't working, when in fact all it was doing was getting him high as this guy was playing the ultimate game and knew all the angles. I have seen and known many a manipulative junkie over the years but he was by far the best. But, like all lying bastards he would eventually be unmasked as just another deviant killer of a young kid with learning difficulties. The boy had just left the Post Office after cashing his giro. Mark had befriended him then stolen his money to by some drinks. The kid said he was going to tell his Mum, so Mark beat the shit out of him, then stabbed him in the back killing the child instantly. Another senseless murder by a 2-time loser. This all came out on

Terry Ellis

Marks assessment which was ironic as Mark had been the victim of a child molester and banged on about how much he hated abusers and bullies, that is why he had become the anti-violence rep on our wing. The psychologist said the reason Mark had taken on the anti-violence rep job and was a vehement proponent against bullying was to hide the fact he was a bully himself and a sexual predator .

After listening to his assessment, I wondered if I could ever trust anyone ever again as Mark was the bully rep and look what he was hiding. It seems everybody lies to defend their position. An example of this was when Britain's Catholic Leader Cardinal Keith O'Brien, who was an outspoken opponent of gay rights and gay marriages, had to resign over a gay sex scandal and what a fucking bigot he turned out to be. He like most predators always strenuously deny their deviant behaviours by saying they have nothing to hide, even Jimmy Saville used that old chestnut. So, to say I was having trust issues since I'd come to Grendon was an understatement and my trust in human nature was being tested to its limit and the way things were going I could see the cast of Coronation Street being in here with us by the end of the week.

However, I was starting to see that the bigger defence someone put up the guiltier they looked as most screamed and shouted to protest their innocence, it was a common trait of someone who was embarrassed at being found out. The more I saw of this behaviour in my small Group and on the Community meetings the more transparent it became and when a deviant was put in this position most turned into spoilt little children caught out by their headmasters. But, seeing this behaviour played out on a daily basis the smarter deviants on the wing evolved like rats resistant to poison after seeing the outbursts for what they were, an admission of guilt. So instead of coming clean, they built up a resistance making it impossible for the psychologist to notice, as the staff disregarded the deviants ability to learn from their mistakes by mimicking their peers. They saw how Smitty lied when he despatched Eugene as he never showed any emotion or anger under interrogation. They learnt to control their emotions and anger through manipulation, so instead of real change they were actually making better deviants as they were now capable of perfecting their skills under interrogation which made them harder to detect in the real world. What better endorsement by a Grendon Psychologist to a deviants Probation Officer than their client had changed all because he'd learnt to be subservient on command and was prepared to obey his masters unquestionably and would be subservient to the point of self-flagellation, as it made him more manageable in their eyes to be released back into society, this was a joke. This endorsement by Grendon that their deviants had changed was an absurdity to some of us as we lived on the wing with them and saw first-hand all the manipulation and the crocodile tears. It was sickening to see

Living amongst the beasts: The rise and fall of the Grendon experiment

but the Psychologists would never admit that anyone could manipulate their way out of prison.

However, I was also learning to control my own anger and emotions in the same way as the deviants. You could say it was a double-edged sword of good and evil, but it still didn't detract from the fact that some of the beasts were slipping through the therapeutic net under the guise of change to rape and kill again. No better example of this was Alex who had been through Grendon twice for rape and let's not forget x2 Steve who, like Alex, had both been passed fit to live back in the community but within weeks had raped and ruined lives again. All this because the psychologists had made them look subservient in the eyes of their paymasters to the detriment of the families, which in the 21st century was unacceptable because we have the technology through lie detectors like the one they use in prisons in America for all their paedophiles and rapists, so why don't we use it here? I'll tell you why, it is because we rely on the goodwill of the paedophiles and rapists to tell the truth, that they have changed and we believe them. You see, the trouble with this country is that we treat paedophiles and rapists as if they are mentally ill and can be cured by medication or therapy this is ridiculous, also giving them sentences the same as someone who has been caught shoplifting. This sends out a message that if you rape and molest children and destroy life's it's not as bad as someone who steals a few quid. Time and time again over the years I have seen deviants getting between 18 months and 5 years, these sort of sentences send out a green light to the perverts that no matter what they do they will get a lenient sentence in a cosy prison and only do half their sentences, as most get out for good behaviour. They are given all the best jobs as they are seen as being more compliant than your average con who ducks and dives, only because they are master manipulators. We need to bring in sentences that reflect the hideous nature of their crimes, like life sentences. Even though I believe what I am saying I still had to carry on at Grendon because I wanted to see first- hand if it had anything to offer me other than what I had already seen. So, it was fingers crossed again as I had to keep an open mind which was becoming harder and harder the more I saw of this community.

Terry Ellis

CHAPTER NINETEEN

My Small Group was also going through a few changes. Shaun had joined our Group and like me he took an instant dislike to Bilal. Also, Dan wasn't too happy that Pauline was our new Facilitator and showed his distain by staring at her intently which seemed to put her on edge. After our Group that morning she asked me to stay behind as she was scared to be alone with him, so I waited then walked down with her to the office on the ground floor. When I went back I had a chat with Dan about his behaviour but he said he had no recollection and denied it until he was blue in the face. I brought it up the next morning on our Group, but once again he tried to deny it but we wouldn't relent and after 20 minutes he broke down and then confessed. He hated all women especially fat ones as they reminded him of his Aunty Pat who he loathed as she beat him when he was a child. He said he had gone to live with her after his Mother died and no matter what he did or said she always put him down and constantly picked fights with him. She also regularly beat him with her belt then banished him to the back garden and made him sleep in the shed at weekends and by all accounts she was a right bitch. Dan also said he had a disabled brother but Aunty Pat treated him as if he was her own, this was down to the fact she was paid to care for him. She also received a new car and extra money for his disability. We spoke with Dan all morning regarding his thoughts and feelings and gradually persuaded him that Pauline wasn't the enemy and eventually he saw sense and apologised, which for me made the whole process seem worthwhile which was great to see. But, unfortunately for Dan the damage had already been done as Pauline had been traumatised by her encounter with a real-life psychopath and, true to form, 2 weeks later she had a nervous breakdown and was replaced by a new Officer called Richard.

Richard looked so nervous on his first day but narcoleptic Andy was on hand to help him out but as usual he nodded off after 5 minutes leaving baby faced Richard to fend for himself in what would be a therapeutic shark pool. We fired question after question and, being rather gullible, Richard answered them all with the honesty of a man on trial who was fighting for his therapeutic future as a Grendon Facilitator but regrettably to no avail as honesty is not necessarily the best policy as any creditability he might have had went out the therapeutic window as he explained that only 6 weeks previously he had been on the dole. Before that he used to work as a forklift driver adding he was surprised that after only 6 weeks training he was now a qualified Officer working at Grendon in the therapy Groups. And as he sat there with a grin that stretched from ear to ear, we as a Group were dumb struck as we took in the enormity of what he had just said. This young kid of about 25 was now a Facilitator after only 6 weeks training and would be in a position to write reports on us that could possibly have a major bearing on all our futures with little or no experience at all. This was the last straw for us. After the Group we all complained to Smitty that we needed a Facilitator who could do his job or none of us would continue with our therapy. We understood the country was going through a tough time, what with all these austerity measures, but these efficiency savings by Chris Grayling were having an adverse effect, because how could he or Grendons hierarchy expect us to do any worthwhile therapy in these conditions? The whole situation was ridiculous. However, out mini revolt seemed to work as Richard was moved the next day and replaced by our old Facilitator Monkey Boots, who we told would be back on a short-term contract until our Group was back on track, which was music to our ears as we could all now fulfil our therapeutic struggle in the pursuit of perfection hopefully becoming the crème-da-la-crème of our community with Monkey Boots now back at the helm.

The next day Bilal was up for his commitment and as always when there was a commitment vote everyone was buzzing about with the enthusiasm of a large buzzard circling its prey. Some would hover in the background but as usual most used the two-faced approach wishing Bilal well, leading him into a false sense of security as most had already made up their minds that they wanted to vote him out, as even the deviant hierarchy had its own standards and anyone like Bilal who kills children has a very low status even in their eyes. Which, I found funny as even in the low echelons of Grendons hierarchical system according to their own imaginary place on the deviant board of what was deemed more heinous than their own crimes, Bilal came out bottom as his offence was deemed more odious which aroused disdain towards him on a daily basis. So, to see this sort of double standard approach to what the deviants saw as acceptable as far as whose crimes were worse made me feel uncomfortable. I felt as if I had to be the Kofi-Annan of the wing and help him out as I would rather see Bilal get the help he needed than none at all, which surprised me as I hated the sight of him and everything he stood for. But, I also hated the thought that the other deviants put themselves above him as if their own perversions were of a lesser category, devaluing their own positions on their imaginary board of what was acceptable and what was deemed repugnant in their own eyes as to me they were all the same. So, to see them judge Bilal as a lesser person was a joke as it brought the whole process of having a commitment vote based on honesty into disrepute as it wasn't about helping the inmate, it was about rank opportunism which I believed undermined the whole foundation of therapy in Grendon turning the whole process into a kangaroo court of the worse kind.

As I took my seat in the Community Room looking at the faces of Bilal's' executioners, as he the condemned child killer took his place, I noticed that no-one gave him any words of support for fear of being labelled a child killers friend. Instead they all sat there nonchalantly not meeting Bilal's gaze as he looked around the room pleading with his eyes for a fragment of encouragement at this stage in the proceedings as he needed some hope that he might get a reprieve, but none were forth coming. So, he just sat back and waited for the inevitable onslaught.

The first to speak was Smitty who read out the charges with all the pomp and ceremony of an administrating judge. At the same time, he gave his own recommendation that Bilal should go as he had stepped over the mark which then prompted all and sundry to look at him with disapproving eyes before they all took their turns to give it to him in what was a period of prolonged questioning. It looked and sounded like a right ecclesiastical tribunal of deviant pontificators expressing their opinions as if they were righteously ordained to pass judgement on one of their minions.

I felt the whole process was one of one-upmanship as everyone was trying their best to impress Smitty with their fake indignation that what Bilal had done was the crime of the century. At the same time, they were trying to prove a point that they had all changed and to hear them all talking this way made me sick to my stomach as I saw each and every one of them on a daily basis manipulating the staff and Smitty knew first-hand what was really going on in here today. It was all about pay back and believe me he got it.

Bilal was still in the hot seat and no matter what he said it wouldn't get him off the hook as Smitty and the staff wanted him out also most of the wing hated him. So, no matter what I or anyone else said to help him nothing could change his fate as it was already written in stone before we came in here today, as Smitty and the staff took it in turns to vote him out, as one by one everyone raised their hands Bilal's future at Grendon was brought to a shuddering end. Another casualty of the deviant mafia and their hypocrisies.

I was starting to understand the reality of the wrongs and rights of Grendon. It was all about having the right friends so when it came to a commitment vote you wouldn't be voted out, it had nothing to do with democracy in fact it was quite shambolic if I'm honest. However, it only took me a second to get over the fact that Bilal had been voted out and as I passed him on the landing I couldn't help but think good riddance to the little prick, for what goes around comes around as I'd seen him vote people out for no other reason than he didn't like them. Plus, if anyone deserved some pain and distress he did, especially after what he had put that little child through. Even though I thought the commitment vote was bollocks I still went along with the general consensus that he was a deviant child killer and for that, and no other reason, I voted him out and that's why I believed the whole commitment process was flawed. Anyway, another lesson learnt through Bilal's demise.

The next morning Jamie, a new Officer, put Mack in the book for telling him to 'fuck off' which was a blatant lie as I was standing with Mack. Also, quite a few of the other guys saw and heard what was said as they were all waiting to go to the gym. Mack was talking to me when Jamie poked his nose in and said something sarcastic so Mack told him to grow up, adding "if you haven't got anything to say or contribute to the conversation then keep your nose and mouth shut", with that Jamie went bright red and stormed off. Jamie was a very immature Officer but we thought nothing more of it until the next morning at the Community meeting when Jamie thought he would get his own back on Mack by putting him in the book and saying Mack had told him to fuck off. He then gave a detailed account of what was said and his version of what happened, then sat back as calm as you like believing he had got his own back on Mack. You see Jamie had just come to Grendon after working in a main stream prison and believed he could say and do whatever he wanted and his fellow Officers would back him up. But, as I said he was new to Grendon and didn't really understand the consequences of his lies as one by one everyone who was standing there the day before including me and the wing Chairman Terry P said he was lying giving their account of what really happened, which sent a shockwave through poor old Jamie as he did not expect anyone to go up against him. He must have thought he was back in the system and that his word would be final, plus he was up against a few bacons, but he was mistaken as Mack, myself and Scouse Micky were none of the above and plus we had the wing Chairman on our side who said Jamie was lying. After about 20 minutes of taking questions James was on the back foot as none of his fellow Officers could back him up as they too could see through his lies. He then tried to back track by saying he might have been mistaken, he even tried to change the subject and wriggle out of it that way, but if he thought it would be that easy he was well and truly mistaken as Mack and myself took in in turns to ask him questions like why he thought it was OK to lie and did he think he would actually get away with it? What was he thinking, where did his head go, did he do it out of embarrassment? Was it to do with his ego, what did he expect to achieve, had he lied before? Everyone took it in turn to ask him questions even Smitty which didn't go down too well as he squirmed in his seat and by the end of the meeting he was a broken Officer and we all knew he wouldn't do it again. He had just had his own baptism of fire, a mistake he would never make again, even the other Officers seemed to take pleasure from seeing him put in his place as he was a bit of a know-it-all but this experience had well and truly curtailed his behaviour.

He had now experienced what we all had to go through because if you were caught out in a lie you learnt early on at Grendon that there was no hiding place as there were eyes and ears everywhere, be it staff, inmates, psychologists, anything you said and what you were even thinking would be picked up on and used against you. You couldn't lie your way out of trouble, so lesson learnt for poor old Jamie.

That afternoon I found out that Robbie the little Scottish guy on our Group had pulled out of therapy as he'd gotten his D-Cat. He had told Daryl he would be leaving next Tuesday so needed a few days off of the Group to acclimatise. So now we as a Group were down to 5 members, me, Daryl, Dan, Terry P and Shaun, which meant I would now be under more pressure to open up and talk about my childhood. As much as I wanted to talk about my thoughts and feelings regarding that period of my life, it still felt awkward and embarrassing. I had seen the others breakdown after speaking about their families and I found it uncomfortable to watch, so the thought of them seeing me like that was mortifying.

I had spoken a few times about my criminality as I found that topic easier to deal with as I didn't feel any shame or guilt about it, but I could see now my biggest problem was my ego. It was really holding me back so I had to dig deep if I wanted to make any real gains in therapy so I went to see Daryl as he was a senior member. I told him how I felt and the reasons why I hadn't used the Group for the last month or so. He said it was normal as he had also gone through the same turmoil. He had bottled up his emotions for years as his dad was a hard polish man who never showed any love or affection towards him as a kid. With that sort of upbringing he had developed his own dad's traits which was characteristic of that generation who believed that crying or showing any sort of emotion was a sign of weakness. I too had been brought up in a care home and as I got older I was placed in a community home and in those sort of places if you showed any emotion it was seen by the staff and the other kids as a weakness so you learnt very quickly to keep them hidden, which meant bottling them up. However, on the few occasions it became unbearable I used to lock myself in my room and just cry my eyes out until I was all cried out which helped to release all my feelings of abandonment.

As I left Daryl's cell with his advice still ringing in my ears, I made the decision to use the Group the next morning regarding my thoughts and feelings surrounding my time in care but first I wanted to speak to Brian as he had been in therapy for years as he had killed his Mum and Dad. But I didn't want to talk to him about his crime, I wanted to enquire about an article I'd read in the paper. A reporter had been allowed to sit in on a few of the wings meetings a week previously where someone had mentioned the fact that Brian had just started working in the gardens and that since he'd started a number of rabbits had been found mutilated. Brian was asked if he knew or had anything to do with the deaths, his answer was cold and shocked most of the guys as he said he was glad the rabbits were dead as they were pests as they fucked up the lawns which was now his job to maintain. However, he vehemently denied any involvement in the bunny-gate murders so the meeting was moved on. However, after the meeting the woman reporter had asked Brian his full name and a few questions regarding said matter. She also asked him what he thought of Grendon and its ground- breaking therapy and Brian being a bit gullible around a woman reporter opened up believing he might get a mention in the paper. True to form he did as a few weeks later an article came out with the headlines 'serial killer on the loose in Grendon' and, it appeared the number one suspect was Brian as he had form for wiping out his own family warren. Which left Bright Eyes Brian in a state of shock as he, like superficial Smitty, believed the reporter was on the level and was going to write something positive about Grendon and its therapeutic deviant geniuses.

Smitty, Brian, all the staff and deviants asked for an emergency meeting to discuss the situation. Smitty never said much as it was his idea to bring the reporter on the wing in the first place so he just sat red faced in the corner. The staff tried in vain to calm things down but it was too late as Brian and the deviants had gone into melt down. Brian was on the verge of killing himself and a few of the others were threatening to pull out of therapy but after an hour or so the staff talked them down but the damage had been done as someone had written 'Rabbit Killer' and 'Save Watership Down' on Brian's door. This didn't go down too well with Smitty as he threatened expulsion if the jokes continued and, at the same time, we all took a vote to never allow a reporter on the wing ever again.

It had now been a few weeks since the article had come out and Brian was now in a better mood and like most of us could see the funny side of it all. If I am honest I found Brian easy to talk with as he was quite a sensitive sort of guy. He was about 29, going bald, 5' 9", thin and quite effeminate. You would never have thought he was capable of killing his Mum and Dad with a cricket bat and dumping their bodies in the back garden while he went on holiday with his new girlfriend. He was an intelligent guy but never had any social skills as his parents never let him play out with other kids. Also, at the age of 21 his Mum still used to bath him and wash his hair. Also, they wouldn't let him have a girlfriend which he said was the reason he finally snapped and killed them. He told me he met a girl at his local tennis club, they had formed a none sexual relationship and thinking he might lose her he had decided to kill them. He was very naive and thought

Terry Ellis

everything would be alright and plus no one would miss them so he just threw them out in the back garden like rubbish believing all his troubles would just go away. But as it was the middle of the summer the bodies started decomposing and the smell came to the attention of one of his neighbours who phoned the council, who then discovered the remains and reported them to the police. Brian was then arrested on his return to England from his week- long stay in America and given a life sentence.

Brian was an interesting guy so I spent about an hour with him discussing therapy. He told me about the gains he had made but I took what he said at face value as I didn't know him or what he was like before he came to Grendon. Plus, all the guys here were very manipulative and I really didn't trust anything they said but I still soaked up all his enthusiasm as I needed to give myself a push as the next morning I was going to use the Group.

I spent the best part of the night in self-reflection trying to make sense of why I was here and also asking myself if I really needed to put myself through all this shit by raking up my past just to appease Monkey Boots and the rest of the mugs on my Group. It didn't feel right me airing my dirty laundry just because Daryl and Brian had told me that I needed to reach rock bottom if I was ever going to release all those years of pent up anger and frustration by me being put in care as a kid. But, this was why I was here as I already knew the aim of therapy was to strip away all the barriers that I had put in place to protect myself over the years. I wondered if my ego would allow me to open up in front of my Group as my pride and anger was a big part of who I am. It kept me safe, it's why my kids and family love me, my humour and sarcasm are what makes me who I am, but I also knew my sarcasm and humour was something I used as a weapon to protect myself. If I had to relinquish that part of me would I then turn into a jellyfish like the rest of these spineless bastards or was thinking like this my way of protecting myself still. As I tossed and turned that night I wondered if I would bottle out and not do any therapy tomorrow morning or would logic and common sense prevail.

For years I had done it my way and look where that had got me, 17 years in prison away from my kids and the people I love. I was still angry at myself and the world but I had never been frightened of anything as I was now opening up in front of my Group tomorrow. This anger was coming out of me on a daily basis, from the way I treated others I could see that more and more each day. This made me feel better calling everyone here a deviant and monsters to make myself feel better by psychoanalysing everyone. Also, character assassinating them all in my head making myself look superior deflecting ay responsibility away from myself for being a useless fuck up in the eyes of all my kids and family in the first place.

Living amongst the beasts: The rise and fall of the Grendon experiment

In the morning when I entered my group room I hoped someone else would use the Group instead of me but Daryl put paid to that, he made sure I wouldn't bottle out. He took the first minute and said we'd had a talk last night and we felt it would be a good idea if the rest of the Group let me use the Group today to do some therapy. I tried pleading with everyone with my eyes to say no but all said yes it would be O.K. Even Monkey Boots sat up in his chair at the thought of me finally taking the plunge. With nowhere to go I took a deep breath and started to spill my guts.

I started talking about getting into trouble as a kid but Daryl and Monkey Boots were wise to that one and both stopped me at the same time and said that I was just trying to talk about things I felt comfortable with which I knew wouldn't upset me as the real issues with me were to do with feelings of abandonment and being taken away from my brother and sisters and they felt it would be better if I spoke about the real issues that got me emotional. Of course, they were right, I had tried to stay in my comfort zone by talking about trivial matters as it is common in therapy to try and evade talking about anything that would normally upset you and that's why it was so important to have an experienced facilitator and senior members in your Group to steer you in the right direction.

So, I started again and by the time I had finished I was emotionally spent but at least I had experienced what Daryl and the rest of my Group had been through. This joined us all emotionally together as a Group and I now realised why the first subject we were asked to talk about was our childhood experiences as we were told that it was only through revealing these traumatic, and at times deeply disturbing events, that we were able to remember what we felt as children enabling ourselves to reconnect with the pain and emotion of our pasts. As this was the first time I had used the group all the memories that I had blocked out for years completely overwhelmed me but I was informed my reaction was normal and a sign to the rest of them and the therapist that I had started to engage. They were then able to guide me through and ask me all the relevant questions but there was so much going on inside my head that I couldn't speak and as much as I tried to stop myself the worse it got. I was having involuntary reactions which I had no control over and as the tears started I put my head in my hands, all I could do was picture myself as a little kid waiting for my Mum to come back and get me from this empty room where I had waited for her as a child. I could even smell the distinctive unpleasant aroma which brought back so vividly the pain of being that child again. It was more than I could bear. I felt like running out of there but I couldn't move my legs. I felt self-conscious and awkward as I sat there breaking down in front of them all, this embarrassment stopped me from really letting go. My inner child just wanted to stand up and scream and shout

Terry Ellis

out loud. This extreme emotional pain I was feeling at that moment was enormous but I had to fight it with all the strength I had left inside me to gain some composure.

Even though the whole experience made me feel uncomfortable I felt as if I had benefited from it emotionally as I was drained and couldn't wait to get back to my cell. When I finally did I sat with my back to the door, sitting on the floor and I just cried like I had never cried before. After I had finished I tried to rationalise what had just happened.

Intellectually I understand the pros and cons of putting myself through it, but there was a part of me that was fighting it.   I wanted to disprove to myself the validity of it all on a rational level. But, I couldn't at that moment as it felt so real and at the same time I had enjoyed the pain of reliving it as I felt calmer and the anger I'd felt for years seemed to have gone and been replaced with an inner peace and a freedom from all the shit I had been carrying for years.

I spent the rest of the day reflecting and talking to other members of the community and, as I went to bed that night and for the first time in years, I thought of my brother and sisters, also my Mum and Dad, then the tears came again.

CHAPTER TWENTY

It took me a few days to get back to normal and accept the fact I was now one of them. For months I had been able to control myself and on the few occasions that I had nearly cracked I'd been able to swerve it. But, because the group had been relentless over the last couple of months making me work and look at the relationship I had with my kids and their mothers. I worked on my lifestyles and associates, my attitude. I worked on sarcasm, my awareness on others and actions on my victims. I worked on fear and intimidation, control, manipulation, my index offence, my family dynamics, infidelity and bringing the odd issue into the Group. I had been brought to this point incrementally by my Group and a skilled Facilitator pushing me towards a crescendo and an out-pouring of emotion, which was their agenda in the first place. So, now it was up to me to continue in the same vein if I was ever going to reach and fulfil my true potential.

Over the next 2 weeks we received 4 new community members and our Group was the lucky recipients of 3 of them.

The first to enter our Group that morning was Mark a tall black guy who was doing a life sentence for a gang murder. He was about 6' 1" tall, well-built and as fiery as they come but honest with it. He wasn't a criminal, he was just in the wrong place at the wrong time. He and his family had moved away from the area where they used to live and Mark had returned a few months later with his new car. On seeing his new car his mates asked him for a lift and not knowing that one of his mates had a gun on him they drove into a block of flats. His mate saw an old enemy and decided to take a shot at him. His mate was in the lead car and there were 2 cars. Mark was about 200 yards away just pulling up and not knowing what was going on was driving his own car which was registered to him. On seeing what had just happened he drove as fast as he could to distance himself from the incident but his car was caught on camera and unfortunately for Mark the guy died and it looked like a premeditated gang murder. Mark was given a life sentence through joint enterprise and that was why he was so angry.

Terry Ellis

Mark's anger came out about a week later as he told Pete the arsonist to fuck off or he would bash him up. This upset poor old Pete so he tried to put Mark on a commitment for threatening behaviour but couldn't prove it even though Daryl, Terry P, Mac, Mick, Ian and a few of the others were there they all copped a deaf ear as none of them liked Pete. Even though Terry P was Wing Chairman he still lied, also the rest of the two-faced fuckers lied. This sent Pete on one as he accused them all of lying. So, to get their own back on Pete they all put him in the book for abusing the therapeutic process which sent Pete into hibernation as he wouldn't come out of his cell. This pleased everyone on the wing as Pete could be a right pain in the neck. However, this was a perfect example of a corrupt democracy, if you didn't like someone and there was more of you then you could gang up on them and use the therapeutic process against them.

Next to come into the Group was Barry who was in for arson. Barry was quiet and never spoke much but when he did his speech was slurred as if he was on drugs, which for him was most of the time. He kept himself to himself and was a short fat guy, about 5' 6" tall, cropped hair and came from Manchester. He was another one who was always angry. I kept away from him as he was a bit crazy. I knew from the start he would be a pain in the arse, but not as much as John.

John was a gypsy and as thick as shit, 5' 7" and skinny. He was in for robbing a security van of its' money box. He and his mate drove straight from the van to his girlfriend's flat to open it, not realising someone had followed them and to make matters worse the box had a paint dye pack in it and it went off covering all of them in dye from head to toe. When they left the flat the old bill were waiting and nicked the lot of them red handed, which was funny as that was the same colour as the dye. I could see from the look of John that he was a life-long drug user as well.

Now our Group was back to full capacity, 8 of us and Monkey Boots which made 9 but because Sean, Mark, Barry and John were new it put a bit of a strain on the Group as none of us wanted to use the Group as we didn't trust the guys yet, making the atmosphere cordial but unproductive.

The 4th guy to come onto the wing was Tony, who was now my next-door neighbour as Rob had moved the day before. Tony was doing a life sentence. Tony was a drug dealer and one night a guy he used to deal with tried to rob him, so Tony fought with him taking the knife off him and stabbing the guy to death. Unfortunately for Tony he was charged with murder instead of manslaughter which left Tony very bitter and angry. When you mixed that with Neapolitan Syndrome you were left with a little black guy of 5' 5" tall with plenty of attitude and a temper to go with it. However, Tony was one the of best guys I had met at Grendon and within a few days we were the best of friends as we were the same age and both came from London. Also, we had the same sense of humour.

It was a therapeutic match made in heaven and from that first day I took Tony under my wing I was able to predict every situation as they were just about to happen as Tony made all the same mistakes as I did, like using people's offences against them when he was losing an argument or to back up a point, which we all did when we first came to Grendon. Seeing this time and time again when new guys came on made you see how pathetic they and you looked when you started using profanity to back up your arguments instead of articulating a response. This would then reinforce in you that the only way forward was to keep calm, never swear and always think before you spoke. This new tool of communicating brought about a new maturity in the way you responded to others and of course a new respect from your peers, which meant you could argue with the best of them without ever losing your temper. It was only by seeing Tony's responses that I could see how far I had come. As we worked together over those months I could also see the change in Tony as he went from bitter and twisted to a calm and articulating fighting machine. This miraculous turn around in him gave me a renewed optimism that I was also making the right changes in my life which showed in the way I spoke to my kids on our visits as I was now communicating so much better with them and also with my Group members. So, all in all things were looking up.

There was a consequence of the new arrivals, it meant I would lose my job cleaning the toilets, thrusting me into the spotlight as the new canteen rep making me responsible for representing the community on all the canteen meetings ensuring that the community was aware of future meetings so members could make suggestion for the agenda, then feed it back to the community. Also, I had to help D.H.L. staff distributing the canteen every Thursday night, which was a pain in the neck as I had to eat my tea in 5 minutes then sort out all the canteen before everyone else had finished theirs. I also missed my gym all because the job was seen as a responsible one meaning everything else I did came second but I had to do it.

I was also given a new wing job cleaning the dining room which would put me under even more scrutiny as the job had to be done twice a day and entailed more effort on my part as every member of the community was fastidious when it came to the cleanliness of their beloved dining room. This meant that I had to up my game as failure to do the job correctly would end up with me being winged and put in the book to answer for all my indiscretions, in front of the whole community, a prospect not for the faint hearted as I had already been up on one for my sarcasm. On that occasion I was given a forfeit such as

Terry Ellis

having to write a diary and feed it back to the whole wing about my feelings and thoughts. I also had to read it back to my Small Group once a week. I also had to write a speech about using sarcasm and why I used it as a weapon, which didn't go down too well as my opening line was 'the reason people here don't like my sarcasm was because they were not sharp enough, because to use sarcasm you had to be as sharp as Jack the Ripper's knife'. Unfortunately, Smitty didn't find if very funny. He made me write it all out again without the sarcasm plus I was also banned from the gym for 6 weeks as they thought that would be a better punishment for me as they knew I enjoyed the gym making me think twice about being a sarcastic twit ever again, which in my case worked. Losing my gym was like losing my TV, I needed it every day, so, I did learn from this lesson. The punishment by loss of privileges was a way of reinforcing good order and discipline on the wing.

    The environment at Grendon was one of self-reflection so to make the same mistakes twice was seen as a failure on your part so you had to change your behaviour. If you failed to change your behaviour you would then be asked to use your Group on why you were still fucking up. This then brought you into conflict with your Group members who would then chastise you into not making the same mistakes again, otherwise they as a group had the power to put you on a commitment vote which was a sign to the whole wing that they had lost confidence in you, giving the whole wing the green light and no other choice but to vote you out. This was a good enough incentive for you to learn very quickly that your behaviour would not be tolerated. This lambasting and the prospect of losing out on family day and eating toast every morning was more than most could bear. Even I was beginning to like the atmosphere here especially the fish tanks. I also enjoyed the easiness of our living conditions and it didn't take much to see it was better to toe the line than to step over it. Another way to show your Group members and staff that you were becoming more empathetic regarding your surroundings was to be seen mixing with the beasts of the wing and as Bilal was now an ex member of my Group I decided it wouldn't hurt if I was seen in his company. This gave him the green light to come into my cell most days after he had come back from dialysis which brought me into conflict with Tony as he hated the sight of Bilal. Every time he came into my cell and saw Bilal Tony would turn around and walk straight back out making Bilal feel like a leper.

    Tony's behaviour only lasted a few weeks until I explained the advantages of having Bilal around as he had a wealth of knowledge as he had already been in therapy for 2 years and what we could learn from him was invaluable. Tony apologised to Bilal and we all milked Bilal for all he was worth. It was a win-win situation for both of us as we both needed our C-cats and to cut so many corners without making so many mistakes would put us in good light as far as Smitty was concerned. Tony and I were the only ones on the wing who were talking to Bilal at the time which was mentioned in dispatches on the community meeting. This made Tony and I look like we had converted to the dark side, making us more accepted in the eyes of the deviant community thus leaving poor old Mac, Mick, Martin and a few of the other deviant haters in the spotlight.

Tony and I could then blend into the background which seemed to work as all we kept hearing was that Mac was bullying everyone and Mick was his right-hand man. Both of them were winged for bullying, putting them both in the hot seat where Mac broke down and had to go to Healthcare as it seemed his only way out. When he came back and over the next few weeks he had changed into a model prisoner and in the eyes of the staff and Psychologists he had been broken, which was their aim in the first place. But, after I talked to Mac I found out he was just playing the game and had manipulated them all into letting him stay. A master move as I thought he was on his way out and as we laughed about it in my cell he told me that Smitty had said that "what had happened to him was that he had let go of his past". Which Mac lapped up as faking change was important to him as he was doing 37 years and any Psychologist report that he had changed wouldn't hurt him.

We kept our heads down after that and let the new guys make their mistakes as we were now senior members of the community hoping they would take the diary of us. This didn't take long because on the Tuesday while we were all in our Small Groups, one of the Officers had found some drugs hidden on the landing under the sink and once they were tested it came back that they were prescription drugs, the ones Grendon handed out on a daily basis like confetti. They were called Tramadol. So, being the finely oiled machine Grendons security was we were told that at 2 o'clock sharp a wing special meeting would be called which gave everyone a chance to get rid of any drugs they had in their cells before they were searched which I thought was a bit counterproductive. So, as the toilets were being flushed all over the wing, I went and sat in my cell with Tony and Bilal to discuss the ramifications of the potential fallout from what we were now calling 'Drug Gate'. As Tony and I were not drug users it would be a pleasant distraction from the mundane routine of the wing to finally have a bit of controversy which we were not involved in. We could just sit back as spectators instead of the protagonists for a change making the whole experience a more pleasurable one and of course a learning experience on our journey to enlightenment. However, I still felt a bit of anxiety as we were not out of the woods yet, we could still be accused of it as you never knew if one of the deviant manipulators had planted anything in your cell and as I already had trust issues regarding the inherent nature of the beast, I wouldn't put anything past them.

Terry Ellis

As we finished our cuppas and made our way down to the community room I wondered if the others felt as I did, or was I just being paranoid. As we took our places I could see the look of apprehension etched across the faces of my fellow Grendonites which brought a wry smile to my face as they all looked worried. I wondered how many of them would be implicated or would anyone own up to it as we all knew the outcome of drug dealing on the wing, expulsion would be the order of the day. I just hoped it wouldn't be anyone on my Group as they all seemed to be working well and also, we didn't need any more upheaval as we were just starting to gel.

Just as I was pondering that thought Smitty walked into the room stony faced by the thought that one or more of the wing had infiltrated the induction process and was still abusing drugs and maybe even worse, corrupting some of the weaker and more vulnerable members of the community undoing all the good work he had done.

Smitty was followed by Cry Baby, the Governor, the head of security Miss Hitler, our very own Senior Officer Miss Piggy and 4 of the screws, Jamie, John, Andy and Dave, all looking just as perplexed, as someone had got through the rigorous process of selection and was now pedalling their own prescription drugs on the wing, the same drugs that had been prescribed by their own Healthcare Department in the first place. It was laughable to see the forced indignation of the whole sorry drama being played out in front of us. What did they expect a grown man to do, a man who had just been prescribed a week's worth of Tramadol in his cell. Did they honestly think he wouldn't abuse the trust they placed in him for a night out on the town?

I thought it best not to voice my opinions as I could feel a little bit of tension in the air, so I just thought I would air on the side of caution and keep my gob shut for a change and wait to see how it all played out.

As the last screw took his place, the Chairman thanked everyone for being on time and asked Smitty to take the helm and as he regurgitated what we already knew with the exception that Barry's cell had been searched and that his weeks supply of Tramadol was missing and what did Barry have to say about it. With that Barry went as bright as a belisha beacon as he spurted out the reason for the absence of his weeks supply of Tramadol saying that once he heard of the finding of the drugs he had gone back to his cell and flushed his down the toilet as he didn't want to be implicated in anything to do with drug dealing on the wing and that he was innocent of any involvement in the issues and that was the reason why there was no Tramadol in his cell. In hindsight he had wished he hadn't done it as it now made him look guilty, but that was not the case as he knew who the Tramadol belonged to that were found on the 3s landing but didn't want to grass them up, but if they were not forthcoming here today and it looked like he was going to get the blame then he would expose the culprits to the whole wing. However, before that he had to go through his own mini inquisition brought on by his own stupidity by panicking and throwing his stash down the toilet, which everyone at the moment found hard to believe, even me. But he kept to the same story and didn't budge an inch and when he was asked to name names he refused to say who they were as he said he wanted them to own up in their own good time and wouldn't give them up until tomorrow. Smitty and the rest of the wing asked if the 2 vagabonds wanted to come forward on their own volition but nobody was forthcoming and I wondered if Barry was playing for time as the 2 ignoramuses surely knew they would be exposed in the morning. Or, would they just try to blag it and carry on with the charade that they were the innocent parties and put the blame back on Barry hoping his excuses would be ridiculed as a blatant attempt to muddy the waters before he admitted he was guilty. Only time would tell so we were excused until the next morning when we would have to go through this again.

As we left the community room you could have cut the atmosphere with a knife as everyone went to their perspective corners wondering who were the two unlucky culprits who would be unmasked in the morning. As the gossip mill went into overdrive and speculation mongers pointed their fingers I couldn't help but wonder what Barry must be going through as he had only been on the wing a week and now his head was on the therapeutic chopping block and the likelihood was he and his 2 accomplices would be out on their ears by the end of the week. Or would Smitty drag it out making an extravaganza out of it hoping it would deter anyone else from the community from ever doing it again? I could only assume Smitty would drag it out as he believed it would act as a deterrent but like most of Grendons ideology it was flawed as all it really only taught you was never to trust anyone, as one minute they were your best friends and the next minute, just to save their own arses, they would sell you down the river. So, by making the whole community sit through days of this sort of kangaroo court you realised very early on that it was a weakness for you to ever to have an accomplice and that the only way to keep yourself safe was to keep your mouth shut and always work alone.

This sort of reinforcement that safety was only attainable through never letting anyone into your confidence again was paramount if you ever wanted to survive at Grendon. This reinforcing that life only evolved around you equated to you being a more manipulative criminal as it never brought about any real change in you which was supposed to be the desired effect because on the surface through your engagement on the wing to look as if we were all participating in the process it looked to all and sundry that real change was taking place here. But that couldn't be further from the truth as I was learning, so were the vast majority of senior members who had made it this far, because if you acted accordingly in front of the Psychologist and staff at the cost of the more inept members of the community to learn from their mistakes was all that was required of you, making a mini society of elitist on the wing at the detriment of weaker members who were fodder that could be discarded to make way for the more intellectual of us. This cohesive look on the surface would then look to the outside world more structured, giving the impression through this cloned conformity that we all had the same identical beliefs, which was Smitty's goal, so for him it was a win-win situation as we would do his job for him while routing out the offenders from our own vast experience of criminal behaviours. Then Smitty, the Governors and the staff alike would see our actions as one of change in our moral beliefs then reports would be written to that effect and everyone would live happily ever after. As much as we all knew it was a load of bollocks, none of us could admit to it as all of us wanted and needed our Probation Officers to see us in this light, so we just carried on with the pretence.

With this in my mind I went for a run with Tony and spent the rest of the day talking about therapy and just hoped no one else in my Group was involved.

The next morning as I sat there with that overwhelming feeling of déjà vu watching everyone take their places, I wondered if any deals had been done the night before. That all changed when I saw Barry's face as he looked like a man on a mission and I could only wonder what his conspirators were going through as they saw Smitty and his side kick Cry Baby enter the room with all the staff.

The door was shut at the stroke of 9:00, bringing the room to silence before Smitty uttered those immortal words "good morning everybody" before his eyes moved to Barry's. He asked everyone in the room if they wanted to own their behaviours before they were exposed. Once again there were no takers so the spotlight fell back to poor old Barry who took a deep breath and said "you know who you are why don't you just come clean as I don't want to do this to you but your silence leaves me no other option or alternative?" Then he just sat there for a few minutes looking down to the floor and talking to himself at the same time taking more deep breaths before he blurted out who his fellow collaborators were. The first name out of the bag was Gypsy John and the other was Jamie Q, the young guy who had killed the old man with his gay brother. These revelations brought gasps from the staff and Psychologists and a few wry expressions of disgust and disappointment from Group members, as they showed their annoyance with twisted faces and frowns. However, gypsy John was not having any of it as he went straight on the attack calling Barry a fucking liar and saying how could anyone believe Barry when he had already admitted in here yesterday that he had panicked and thrown his own medication down the toilet. He then said that the drugs that had in fact been found were Barry's and no one else's, and that everything Barry said was a fucking lie and that was all he was going to say on the matter.

However, if he thought that was going to be the end of it he was kidding himself as now the whole wing took the opportunity to take John to task and by the end of it he was spitting blood and looked as guilty as sin, but he kept the pretence up. Barry just kept quiet and put his head down and Jamie took his turn. He also said that Barry was lying and asked him why he was lying trying to put the dairy back on Berry himself. The game was now afoot and the questions started coming but no matter what they asked, he like John, was not forthcoming with the truth. So, Smitty brought the meeting to an end, asking John and Barry to work on it in their small Groups and also Jamie on his Group. With that the meeting was over, for now.

Over the next few days John and Barry argued on their Groups relentlessly, but a picture was starting to emerge that they were both lying, putting both of them on the back foot as both threatened to put their papers in and leave.

By Monday we had a stalemate as both men now refused to talk to each other let alone admit their part in it, but if they thought that was the end of it they were mistaken as the screws were just about to be tightened as word had got round that if nobody admitted their part in it, we as a wing would lose our family day which was not an option as far as the wing was concerned. So, the pressure was put on them behind the scenes and after a few well-placed threats which always beats therapy hands down, we all waited until the Monday for something to develop and as always in these cases someone would crack as there is no honour when it comes to druggies, especially where family day was concerned.

The word on the wing was that all 3 of them had been arguing amongst themselves all weekend but as far as any admissions of guilt were concerned none were forthcoming and we were none the wiser, apart from one of them would be making a speech in the morning.

So once again we all took our places and waited for Smitty and the rest of the crew to make their way to the community room. As I looked around the room at their faces I realised one was missing, it was the old man killer Jamie, he had either pulled out of therapy or had gone sick, which was funny as he was seen as the leader of this band of merry twits and I had it on good authority that he was the main player as the drugs had been found outside his cell, in fact right opposite. Also, a mate of mine had told me that Jamie was buying Tramadol off one of the guys on G-wing, a guy I had been in Pentonville with and who had told me that Grendon had changed his life and that he was now a born-again Christian, he had even been baptised.

After learning Cookie had supplied him I felt a bit cheated as I had believed him when he said that he had finally turned a corner in his life, but like most people I had met in Grendon most on the surface projected that they had changed, this was to promote themselves in a better light. This sort of behaviour was common in front of the cameras and I was starting to see it more and more on a daily basis but it was seen as the acceptable face at Grendon, one for the cameras and the other one for the landings and I could only imagine historically this had been going on for years and passed as change to the untrained eye as the norm.

As we all sat there and waited for Smitty to walk in and start this morning's proceedings, bang on cue as always, he and his posse entered the room at 1 minute to 9:00 followed by a sullen faced Jamie Q with his tail between his legs and the look of someone who was just about to unburden themselves of any wrong doing. As they all took their places with Jamie by Smitty's side, I took a quick look at Barry and Gypsy John and from the looks on their faces they were as bemused as the rest of us as to what was going on in here today, but it looked to all like a deal had been done. Another case of the survival of the most manipulative and as Jamie was a senior member he knew that if he had any chance of staying he had to come clean first, even though he was the main player it would be seen as him breaking away from the bad elements of the community, which in the eyes of Smitty was a major breakthrough, which was naive and lacked any judgement or wisdom on his part to the fact that Jamie would sell his own Mum down the river to stay at Grendon. This sophisticated technique was all that was needed in the eyes of the Psychologists to show the powers that be that he was making real inroads into the psychology of the deviant mind which was laughable to say the least.

So, I was not too surprised when Smitty said that Jamie had something to say which would take a great deal of courage and asked Jamie to take the floor. As the crocodile tears started to flow and in his most 'eat humble pie' voice he grassed the other 2 up. Not just by saying that they were involved but he started from the beginning, the first time he had met John to the part he played in the distribution, also Barry buying off him as well leaving no stone unturned, days, times, places, when the contraband was taken in front of him and by who. This made John and Barry look like Pablo Escobar. Then Jamie apologised to the whole wing and carried on crying with his head in his hands. The smart move had been played and Jamie had won hands down. A performance that Shakespeare and Sigmund Freud would have been proud of, also the rest of the wing lapped it up apart from me, Tony, Mick and Mac as we saw it for what it was.

However, Smitty was reading it from another page and looked at Jamie like a proud father but before the applause started Gypsy John went on the attack once again, which lacked any real substance as Jamie had covered all of the bases so his retort fell on deaf ears. Barry took it on the chin with the dignity of someone who knew that they had been beaten by a master deviant manipulator in Jamie. Barry even said he was sorry and asked to be voted out, which also signed Gypsy Johns death warrant, but we still had to go through the voting process.

First up was Barry and most concurred with his wishes and voted him out but once again Gypsy John was not having any of it, he just walked out and told everyone to go fuck themselves.

Then it was Jamie's turn which was a different outing all together as Smitty made a speech on his behalf to the fact that he had turned a corner, blah, blah, blah, which sent a message out to anyone that if you ever got caught then make a deal as quick as you can as you would then be exonerated of any blame and released from any obligation to take your medication, which was a fact as far as Jamie was concerned, as all the deviants voted for him to stay. His Group patted him on the back saying he had done the right thing but my thoughts went to Barry and Gypsy John, my now 2 ex-Group members.

CHAPTER TWENTY- ONE

Afterwards I went for a run with my old mate Tony and wondered what was going to happen now because living here was becoming a bit precarious, I decided to phone my Probation Officer to let her know that I was at Grendon as she was now my 3rd Probation Officer. So, I put on my poshest voice and started talking like Smitty making sure that my pronunciations were all spot on and after a few minutes she was eating out of my hand. As I rattled on in my best Oxford English dictionary voice with a few pages of Thesaurus thrown in, I convinced her that I had turned my life around and with that I promised to phone her once a month as this would help me when it came to my categorisation process. And, just when I thought I had her on the hook I went in for the kill and asked her if she would be able to come up on one of my social evenings, which I explained to her would enable us the opportunity to get to know each other and talk about areas of concern, like resettlement when the time finally came.

Thinking that I had done the business and that there was nowhere for her to turn, she dropped her own bombshell on me and said due to funding she couldn't come and see me but thanked me for phoning her and told me to keep the good work up and that in all probability she would not be my Probation Officer as she was now moving to another department. She also added that to stop wasting my time, I should phone back about 6 weeks before I went home. However, in the meantime if I ever needed any advice I shouldn't hesitate to phone her. It took all my energy not to have a fucking go at her but I took a deep breath and thanked her for her time and put down the phone.

I reflected over the conversation and as much as I was disappointed with the outcome I was remarkably calm in the way I had handled the situation, as normally I would have switched back to my Cockney voice and given her a piece of my mind and probably finished off with a few expletives, putting myself in all kinds of shit when it came to my next recategorization review, fucking up any real chances I might have had of getting any resettlement. So, with this newfound realisation that I could get what I wanted through better communication with my peers, instead of just going into one when I couldn't get my own way, gave me a renewed faith in what I was actually doing here. Another lesson learnt.

The next morning, I went to my Group and asked to use the Group on how I felt about being fobbed off by my Probation Officer and how it made me feel, which seemed a good way of getting the anger out of my system and at the same time let the others know I was managing my anger, which seemed to elicit a bit of sympathy out of them. So, while they were all on my side I thought it wouldn't hurt to ask for backing for my family day and, as Gypsy John and Barry were now out of the equation, then why not take advantage of the situation. I slipped in the names of my 2 girls Terri and Charlene and a friend of mine called Melanie. To my surprise I received a unanimous vote of confidence that I was ready for my first family day. I knew I still had to take my backing to the rest of the wing on Friday and also Smitty. I knew it would only be a formality as I had been doing everything right and plus, after what happened to John and Barry I was looking like a model Grendonite. I also had the backing of my whole group and after the palaver of the last few months it would make a welcome change to finally be able to let the kids see what I was doing here at first hand. Also, it would be good for them to sit down with me and have some dinner and even get a chance to look at my cell and really see how I lived in here as it was so much different to how it's portrayed on the TV in all those silly prison programmes with all those mugs they pick to front them. Programmes never have any real chaps in them or villains, as they would never lower themselves to come across as cunts as that's all the BBC wants the outside world to think of us.

I wanted the kids to see the real Grendon. I wanted them to see the fish tanks on the wing and all the mod cons, the shower facilities and even a dining room, it would go a long way to alleviate any misconceptions the kids might have as I hated them worrying about me, also it would give me a chance to tidy up my cell. It would also give me a chance to introduce Melanie to them as Terri was studying psychology and Melanie was my Psychologist and was one of the reasons why I came to Grendon in the first place as she was a Forensic Psychologist who I had met in Pentonville when I first came to prison and we had remained friends. She had also been visiting me. I also had a great deal of respect for her and hoped that one day I may get the chance to take her out for dinner, but for now that thought was a pipe dream. I still had 5 years to do but if I played my cards right and never put her under too much pressure she might actually be there at the end of all this shit. That's another story as I still had to get through this sentence but I thought it wouldn't do any harm to let them all meet, so I put Melanie's name down as well for my family day. If I'm honest it would do me the world of good to see her as over the past months I had become demotivated with Grendon due to all the constant shenanigans

Terry Ellis

going on the wing as I saw all the shit that happens behind the scenes and the many faces people put on to impress Lord Smitty so that they could get reports done and it also seemed that at the moment that therapy came secondary to all the other shit that was going on. So, seeing my babies I hoped would change all that, with these thoughts I would carry on. I got on the phone and let them all know I had got my backing.

After I came off the phone I went into the community room to listen to feed backs and was shocked that Pete the arsonist, who lived opposite me and who no one liked as he was a pain, started to tell everyone he had been fantasising about Lewis the old man killer and that he had been wanking over him. As soon as he said it the whole wing seemed to explode into laughter, which made Smitty rather angry as I'd never seen him flustered before. He called everyone to order then asked Peter to carry on and at the same time asked him what had brought these feelings out of him. Pete said that Lewis had been coming into his cell after he had used the shower and under the guise of an accident dropped his towel on purpose on 6 separate occasions leading him on with sexual innuendo. Smitty then asked Lewis if what Pete he had just said was true. As I looked over to Lewis his face was twisted and contorted with what looked like uncontrollable rage and he then started vehemently denying Pete's allegations, calling him all the names under the sun, at the same time refusing to even use his Group again as long as Pete was on it. This riled Pete and he started to tell everyone that he had kissed Lewis one night before he left his cell and Lewis had kissed him back. This made Lewis even more angry and he went into one calling Pete a fucking poof and a queer cunt. With that Smitty called the meeting to a conclusion and asked them both to calm down.

They were still raging at each other after we left the community meeting and I wondered if it would all end in tears as Lewis had been exposed as a bum bandit, which most of us already knew as this was the third time he had been brought up to the wing for such actions as he had been found in possession of some love letters he received from one of the guys on A-wing. Another time it was implied he was doing favours for bars of chocolate and that's why he was called the Milky Bar Kid behind his back but nothing had ever been proved or came of it. Smitty seemed to have a soft spot for him and that is why he hadn't been put in the wing book for calling Pete a poof and a fucking queer. If anyone else on the wing had called Pete names or used that sort of language they would have been put in the wing book.

Lewis was very spoilt and vindictive and had been responsible for a few of the guys being kicked off the wing as he had accused them of bullying him. Most of us kept away from him as he knew the therapy game inside out and was always crying on the wing to the staff and Smitty and anyone who would listen to his dribble. I could see from his eyes that this wasn't finished yet.

The community meeting was now over and the argument would save for another day, so I thought. That was until we heard Lewis shouting that Pete had attacked him on the stairs, the noise brought the staff and Smitty out of their offices with concerned looks on their faces. The two of them were asked to go into Smitty's office and then 10 minutes later we were all told there would be a wing special at 2 o'clock sharp. As I was being told this I was starting to wonder if I was in a prison for kids masquerading as grown-ups. I wondered how much of this shit I could take so I decided to go for a run on exercise with Tony and when I came back I showered and hoped that Lewis wouldn't be in there. After that I had something to eat then went back to my cell and banged up over dinner. At 2 o'clock sharp the shout went out saying "5 minutes to wing special", which brought me to my feet and as I opened my door I saw Pete coming out of his cell. As our eyes met he smiled at me for the first time ever since I had come here, he hoped I would respond likewise but I kept my face passive as I like most believed Pete shouldn't be here as he had come to Grendon straight from a mental hospital. That is why he had a poor attitude and lacked any real social skills, which made it hard to interact on any normal level, making any interactions unreciprocal as far as seeing an argument from both sides as far as Pete was concerned as he was one dimensional and made it almost impossible to have a conversation with him. Which I believed in part was a defence mechanism he used to keep himself safe as it was easier for him to be passive aggressive all the time which enabled him to stay on the wing as a token member of the community as he wouldn't be able to function in mainstream prison.

I also believed the only reason why he was at Grendon was to push everyone's buttons, which he did on a daily basis which infuriated most of the community as he was able to do and say anything that would normally result in anyone else being kicked off the wing but, as it was him it was just seen as par for the course and didn't warrant any real concerns until now as he had picked on Smitty's pet project, Lewis. This made it I assumed, untenable for him to stay leaving no other option for him but to be sent back to the institution whence he came from.

Smitty and the rest of the deviant community had to be seen to be going through the therapeutic process in order to get their pound of flesh, making poor old Pete another casualty in the war on bad behaviour, leaving him more than likely feeling discarded and unappreciated, sending him into a spiral of depression bringing about a hatred of all that was good about his stay at Grendon.

Terry Ellis

    I pondered on his impending fate and could only hope that his departure would be swift as to leave him on the wing with his arsonistic tendencies might end up with all of us being toast by the end of the day. With this in mind I would be recommending that he be removed forthwith but first we had to see what he had been charged with or would he just be getting a reprimand off Smitty? This toing and froing of the rules made the outcome of any situation unpredictable, as Smitty had the real power to crucify you at will if you displeased him or you messed with one of his pets. He was the one who defined what was serious and what was deemed just run of the mill, making a mockery of the constitution that had been written in the sweat of its demented past and present practitioners, making me wonder why we had to go through this hypocrisy day after day just to make the deception of democracy seem legitimate so they could write it in a report that he had been voted out of Grendon by his peers for bad behaviour, all because Smitty couldn't do his job properly as he should be asking what was Lewis doing in Pete's cell with just his towel on in the first place, especially when his shower room was one floor down on his own landing. So why was he up on the 2s landing showering? Also, why had he dropped his towel in front of Pete more than once as this linked in with his index offence where he had killed an old man on a gay beach all because he couldn't admit he was gay. He was now re-offending again by leading Pete on with his body, then once he had got what he had wanted he then beat Pete down therapeutically just like he did to that old man, an issue he should be working on instead of being mollycoddled.

    All these questions should have been asked instead of trying to get rid of Pete for talking the truth and expressing his feelings. That was the reason he was here for in the first place and what we were asked to do on a daily basis. This opting out of real issues because of favouritism went unchecked because too much power was left in the hands of one person, Smitty. Even the staff seemed perplexed at times and voiced their opinions to me on a number of occasions but they were over ruled as their own hierarchical system dictated that the Head Psychologists word was final and once again seeing this rank opportunism played out. As these questions were not being asked it made each of us question why we were all playing this game and the only answer I could find was that Grendon was such a sweet little number we expected this sort of shit as part of the payoff, even if it did destroy people's lives like Pete.

    What made it more bearable for me most of the time was that I had a hand in helping to fuck up another deviants life, a trade off that I could handle. So once again I went into the community meeting with an open mind, to get rid of him for no other reason than for the fact that he was a prick. With this in mind I took my seat and waited for another shambolic episode of he kicked me to begin as it was the only excitement we would experience for the rest of the week, unless someone hung themselves, then we might get a day off if we were lucky but for now I would play my part in the downfall of poor old Pete by pretending I gave a shit about him kicking Lewis in the shin. Just then Tony came and sat by me and whispered in my ear that Lewis and his Group had been soliciting votes and had persuaded the majority to vote with them and could they count on our votes. With that I looked over to Lewis and nodded my head to the effect that we would party to their deception as this was the way things were really done at Grendon especially if you fell out of favour with your fellow Grendonites. That's why you couldn't voice your true opinions as the collective would find a way to get you out. That is why it was always important to give the impression that you were neutral and playing both sides at the same time, respectful to the deviants and courteous to the staff and Psychologists because the only other option was what Pete was just about to get.

As Pete walked into the room you could almost smell the fear on him that his time was up as he avoided everyone's gaze and looked at the floor ready for the door to shut.

Smitty took the floor saying that the no violence rule is the most important in providing a safe environment for therapy to take place at Grendon with no fear of systemised pressure and must be strongly upheld for the common good of all the community members. All areas surrounding violence will be looked at thoroughly and anyone who commits an act of physical violence towards another person is to be held accountable to the community and will automatically be put up for their commitment and today we must address the situation that has occurred between Pete and Lewis in a therapeutically supportive environment. This is everybody's responsibility so I will be dealing with this matter by way of removing the person or persons off the wing straight away for the safety of the wing if it is proved that an act of violence has taken place.

This sent out a clear message that Pete was definitely gone as Smitty had just signed Peters death warrant. Even I would say I saw him kick Lewis if it meant he would be gone today, even though I was actually sitting in the community room at the time of the incident. I could only imagine how many of the others were thinking the same thing as me. As I looked over to Pete I couldn't help but mouth 'goodbye scum bag, it's been emotional' with a big smile but he was looking at the floor with his head down and never saw me.

Smitty asked Lewis to explain the whole thing to the wing, what had happened and with youth on his side and in his meekest voice, looking all angelic and submissive he started laying it on thick that Pete had followed him out and tried to engage him in conversation and because Lewis was not having any of it, Pete then lashed out at him without any provocation kicking him in the back of the leg and that there were witnesses to that fact. He then went on to mention all their names and one by one they all concurred with him that they had all seen Pete kick him and because they were all on his Group it didn't look too good for Pete who was now spitting blood and professing his innocence, but once again the deviant mafia won the day. It was only a formality that he would be going now. As soon as he calmed down Smitty asked everyone to vote on whether Pete should be voted out and one by one every hand went up and Pete's fate was now sealed, with that he broke down in tears.

I looked over at Lewis and I could see he was visibly moved by Pete going and I could see he was regretting what he had just done to his friend as they spent a lot of time in each other's company. Also, they had come through the induction process together and all because of a moment of madness the friendship was now over. It was a textbook case of how passion and vengeful feelings can overwhelm everything else

I came across this frequently in Grendon with the gay boys as they could be quite spiteful to each other and very unforgiving and when in that state of emotion mixed with anger their judgement goes right out of the window. These vengeful feelings are founded in a gut reaction that is all about fight or flight and instead of Lewis just fleeing back to his cell he chose to fight because for him it was about immediate hurt and not about looking down the road and realising you are digging 2 emotional graves, one for himself and the other for Pete, the target of his pain and anger as I could see Lewis wanted to turn the clock back.

It was also obvious that he couldn't see that seeking revenge would affect them both but Lewis should have known better as he had been in therapy for over 2 years and should have also been aware that vengeful feelings are incredibly dangerous and need to be understood and managed as there are rarely any winners in these situations, especially when you consider Lewis was a serial liar and the architect of his own humiliating downfall as he couldn't admit the fact that he was gay and when you considered what he had done to the old man that he had killed, he was in fact still acting out here.

Seeing this going unchecked was a damning indictment of the therapeutic process that was taking place here because what hope was there of Lewis changing if Smitty couldn't see through today's events as Pete had only spoken his mind regarding his feelings about Lewis and should have only really got a rap on the knuckles but Smitty had let it get out of hand as what I had seen in here today was a bit harsh because the real crime in here was letting Lewis twist the facts and literally get away with it because no one liked Pete and I could only assume Lewis wouldn't be humbled for long as he would take it in his stride. That was Grendon for you.

Living amongst the beasts: The rise and fall of the Grendon experiment

As the screws escorted Pete to his cell and waited for him to pack his gear, I started to regret that fact that I didn't stand up for him as normally I would have backed the underdog but maybe I was learning to keep my mouth shut. Also, a deal was a deal, Lewis and his group owed me one now which I would get back on Friday when I asked for backing for my family day. When I looked at it like that, losing Pete didn't seem such a shame after all.

A few days later we heard that Pete had been moved back to the mental hospital so everyone got what they wanted. I got my backing for family day and helped to get the wing up to scratch for the big day. Except for one little problem, a week before family day I phoned Melanie and she was a little distraught and said that Grendons security had been in touch with her bosses and that they had found out that I used to be one of her clients and she was forbidden to come and see me and that if she continued she would be struck off from ever working in the prison system and practicing forensic therapy ever again. With that they investigated the matter and she was suspended which also meant I couldn't phone her or see her again which cut me to the bone as I enjoyed talking to her. I couldn't put her livelihood in jeopardy so I kept calm and told her to tell them the truth that we were just friends and that she was just doing follow up work on me and that is why she had been visiting me and if and when it died down she could always drop me a line if she wanted to.

For now, I had no other choice but to let her go, even though it felt so wrong. So, I said my last goodbyes to her and put the phone down and consoled myself with the fact that the times we had spent together were enough but deep down I knew that without physical contact or any mental stimulation from our letters or from talking on the phone, the relationship was now doomed. I told her to be strong and that was it.

I couldn't let anyone at Grendon know how I felt as it would all be blown out of proportion and that would be the last thing she needed, so I bottled it up and took a deep breath and hoped that one day she would get back in contact with me. With my heart broken I had to soldier on plus I had my family coming up and I couldn't let the kids down as I wanted it to be a day they would never forget so I had to pull out all the stops.

Terry Ellis

CHAPTER TWENTY-TWO

On Wednesday when I got my canteen form I ordered everything that I thought they might like, bottles of coke, biscuits, chocolates, cakes, crisps, brown sauce, tomato sauce even some fruit for the table and with a heavy heart I would get through it, plus I had a lot to be thankful for as Charlene had just opened up her first hairdressing saloon which made me so proud and Terri was now going to university. Also, Chloe was starting college and my son Tony was expecting with his girlfriend making me a Granddad and my other son Kyle was doing really well in the Army, which made me even prouder. Also, my 2 Mums and Dad were still healthy and the rest of the family were in good condition and I was healthier than I had ever been in my life, so fuck the rest of the world I thought. A little bit of heartache wouldn't get me down.

I carried on in therapy as if nothing had happened and by Friday when the kids would be coming up I was back in the game and on good form again. As I arose that morning and looked out of my window to see a beautiful sunny day, I wondered if the kids were already waiting outside of the prison or would they be fashionably late. It's funny how many crazy thoughts went through my head that morning as I got myself together but a soon as I heard the click of the door sound I heard everyone rushing about and I knew they would be outside waiting. But, to be on the safe side I phoned their Mum, Kelly, she allayed all the fears I might have had by saying "are you sure it's today as they are still all in bed Tel, do you want me to go and wake them up?" Then she started laughing and told me of course they had left and if I know those 2 then they are probably outside already. She told me they had left about 7 o'clock in the morning which would give them plenty of time to get here.

So, with my fears of a no show averted I had some breakfast and jumped in the shower and then put my best shirt and jeans on with my timberlands and soon I looked the dogs bollocks. I even put a splash of aftershave on and made sure that my cell was immaculate and that nothing was out of place. I then picked up my bag of goodies and went downstairs to dress my table with a nice cream sheet laid out on it and then placed all the stuff down. When I had finished it looked the business.

As I surveyed the room checking the other tables I could see that mine was the best as Martin's table was to my right and he hadn't made too much of an effort as he said it was only his Mum and Step-Dad coming up. Opposite him was Mac who like me had made an effort as his Mum had flown over from South Africa, also his brother who lived over here would be coming up. Which left table 4 for Geordie Gary who said he had 3 of his mates coming up.

We had the best room as far as being away from all the others who had set their tables up in the community room, which sat 11 tables and didn't leave room for privacy, as the tables were very close unlike in the room we had but that didn't change the fact that everyone seemed happy and the atmosphere was cordial.

The staff were wearing their best white shirts and Smitty and Cry Baby both had smiles on their faces as big as Cheshire Cats, there were even a few Governors on parade with matching smiles. Falkland's Steve was cooking in the pod preparing the food for dinner, gay Ian who we called Scotty, was doing the teas and Nick and Derek would be our waiters for the day with fat Mark doing the washing up.

With me included there were 22 of us with visitors with between 2 and 3 visitors per person. All in all, with the staff there would be about 80 of us on the wing hopefully making it a day to remember.

As the time was now fast approaching 9:00, we all started making our way towards the wing gates to see whose visitors would be first through the door and to say I felt a little bit apprehensive was an understatement as they started letting the visitors onto the wing one by one. As the guys recognised their spouses and friends the noise level went through the roof as everyone started talking at the same time.

As I saw Terri and Charlene the noise seemed to fade into the background as the 2 tango twins made their way towards me with their new spray suntans lighting up the wing as they ran into my waiting arms, hugging and kissing me until they nearly knocked me over. Once they had calmed down and regained their composure the questions stared coming fast and furious as they pointed to the deviants on the wing, which I had to put a stop to straight away and tell them both to be a little bit more discrete but they wouldn't take no for an answer. So, I had to give in and explain what most of them were in for, as they pointed a bit more subtly I gave them the run down.

Terry Ellis

First was Terry P who they both said looked a bit weird as he was smiling with his false teeth, grinning from ear to ear. I told them he tipped petrol over his girlfriend and set her alight.

Next was gay Ian who we called Scotty. I told them that Scotty had been to Grendon twice, the first time was for rape which was a bit weird as he way gay and used to be a rent boy, but now he was doing a life sentence for killing his wife, which sounded even stranger but I explained that he was a fucked-up individual because even though he knew he was gay he got married. One night when his wife went out he dressed up in her wedding dress and was dancing around the room to 'It's raining men'. She came home unexpectedly and caught him bang to rights, he even had her knickers and bra on and upon seeing him she went into one calling him a freak and threatened to tell her family and friends that he was a deviant. She started throwing all of his prized records at him which made him see red, so he gave her a right hander to calm her down and tried to explain to her that he was actually gay and he was sorry, with that he said he wanted to play her a record but she didn't want to listen to it. She got up and tried to go to her bedroom but with him thinking she was going to leave him, he took the bra off and started to strangle her to death. He then said he carried on playing records and once he had finished listening he then took off the wedding dress and put it on her, dressing her up in it, even putting makeup on her so that she would look her best and then he went to bed. But, one of the neighbours had heard all the noise and had called the police and when they turned up he said that she had gone to bed but they insisted on talking to her. Knowing that the game was up he let them in and they discovered her body and Scotty was nicked on the spot.

I then told the girls about Brian killing his Mum and Dad. Also, about Chris killing his wife and baby daughter with a golf club, and Lewis and Jamie killing the old men. I even told them about Bilal killing a little baby. After that they were asking me to stop as they couldn't take it anymore and asking me how I could live here with all these monsters and not beat the shit out of them. I explained to them how hard it was and that I was here to make some fundamental changes in my life and that price of change meant that I had to test my tolerance to the max and what better place than here to do that, as most if not all of the deviants would be easy targets back in the system. Instead of looking at them today as monsters, look at them today as helping me sort myself out, that way they could enjoy their day and also it would take their minds off the deviants.

Living amongst the beasts: The rise and fall of the Grendon experiment

I then introduced them to Tony, Mick, Martin and Mac who I classed as normal and that seemed to change the girls moods a little bit and with that I asked them if they wanted to have a good look around.

First, we went to the dining room where they got a cup of tea and I showed them where I ate and where the food was cooked. Then, we looked at all the stuff that had been donated for the raffle like the books, cd's and cuddly teddy bears. I showed them the community room and how it operated with the backing process and how we voted people out and how we got our jobs. I then showed them the laundry and like me they took the piss out of the prehistoric machines and dryers. I also showed them where we washed our cutlery and back into the hallway to see the fish tanks, then the phones which would give them a focal point for when I phoned them in the future. They then asked if they could see my cell but I told them we had to wait until the Officers gave us permission as they needed an Officer on each landing to make sure we kept all of our doors open as in the past a few of the lifers had got their wife's pregnant, so there had been a clampdown on wives and girlfriends in the cells.

I took them into the small room and showed them all the stuff I had bought them and we had another cuppa and just chatted for a while , which felt good as I had missed our little talks over the years. While we were all talking Mac came over and introduced his Mum and brother to us, also Gary introduced us to his mates. Terri said to me "how could his mates come and visit him knowing that he had killed an old man?". I just gave her a look and shrugged my shoulders.

Martin came in with his Mum and Stepdad and seeing that they didn't have anything on their table to eat or drink, Charlene and Terri asked if they could give them some of ours as we had plenty. We topped up Martins table and after a few minutes we were all laughing and joking with Mick, Mac and the other families which made me smile inside as the kids were really enjoying themselves and seemed to have settled down, taking the edge off me as I was worried that by them coming here it could freak them out but like me they were resilient and took it all in their stride.

At 10:30 the screws came in and said that they were now ready to let our visitors see our cells. With that the whole room rose to its feet and we all headed to our respective landings. Mac onto the 1s landing, me and the kids onto the 2s landing and Martin and Gary went up to the 3s, leaving me to show the kids the toilets and showers first. Then we were home to my abode which seemed to shock them as it was so small but as soon as they got a look at the view I could see that they were impressed, as you could see the farm house in the distance as well as the trees and a few cows, which made up for the cramped conditions, also my bed was comfortable. I had all their photos up on the wall, my PlayStation and TV. Once I explained how the nightstand worked I had won them over, the carpet tiles actually swung it for them as it made the cell look warm and cosy.

All in all, the experience was a positive one and after 20 minutes the shout went out that we had to return downstairs, so I took the opportunity to show then the pool room and the other fish tanks on my landing. Then we sneaked up to the 3s landing to have a look at where I did my therapy. We then headed back to our little room as it was now time for an early dinner of chicken and chips and strawberry gateau served by Mick and Derek, which the kids found funny as Del had a bow tie on. He also made a few jokes which made the girls laugh until I told them what he was in for. He had killed his wife by poisoning her, which put them both off their cakes until I told them the truth that he had only killed his wife by strangling her which shocked them even more as Derek was a funny old git and you would never think that he had it in him. After seeing their faces at this news, I told them that's why they should never judge a book by its cover or trust anybody apart from me. Once dinner was served we went outside to the garden to have a cigarette and walk around. The girls looked so healthy with their suntans and I could see that my babies were growing up and as we waited Craig and Bradly popped their heads out of the window from B-wing so I introduced them to the kids and while we were talking Kat came out with a camera and asked me if I wanted a few photos with the girls to put on my picture board and of course a few to take home. So, we stood in the middle I cuddled them both and we had a giggle, then it was time to go back inside for the raffle.

As we started to walk back to the gate I couldn't help but wonder what all this was in aid of today and did they actually think that by giving paedophiles and child killers family days that the gesture would turn them from deviants to born again saints? If they thought for one second that was indeed the case they were kidding themselves, as most of the morons here saw family day as some sort of reward for committing the most heinous of crimes and that being treated with sympathy only reinforced this belief that whatever crimes they committed in the future would be rewarded with them being put in places like Grendon as Grendon believed you could actually change a deviant through kindness, which was bollocks and couldn't be further from the truth as you can't change a deviants nature.

Only a criminals behaviour can be changed as criminal behaviour is brought about by nurturing which can be changed through change of circumstance. For instance, if I had a good job that paid really well, for that I would pack up crime tomorrow but if a deviant came into money he would only be a richer deviant, or maybe family day was a way of showing the deviants families that their deviant sons were on the mend. I couldn't understand it's purpose or objective but I'm sure there was one.

Now it was time to win the kids a few CDs that I had my eye on so we took the long corridor back to the dining room and took our places at the back of the room with our backs to the wall so we could see what was going on, plus there wouldn't be any deviants standing behind my girls as keeping them safe was still a concern for me as you could never trust any of them, as once a deviant always a deviant.

Daryl would be our compere today and as he picked up the microphone and started calling out the raffle numbers one by one over the next hour we clapped out way through it, laughing and joking at the prizes they were giving away. When it was all over it was time for a few speeches, one from Terry P and the other from Scotty who both seemed to go on and on about how much Grendon had changed their lives. This was the only part of the day that made me feel sick as Scotty had been to Grendon twice. Once for rape where he had been passed fit to live back in the community, then went on to kill his wife after being found out that he was a dancing transvestite and the other lying fucker was Terry P, he had lied his way through Grendon minimising his part in setting his girlfriend on fire. To see them both up there talking shit only reinforced in me the hypocrisy of this cesspool of scum I found myself living with and I was starting to wonder if there really was a crock of therapeutic gold at the end of all this madness or was it just like all the other courses they send you on in prison that are not worth a wank? I also wondered if Grendon would end up like the 'serious personality disorder units', not fit for purpose. I could only assume the latter as up until now there was not really much depth in what I was learning here apart from getting better at manipulation through spilling a few tears from time to time for the benefit of the Facilitators so that they could write that I was engaging well in therapy.

It was now 3:30 and I only had half an hour left with the kids so we went and sat at our table and spoke about Charlene's salon and how well she was doing. We also caught up on all the gossip that was happening in Camden Town where we lived. We even had time to finish off all the cakes, spreading the last of the Philadelphia on them before the last shout went out that the day was now finally at an end. We said our goodbyes to Martin and his family, also Mac's, then I hugged both my kids and we said goodbye as we walked to the gate. I than waited and waved at them until they were outside.

This seemed to hit me like a sledgehammer and for the first time in years I really felt the loss of their departure. When I went back to my cell and laid on my bed the full force of the remaining years I had to do hit me like a ton of bricks and no matter how hard I

Terry Ellis

tried I couldn't shake off the fact that the next time we would all sit together again as a family I would be 50 years old or more and they would be grown women, most likely married with their own kids and they would not be my babies anymore. With those thoughts in my head I went to sleep hoping that those feelings of self- pity would be gone by the morning. As I kissed the photos we had taken this afternoon I only hoped that I could make it up to them all one day for the pain and misery I had brought upon them over the past 4 years of my incarceration, which brought the whole day down on my head and made it seem like an anti-climax but the whole day had the desired effect of making me think of my family, so well done Grendon.

The weekend passed without much to talk about as most, like me, were feeling the after effects of family day and were coming down from their highs of seeing their loved ones. Just to give myself a boost I phoned the kids and listened to them go on about how much they enjoyed the day and how much they enjoyed having dinner with me and being able to see my cell and where I phoned them from, which made me feel good as I knew they didn't have to worry so much about me anymore.

CHAPTER TWENTY-THREE

Monday morning, I was feeling alright until I heard that Mick's Dad had died that morning. Mick was distraught and had stayed in his cell with Mac as they were really close and also Group members, but Smitty seemed a bit put out as he believed Mick should be in the room explaining to everyone how he felt about his Dad dying, which I thought was a bit cold and if I am honest lacked any real understanding. I knew once Mac heard what he had said, he like me, would hit the roof so I thought it best to keep out of the way for a few days after I gave Mick my condolences.

The next morning Mick still hadn't come to his Group but his Facilitator had made a point that he should be sharing his thoughts and feelings with them which didn't go down too well with Mac, Martin and Jamie who all showed their contempt by refusing to discuss the matter. Mac even went as far as to tell the Facilitator to grow a back bone and stand up to Smitty as he like the rest of us could see it was an absurd idea to ask Mick to use the Group so soon after his Dad's death. Smitty tried to raise the subject again on feedbacks but was told in no uncertain terms by all the Groups to jog on. Even Martin had words with him saying it was the most half-witted thing he had heard Lord Smitty say since he had been at Grendon and also added that it was annoyingly insensitive. Also, black Mark, Tony and myself said that the very thought of Mick having to use the Group the very next day after his Dad had died was ill conceived and we asked the whole wing to take a vote on the matter as we felt it was important that no other member in the future should be subjected to this moronic bullying by staff and the Psychologist to bring such a sensitive subject to the wing just to appease Smitty. We also asked if we could take a vote to give Mick a few days off and then proceeded to ask the wing for a show of hands on the matter. All at once everyone's hands went up but Smitty said that this was not the time or place to vote as it wasn't a community meeting, he said it was only feedbacks. So, we asked the Chairman if he would over-ride Smitty as we as a community felt that we needed to act immediately. The Chairman was not having any of it as he knew he would be in deep shit if he sided with us. After much jeering and a few taunts and shouts of disapproval from us Smitty had no other option than to call an end to the meeting as he was fuming. As he walked out you could see that he had lost all credibility and was incensed to have been questioned about his methods regarding therapy but none of us gave a fuck as we were all right and Smitty knew it.

It took Mick just over a week to pull himself together and on the Monday of his Dad's funeral he left early as he had to get back to Liverpool. By the time we all got up he was already well and truly gone so we all went about our business and got ready for the community meeting.

The atmosphere seemed strange as Smitty said that he had some upsetting news for us all. He told us that Mick had left early this morning at about 5 o'clock so that he could get to the funeral on time but due to mechanical problems the taxi taking Mick had broken down on the motorway and Mick had to be taken to the nearest police station and had missed his Dad's funeral all because the taxi was the only vehicle authorised to transport Mick. No other taxi could take him which we all thought was a fucking joke and typical of the red tape bureaucracy that was put in place to cover up the fact that they had fucked up.

Mac and the rest of the group were livid and after 10 or so minutes the subject got back to Mick and how he must be feeling, so it was agreed that Mac would meet him on this return and try to console him, as we all knew that Mick could be quite fiery. If it could really be said though, we all thought that Smitty could have done more as he had the power to get the taxi changed so that Mick could have got to the funeral. But, he was a vindictive bastard and none of us put it past him to have got his own back on Mick because he hadn't used the Group. Plus, we had all gone against him and all of us knew what a spiteful cunt Smitty could be. So, to be honest, I wasn't too surprised when I heard about what had happened to Mick and how unhelpful Smitty had been to him.

To our surprise Mick came back and was as cool as a cucumber and took it all in his stride and even used his Group regarding the matter the next day. By the following week Mick was given the job of wing cook to take his mind off things. To be honest the food tasted much better and I even put my name up to be the second in command as I really needed a job that would tax me as I was bored of cleaning, so I decided that I would ask for backing and try to get a job in the pod as my next job.

CHAPTER TWENTY-THREE

However, we had bigger things to contend with as a phone signal had been detected on the wing, meaning that someone had a phone. A wing special was called and the whole wing was summoned to the community room where Smitty informed us all that a signal had been detected by a hand- held scanner which showed a phone had been used while we were on association. Which meant that whoever had it was a smart cookie as the scanners are not normally used while association is on but due to an overzealous screw who had turned it on while he was sitting in the office by mistake had in fact brought to light that an unauthorised phone was now on the wing. Smitty asked for the phone to be handed in or there would be repercussions as this was the second time this week we had heard of a phone being used. B-wing had a signal which was interfering with the TVs on the wing but thankfully the scanner had exonerated C-wing from any involvement on that occasion. Also, on D-wing a prankster had decided to place a phone case in the middle of the community room on the carpet which got a big laugh that morning when it was discovered by the Psychologist, who was far from impressed and had decided to ban family day on D-wing. As the invitations had already gone out there was nothing they could do about it anyway as peoples visitors were flying in from all over the world, so they decided to put their therapeutic foot down by not letting their visitors view their cells which we all thought was a bit juvenile but at least they had got their family day.

We had only just had our family day so the threat wasn't taken too seriously on our wing but I never much cared as I had decided that I wasn't going to have another family day as the last one seemed to have fucked up my head, also I didn't want to put my kids through that again.

I sat back in my seat and took a good look around the wing and wondered who might have the phone but I thought better of it as it could be anyone. As always with cases like this the new people on the wing would be first to have the finger pointed at then, which meant Mark and Tony would be on that list as they were the latest 2 on the wing, but as I said it could be anyone. Also, we had just had our family day so one of the visitors could have brought it in and if that was the case that would exonerate Mark and Tony because they didn't have a family day.

We were really all in the dark so to speak and because of the lack of evidence and someone to point the finger at, the meeting was brought to an end and as Smitty would be taking a few days off due to outside commitments he would be leaving Cry Baby in charge, which was a fuck up waiting to happen. But, we had to give her the benefit of the doubt and I only hoped that she could handle the situation.

The next day nothing was said so we carried on with our Small Groups as usual, even discussing the pros and cons of having a phone. And from my own experience of having one when I first came into prison they were more trouble than they were worth as you had to bottle it most days and nights as the screws were constantly searching you and your cell and creeping about all night with their scanner trying to catch you out. I also found myself having the same conversations every night and having to keep asking my family and friends to keep buying me top-ups, which didn't sit well with me as it made me feel like a ponce. So, I got rid of mine when I went to Rye Hill, partly because they had a BOSS chair and also, I wanted a fresh start and after a year of playing cat and mouse with the screws I was happy to get rid of the fucking thing.

Daryl and the rest of the group concurred with me. Daryl then said that he had been caught with a phone some months earlier on the wing. He told us about his thoughts and feelings on the subject and also said that when he was accused by the wing, he denied it until he was blue in the face but had got fed up with all the shit that was happening on the wing, so being a bit smarter than the rest of the guys who had all been using it, he came clean and grassed them all up and because he was the first one to break rank, his move was seen as change by Smitty so he was kept on and all the others were kicked out. This sort of grassing to save your own neck was expected of you but it wasn't real change because you knew it was only a matter of time before someone put you in it, so to strike first was seen as the smart move. The other was to never compromise yourself in the first place.

This is what most learnt to do at Grendon as you started to mistrust everybody which was the desired effect of the process, because if you never trusted anyone you were less likely to get into trouble in the first place. Which again was a false economy because as soon as most got back into the real world they would just revert back to type as the scrutiny wouldn't be on you, or be so intense but like most of the things that happened at Grendon they couldn't see as far as their noses as far as therapy was concerned, just as

Living amongst the beasts: The rise and fall of the Grendon experiment

long as the game was being played their way. It really was a joke as they really saw it as change and not the deviants manipulating them, which was actually the case on so many levels.

Daryl was a lifer and a survivor who wanted to get out of prison at any cost and if that meant grassing up a few paedophiles or rapists to get through the therapeutic process, then so be it. And, if I'm honest I didn't blame him if it was at the cost of the deviant mafia or their kind.

On the Saturday morning I was up at 6 o'clock and had decided to boil the kettle for a cup of tea and as I looked through the glass in the doorway to the stairs, hidden in the corner I could see that they had left the scanner on the wing. What idiots I thought, I couldn't believe the stupidity of the night screw or the security screws, it was beyond comprehension. When the nightstand ended and all the doors opened up I showed the guys on the landing the scanner and one of them promptly took it down to the office to show the Officers. They looked pretty shocked but made light of it and by the time breakfast was finished the whole wing knew of the inept attempt to try and triangulate the signal but the Keystone Cops were on the case and Sherlock Holmes would have his man by the end of the week.

It was no surprise when Dave one of the screws, came into the community meeting and said that there had been a signal and that a phone was being used on the wing. The signal had been narrowed down to 4 cells which were Mick, Chris, Neil and black Mark's which seemed to ignite a debate of whose it may be. Mac was saying it couldn't be Mick or Chris as he knew them 100% also stating that they wouldn't do it to their Group, which only left black Mark and Neil who both denied any involvement in it.

This prompted a response from Tony who said he also knew Mark and Neil and was 100% sure they were not involved, which started an argument between Tony and Mac. Then Mick joined in swearing and saying it wasn't him. Mark then hit back at Mick saying the phone could belong to Mac and who did they think they were, accusing him of shit stirring. Then Neil started and before we knew it everyone was accusing each other. This started Cry Baby off as she burst into tears and lost control of the meeting, so the screws had to take over and the meeting was called to an end.

The damage had been done as everyone was at each other's throats by now and by bang up there was an all-out war of words. Jamie had joined in as he was on Mick and Mac's Group. Tony, Mark, Neil and old man killer Jamie with the rest of the wing were

Terry Ellis

on Mark and Tony's side as they all hated Mac and Mick as they were seen as bullies. As Mark and Neil were on my Group I had to side with them, also Tony was my pal.

The next morning the war of words was still going on, all because of the shambolic way Cry Baby had handled the community meeting.

I asked the first question and said "I was the one who found the scanner outside Mark's cell and if the signal came from that direction and there were 12 cells in that area, then how could they pin-point which 4 cells it came from?" I also added that Alex the rapist had said his TV was playing up, which meant the phone signal was near his cell which was at the other end of the landing, so how could the Officers come in here yesterday and say categorically that it was definitely these 4 cells?

Dave the Officer's response to this was that he never said it was those cells, which was a blatant lie as everyone had heard him say it but he wouldn't admit it and kept up the party line.

It could have been anyone's on the left-hand side of the stairs which got Tony and I off the hook as we were on the right- hand side but because of all the lies from the Officers and Cry Bay I was starting to wonder if they had just singled out Mark as he had failed a drug test that week before, but he had won his commitment vote because it was proved that his medication had stimulants in them. With this in mind Smitty had asked for a commitment vote with the recommendation Mark be voted out. The whole wing however voted for him to stay which once again undermined Smitty's authority.

Once again, I could see how Mark had been singled out but because we had asked the right questions Dave had come unstuck and now even the Security Governor was starting to back us up as he knew they couldn't actually pinpoint the signal with these old scanners. So once again we had a stalemate as it could have been a number of guys on the wing who may have had the phone but no-one was talking and Mick, Mac and Jamie were keeping quiet which I found funny because they looked up for a fight yesterday. I was not going to count my chickens yet because I knew that Mac was a slippery fucker plus Tony had decided not to go after him, so I just kept calm and waited to see how it all played out.

After the meeting I went to see Mac and Mick and they swore blind that they had nothing to do with the phone and said it must be Mark or Tony as they were both new, which was a load of bollocks as I had spoken to them and they too swore blind they had nothing to do with it. I said that if that was the case then why were they at each other's throats and doing the deviants work for them and for that matter also Lord Smitty's as it was really nothing to do with the phones, it was just a personality thing and the phones were just a smoke screen to cover up the fact that they didn't like each other. I said knowing this, they should call a truce and stop throwing shit at each other or they would all end up being kicked out for something they were not involved in. With that they all shook hands and the matter was closed.

Over the next week or so we all calmed down and got back on with our therapy. Mac was still upset though and took it out on Martin who refused to sit at the dinner table with us ever again. So, to remedy the situation I asked Tony to join our table hoping Tony, Mick and Mac could all bury the hatchet and move forward. After a few days we were all as good as new and the phone situation was dead and buried. Martin was still on his new table with a couple of deviants and was forgotten by the end of the week as we had excommunicated him. However, I did still go and sit with him in his cell and told him I was always there for him if he ever needed me which cheered him up. After a few weeks he was on top form and even packed up smoking and lost a bit of weight, this was to show Mac that he could stand on his own 2 feet which seemed to work for him.

Also, for the last few weeks there had been no signal and everyone was just carrying on and working well in therapy. Mark and the rest of the guys were doing well and seemed to have turned a corner but Smitty seemed to dislike him still and out of the blue one morning he called a wing special to inform us that Mark would be leaving therapy as it was felt that he was not engaging in therapy and by the end of that day he was gone. This put Tony on a downer as they were good mates. However, I still took the 2 Mars Bars off him from the bet we had that Mark would be gone by the end of the month as he had shown Smitty and the staff up on the last commitment vote and because the staff were slightly resentful towards Mark regarding that fact. I could only imagine that the staff had voted him out and what better excuse than to say he was not engaging in therapy to get rid of him. Vengeance at any cost of someone's life was not setting a good example as all the deviants were learning was that if you can't get your own way all you had to do was lie and manipulate to get rid of any problem at any cost. This was not a lesson they should be learning as most had come to Grendon to get away from this sort of behaviour as all the guys I met a Grendon were quite intelligent but lacked any of the social skills needed to act in a reasonable way when it came to dealing with people, so this was the last example they needed by the Head of Psychology, Smitty.

CHAPTER TWENTY-FOUR

It took a few days for the wing to get back to normal and just like in most cases, it would take a deviant act by one of the community to distract our attention away from what we were doing here and todays lucky recipient Brian, the guy who had killed his Mum and Dad, was to be the one.

Kat had made an allegation against him that he had rubbed up against her in the office as she was trying to pass him. She told him she would be making a formal complaint against him when she got back from her break to Poland after visiting her family, but just to be on the safe side before she went she wrote the allegation down in the wing book and told Albino Jamie, Mac, Tony and me what Brian had done, which didn't surprise me as he was a weirdo but for some reason Mac always had him in his cell as they always spoke about university as Mac was doing a degree. I could sort of understand it but now his buddy had assaulted Kat I wondered how he would react to the news. Also, I wondered how Jamie the Albino would react as he and Kat were always in each other's company and I knew it would only be a matter of time before there was a war of words again before the shit hit the fan.

As Tony was in Brian's Group he decided to take him to task over it but Brian was adamant it was an accident and that Kat had blown it all out of proportion and he would explain it to her upon her return. You could see from Brian's demeanour that he was shaken from the whole experience and a darkness seemed to descend over him and for a few days after he would not speak to anyone.

By the Friday he was moved to F-wing. There were Governor's on the wing and secret meetings going on and all of the staff looked on edge but we as a wing were none the wiser as to what was afoot but something was definitely amiss but with Brian off the wing there was nothing we could do, plus Kat wouldn't be back until the end of the week.

Living amongst the beasts: The rise and fall of the Grendon experiment

In the meantime, however there had been a lot of friction between Gary the old man killer, Albino Jamie and Mac as Gary had accused both of them of bullying him and said that they were using therapeutic issues against him regarding his mum. He also accused Kat, his Facilitator, of passing Jamie and Mac privileged information, so a wing special was called but because Kat was not there to defend herself most just thought Gary was talking shit as he was always crying on his Group that he thought the relationship between Jamie and Kat was inappropriate and he brought it up in the community meetings as often as he could. But most of the guys were bored of him as we knew that the only reason he kept bringing it up was because he hated Jamie with a vengeance and today was no exception as Gary was swearing and saying that Mac and Jamie had been talking about his Mum. This was true in part, but what Mac had said was that Gary should be working on the Group about the issues regarding his Mum's death and their relationship and to stop focusing on Jamie and the rest of the community. With that Gary started on Jamie accusing him of having an affair but Jamie just said Gary was paranoid and was seeing things that were not there, which made poor old Gary lose the plot. He then turned on Jamie saying he was going to kill him and beat the shit out of him at the first chance he got. Blinded by his own rage he forgot that he had just made a threat to kill. The meeting was then called to an end to give Gary a chance to calm down. He was then put on a commitment as his anger towards Jamie was seen as deranged.

Smitty stepped in and said that the safety of the wing had to come first and called for Gary to be banged up straight away, which we all thought was a bit strange as he had never got out of his seat which was one of the rules at Grendon. So why was he stopping Gary from expressing himself? Also, in the past there had been worse altercations on the wing with threats to kill and all sorts, so why was Smitty over-reacting by asking the staff to take Gary back to his cell? Something was definitely going on. Maybe Gary was onto something that Smitty did not want exposed on the wing as there was a Governor on the wing and Gary was talking about Kat and Jamie. Surely that wasn't the reason to bang Gary up and make him look like enemy number one, just to hide certain things discussed on the wing in front of the Governor.

That was Grendon for you, they preached one thing and did the opposite so we just accepted it for what it was and hoped Gary would calm down and be back in his Group in the morning.

Tony and I decided to go for a run before dinner to unwind as the last few weeks had been like living in a fucking nut house and we were both feeling the strain from all the bad vibes being communicated by the bad atmosphere of everyone arguing as the wing seemed to be losing control, what with Mark being kicked off the wing for nothing more

Terry Ellis

than Smitty not liking him and now Gary being banged up for doing what was asked of him. Also, Brian had been moved to F-wing in one of the holding cells and also there was a lot of in-fighting within the Groups as we had seen with what happened to Pete the Arsonist.

The place was turning into a battle ground of deviants all turning on each other. Once again, I had to ask myself why was I here?   As I smiled to myself the question answered itself.

At 2 o'clock sharp the intercom came on and the screws told us that Gary was being moved and that we would all have to stay banged up until tea time. I shouted back up to Gary but he had his music turned up full blast, it was still quiet time over dinner so he was being defiant to the end and if I'm honest I couldn't blame him for being upset as Smitty changed the rules whenever it suited him and today was no exception.

As I passed the next couple of hours reading and pottering about, I wondered if there was any validity in what he had said about Kat and if it ever came out in the future would Smitty update Gary's reports as someone who was the victim of an Officer's collusion or would he just leave it as it was, as to update it would mean he would have to admit he was wrong which would be an indictment of the way he ran the wing and the therapy on C-wing. Also, I couldn't see Kat admitting any wrong doing, so we would never know the truth unless something else transpired in the meantime but for now Gary was gone and Kat was away. Also, Brian was now on F-wing awaiting the outcome of the allegation made against him by Kat. So all-in-all just another crazy week at Grendon.

CHAPTER TWENTY-FIVE

As I went down for tea that evening I couldn't help but notice that Mac and Albino Jamie were both smiling from ear to ear as their nemesis Gary was now gone and to say they were gloating was an understatement, as this was the normal reaction when someone was booted off the wing and if you were party to their demise then you saw it as a victory of your own success and another's misfortune. This malignant pleasure under the guise of democracy in therapy brought out the worst in people and only reinforced in me that the everyday politics on the wing wasn't conductive to a therapeutic community as most of the inmates were more concerned about getting their own back on each other than concentrating on the real issues that they were here for in the first place.

This was a shame as over the last few months I was starting to see some good therapy taking place here. Also, seeing the actions of Mac and Albino Jamie I was starting to see that I also used the commitment process as a way of getting rid of my enemies, or some of them, just because I thought they were deviants.

This rank opportunism actually undermined what Grendon was all about and its ethos but unfortunately was characteristic of the culture and attitudes of most of the staff and inmates alike and any aspirations that this cycle of behaviour might change seemed unrealistic as our mentor Smitty perpetuated these retaliated responses by his own manipulative behaviour.

As I was starting to see the consequences of these actions on others for no other reason than retaliation I had to re-evaluate the way I went after my enemies, so I made a mental note that in future I would listen to both sides and make my judgement upon facts instead of siding with other groups like I did with Pete when Lewis asked me and Tony to back him. Also, I would try my best to be more understanding of the deviants when they were up for their commitments which I knew would be hard as I enjoyed their demise as I hated all of them still . If I was going to be neutral and more objective I had to start acting accordingly, so another lesson learnt by another person's demise as this was how therapy really worked as you eventually saw behaviours played out like this time and time again not realising that the first time you saw it that you too acted the same, but incrementally as you saw it repeated by your friends and enemies alike you started to see the consequences of both sides of the coin, i.e. pain and pleasure. If you were on the side of someone's pain you were able to emphasise with them, giving you a better understanding of the consequences of spiteful intentions. After being on the receiving end more than once you started to play the game and keep yourself to yourself and not be part of this destructive behaviour, bringing about a more balanced individual.

It was only through these self- realisations that real change would come about in your mindset, keeping you safe from being the next victim of the deviant Mafia.

By the time I banged up for the evening Gary's departure was a distant memory and I only hoped now that all the fighting was over and that we could all get back to doing some therapy.

The following day I went for backing on my Small Group for the pod job as Mick had asked me to do so as he didn't want any of the deviants getting it. So, I bit the bullet and volunteered for the position even though I had never ever cooked a Sunday roast let alone an apple crumble with custard. The thought of cooking for the whole community and at times the staff was a daunting prospect but it was something that I had to do as it would show I was a team player.

It also meant I had to work 1 week on and 1 week off as C-wing had 2 teams of cooks. This gave me an opportunity to have a lie in, I hoped, every weekend. My cleaning job involved me getting up at 9 o'clock at weekends doing my bit for the community and if I didn't I would be put in the book and winged for dereliction of duty, so with one week on and one week off it would give me a chance to indulge in some shut-eye at weekends.

I asked my group for backing and received a resounding vote of confidence after I promised them extra apple crumble every Sunday. I only hoped that I would get the backing from the rest of the wing which I thought was just a formality as most of the deviants lacked confidence and hated confrontation. Part of the job was serving the meals which anyone will tell you who has been in jail is a volatile job, especially when you are dealing with fat greedy psychopaths. You tend to see a different side to someone when you are dealing with their food. A hungry man is a dangerous man especially here at Grendon plus we had a fair share of gluttons especially when it came to inmates on steroids in their medications as it made them hungry and volatile at the same time.

Living amongst the beasts: The rise and fall of the Grendon experiment

To work in the pod, you had to have good people skills which I had in abundance, my tolerance levels over the last 8 months had been tested to the limit having to deal with deviants. So, ready or not I was up for the job and on the Friday, I got my full wing backing and was ready for work. Monday morning, I would be dressed in my whites with my chef's hat on.

Mick was a good teacher and by the end of the week I was efficient in the art of warming up the food, also I was making the custard along with boiling the carrots and most of the vegetables. Mick taught me how to make roast potatoes to perfection and my roast chicken was the creme-de-la-creme. By the second week I was able to take charge and give Mick a chance to go to the gym.

Part of our responsibility of being pod workers was that the food came first and had to be served on time with no excuses. Having 2 efficient cooks meant one of us could use the gym. As Mick was number 1 and I was number 2 we took it in turns to use the gym. One cooked while the other went to the gym which worked well as long as we both got back to serve the food together.

Martin was our number 3, his job was to clean the kitchen and as we all got on so well we all helped each other which resulted in most days finishing by 5:30, this gave us enough time to shower and make our phone calls before bang up.

After all the shit that had happened over the last few months it was a relief to be working in the pod as it took my mind off therapy, it also kept me out of trouble.

However, my pal Tony was not so lucky as he was overheard by Scottie one evening saying the word 'bomboclaat' which Scottie took to heart, so on the Monday he winged Tony for being homophobic. Tony claimed that he was not homophobic and said that he had gay friends and even mentioned that a guy named Adam on F-wing, who himself was gay, would verify to the fact that they were friends. Scottie wouldn't let it go though as he thought he was the only gay in the village, so every chance he got to use the gay card to cover the fact he was a deviant who had killed his own wife whilst dressed in her wedding dress. Every time he used his Group about killing her he would always try this distraction technique as it was easier to vent his anger on someone like Tony than to just work on the real issues that he was here for in the first place. This technique was used by most of the rapists and killers of women.

Terry Ellis

Even though Smitty knew this he thought it would be a good idea if Tony proved to everyone he wasn't homophobic by going on the next diversity meeting as Scottie would be reading one of his poems out. This would give Tony a chance to see the error of his ways. Tony was a little scared of going so he asked me to go with him but I said no and laughed and went on exercise.

Tony tried to convince Adam his gay friend on F-wing to put a good word in for him on the diversity meeting, hoping it would persuade Scottie that he wasn't homophobic, putting him in a better light. As the last thing Tony needed was any hassle on the wing he could do without all this unwanted attention from the gay contingency as we were surrounded by them on the wing what with Lewis, Dan, James, Mark, Brian and golf club Chris all batting for the pink brigade and we all knew how spiteful they could be.

Tony thought it was best to placate them, as this was better than going to war with them. This also seemed to me to be the better option as Tony was going up for his C-cat so he needed their backing, so going to a gay disco night with Scottie and listening to a few poems seemed a small price to pay to get everyone off his back.

A few nights later I saw Tony waiting at the gate fretting so I promised to go with him as I didn't want him going over on his own. Also, he looked like he needed some help. So, with me as his escort it seemed to take the edge off his anxiety, we waited for the gate to open. Scottie came down with his Timberlands on wearing a check shirt, blue jeans and cropped hair looking just like Monkey Boots but taller. He took a quick glance over at me and Tony as if we were a bit of dirt on the bottom of his shoe. This made him think he came across as aloof but only really made him look like the deviant prat he was. We both smiled back and made polite conversation. I even tried to hold Tony's hand but he wasn't having any of it. Tony was not really a tactile person and saw any form of touching of men on men repugnant which made me laugh. Tony really was a stubborn man.

Looking at him I could tell he thought the whole idea of going to the diversity meeting was distasteful as it brought him into conflict with his religion as Tony was a Muslim. This made the whole situation even more hilarious as I knew he was hating every minute of it and we hadn't even left the wing yet. As for me, I couldn't care less about someone's sexuality as I have always been open minded.

I did however object to the gay card being used at every opportunity by Scottie as I always saw him coming onto people and being sexually suggestive which was irritating at the best of times as his remarks were always a bit near the mark. He just assumed that everyone was either bi-sexual or gay and often said that there was no such thing as a straight person, this coming from him, a gay guy who rapes women only came across as delusional, which in fact he really was.

I could see Tony was resentful at having to appease a degenerate reprobate like Scottie by pretending he liked him. His religious beliefs had to take a back seat all because Scottie was now taking refuge behind something so relevant like human rights, the very same rights he denied his wife before he killed her. To see him now taking the moral high ground over Tony was offensive to me but this was common practice to the deviant mind especially when you considered Mark was also the bully rep but he had killed a young boy and let's not forget Brian who killed his parents and was now the family rep. They were all over-compensating for their deviant behaviours. This behaviour was all an attempt to hide the fact that they were nothing better than monsters. It was so transparent it was a joke; the funny thing was though they believed we couldn't see through their manipulative behaviours as they kept up their pretence. It was on par with Jimmy Saville being the child care rep.

The psychologists and staff encouraged this manipulative behaviour believing the practice to claiming to have a higher moral standard or having more laudable beliefs in the cases of the deviant mind would somehow equate to change. As I was living amongst the beasts though I could see it for what it was, a deviant distraction from the realities of what they were here for in the first place. As Tony was on the receiving end I couldn't help but see the funny side of it all.

We left the wing and made our way up to the Education Department with Scottie walking behind us looking at Tony's bum. I only hoped the rest of the evening would be just as excruciating for Tony, as to see him out of his comfort zone and normal surrounds awkward and spitting blood, but at the same time having to look and keep calm in what would be an agonising situation for him would be worth its weight in gold for me. With a smile on my face I grabbed Tony's hand and dragged him up the corridor singing James Blunt 'You're Beautiful'.

As we came to the entrance of the Education Department we saw a screw standing there with a smile on his face directing everyone to the pink party. We pulled ourselves together determined not to embarrass ourselves or Scottie for bringing us as his guests. We really couldn't afford any more controversy as it was the last thing we needed as Scottie would have a field day winging us if we gave him the chance, especially when you considered the whole purpose of us coming here tonight was to mend bridges and not destroy them.

Terry Ellis

We both agreed that no matter what happened behind these doors tonight we would be on our best behaviour which meant not taking the piss or being sarcastic to anyone. So, with chins up and chest out we stepped through the door to be greeted by Adam, Tony's gay mate from F-wing. Adam was about 6', skinny, wearing a white string vest and came across as camp as they come. As soon as Scottie saw his pal he changed from he-man to she-man as he deliberately started to camp it up. He started talking in a therapeutic feminine way but Tony and I never battered an eyelid as we took it in our stride.

The room was filled with quite a mixed bunch of guys. Adam introduced some of his mates to us. First was a gay guy called Paul from Newcastle who was about 20 stone with cropped hair, he was in for chopping his Mum's head off. He was about 50 years old. One night his Mum took the remote control off him which made him snap so he went into the kitchen and picked up a knife. He then stabbed her and cut her head off putting it in a Tesco bag and placing it in the bin, he then just carried on watching TV. A simple case of remote control rage I presume and living with Mummy for 50 years.

The next guy he introduced us to was a young guy called Justin, he was the guy who walked into a house up in Manchester and took a little girl out of the bath while her Mum was watching telly. Luckily for the little girl Justin was pulled over 5 miles up the road by the police who discovered her tied up in a bag in the back of a van. He too was very camp and I took a dislike to him straight away especially after I found out that there was a little girl involved. I wanted to smash his face in and I don't know how I managed not to do it, it took all my strength not to say anything to him. So instead I just picked up a couple of plates and went in search of the cakes, biscuits and a soft drink as it was the only real reason I had come here for in the first place.

I got Tony and myself 2 large plates of food which I hoped would make up for me having to come here in the first place and having to listen to all this shit. Also, once I got back to Tony and Adam's table, I told Adam not to introduce us to anymore deviants as I could do without the running commentary. Most of the guys in the room were from A-wing and were the worst type of scum, so we agreed to drop them all out.

Now with our backs to the wall we stood there taking in the spectacle that was the pink party. There were transvestites with full make-up on who looked as ugly as sin with jawbones as big as Desperate Dan's'. As I looked around the room I noticed Kevin, a guy I had met on the induction wing and to say I was shocked was an understatement as the last time I saw him he was down the gym with cropped hair and doing dead lifts acting all macho. I hadn't really spoken to Kevin before as he was in for kiddie porn and also grooming kids online, but being the big mouth that I am I shouted over to Kevin and said " fuck me Kevin who dressed you mate?" which brought the whole room to a standstill and everyone looked over at me probably all thinking that I was being sarcastic, but I was only trying to break the ice. So, feeling they were being over touchy I smiled at Tony who by now was hiding behind Adam pretending he was not with me. So, to save face I went over to Kevin and shook his hand hoping he would speak to me and hadn't taken offence which, thank God, was the case as he was genuinely pleased to see me and told me it was a relief to be himself, so with him now on my side the others went back to what they were doing.

After a few minutes what I had said to Kevin was a distant memory even Tony was smiling over at me now. I suffered another 10 minutes of Kevin telling me how liberating it was to finally be accepted as a woman and to be able to wear his hair in pig tails. I wished him well and went back over to Tony and Adam who both rolled their eyes at me as we all laughed it off.

It was now time for Scottie to read his poem out but he refused to do it as there were about 20 people in the room now and he said he felt embarrassed, so I had to convince him that what he had to say was important and he shouldn't let a little thing like embarrassment get in the way of him expressing himself. With that he spent the next 10 minutes reading out his life story in a poem whilst crying at the same time. I was now looking like the saviour of the evening and as Scottie continued we all gave him a round of applause and I even made a little speech myself. I said how welcome everyone had made Tony and I and what an enjoyable evening it had been. We finished up by shaking everyone's hands and also telling them we would come again.

The next morning Scottie said what a great evening it had been, he had forgiven Tony and he never mentioned the remark I made. All in all, we had redeemed ourselves in the eyes of the wing, even Smitty was over the moon at having cured Tony's homophobia, or so he thought.

By the weekend Scottie was Tony's new best friend. Every time we went on exercise we had 15 new admirers and all of them wore lipstick. They would wave as we jogged round the exercise yard which was off putting. Also, Adam was becoming a pain in the arse and would whistle and try and say something funny in his high-pitched voice every time we passed him. Tony had to grin and bear it though as he was on his best behaviour, at least the hostility was over and the wing was back to normal. Even Mac and Mick had

Terry Ellis

realised that if we were going to make it through we had to make certain allowances as far as the deviant Mafia were concerned.

We proceeded to play them at their own game, we would smile and say 'good morning' to them and it seemed to pacify them and the staff. It was to become our new weapon of choice, it was what Smitty had wanted all along, a forced environment brought on by the need to survive. It meant a cease fire between good and evil, brokered by a better understanding of ourselves and our own needs.

All of us wanted to get through therapy and be seen in a better light as people who had changed instead of failures who were unable to comply with a few simple rules. We carried on with the misery of having to live amongst the beasts. At least we were learning to compromise, which was the most important thing Grendon had to offer.

CHAPTER TWENTY-FIVE

On Monday morning albino Jamie was given the wing Chairman's job, making Group 2 ecstatic. Mac and Albino Jamie had seen the job as one that they could exploit and as they lorded it over everybody, Tony and I had dinner. We all had a laugh at the fact all the nutters were really running the asylum as Albino Jamie hated the deviants more than me and showed his contempt to them on a daily basis as his own Mum had been a victim of a rapist. To put him in charge was really putting the cat amongst the pigeons and I wondered why Lord Smitty would make such a ludicrous decision. I knew he thrived on conflict but this was just madness as Albino Jamie himself was very volatile at the best of times.

I only hoped that Lord Smitty knew what he was doing as the wing was now working more cohesively than I had seen it before. The only conclusion I could come to was that Smitty wanted Jamie to fail as Jamie only had one speed and that was to attack.

Over the next week he surprised us all as he turned off the aggression and worked well with all the deviants. He was more amenable than I had seen him before which also showed me like the deviants he could manipulate at will, as overnight he had changed his behaviour from being truculent to saint fucking Cheesy, all because he wanted to get out of prison at any cost.

This manipulation brought about by the pressure to appease Probation Officers, IPP boards and psychologists alike was not seen as change but just a mask being worn by most if not all the inmates at Grendon who were doing life sentences which was a shame. The whole system perpetuated this sort of behaviour and actively encouraged it as even by the nature of therapy it was never designed to work with a captive audience. However, I could not blame Jamie or the deviants for using their number one skill, manipulation, to get out of prison but this behaviour didn't apply to me as I was not a lifer. I still hoped though that the lessons I was learning here were in fact real as I hated the thought that all my hard work over the last few months was for nothing.

On Monday morning I had to do my first feedback on the community meeting regarding what was happening in the pod. I spent 5 minutes telling everyone how I found the job and its benefits. I also explained how I was coping with the rigours of having to juggle therapy and the pressures of having to serve all the meals on time, blah, blah, blah, blah. Also, I praised my two colleagues, Mick and Martin for all their help, which seemed to appease Lord Smitty that I was now a valid member of the community.

My transformation from agent provocateur to brain washed subservient was now complete as Lord Smitty now saw me as someone who could be paraded in front of all the new deviants coming onto the wing as me being a role model, one who had turned from sarcastic hardened criminal into being obsequious. Being seen also as someone who was attentive and obedient was what all the months of being lambasted had been all about and with this new-found realisation that if I acted as if I was one of the indoctrinated the spot light would finally be off me and focused more on the new arrivals. This would leave me to blend into the background to do as I wished.

I grabbed hold of this new-found cloak of invisibility with both hands rejoicing at the fact I was now entering into phase 3 of my therapeutic metamorphose which had taken me just over a year to attain at the cost of relinquishing my sense of humour and of course my sarcasm. This was a small price to pay on what I now saw as my covert mission to fully integrate myself into the belly of the beast.

So, now with Smitty's approval confirmed by the watching staff and deviants on the wing, my place on the community could be chalked down in the history books and the historians could one day tell their students about transformation and how I was broken down and mentally reprogrammed, bringing about the new and improved Lord Frankenstein version of me. To the outside world this would be seen as another Grendon success story which in some respect was true but for all the wrong reasons, as all I was doing was manipulating my surroundings, which in part was what therapy was all about. All I was doing was acting accordingly in front of the psychologists, if they wanted to call this change then who am I to disagree. I just carried on and hoped somewhere down the line that this conformity to Smitty's rules laid down by him and Grendons constitution would somehow equate to me being a more balanced individual.

Living amongst the beasts: The rise and fall of the Grendon experiment

By the end of the meeting the months of me fighting his ideology was now over, I could hand the baton over to one of the new arrivals who in turn would learn from his own mistakes. Right now, it was time for me to concentrate on my therapy.

After the meeting I spent about an hour with Mac talking about what I should work on in my Small Group as I still valued his opinion and classed him as a therapeutic genius. His insights into deviant behaviour was beyond reproach as he had been in prison for most of his life and knew the social workings of the deviant mind better than anyone I had met at Grendon or even anyone I had ever known. With his words echoing in my ears I made my way up to my cell to bang up over dinner. I also made a mental note to speak to him more as we had drifted apart since I came onto the wing for no other reason than I wanted to experience therapy on my own terms without any input from him as I didn't want him influencing my own perception of what therapy was all about as he was very self-opinionated. However, after talking to him today I felt I was missing out on his years of experience which I now saw as beneficial to me and not a hindrance as I had once thought.

Once in my cell I settled down to watch the 1 o'clock news but all I could hear was shouting out the window so I turned by TV down and caught snippets of the conversation between Andy the old man killer and Lewis saying the screws were outside Albino Jamie's cell and something was going on as Albino Jamie was refusing to come out of his cell. A few minutes later someone shouted that the screws had just gone in on him and that he had been handcuffed and taken off the wing by the mufti squad. Mufti squad are screws dressed up in riot gear with shields that move inmates when needed and are only called onto the wing for violent disturbances. Whatever the situation was with Albino Jamie it must have been serious. It could be anything though so I went back to watching the news leaving the rest of the guys to shout out the windows to each other.

At 2 o'clock the intercom came on asking me to go down to the community room as a wing special had been called by Smitty, the door then opened a minute later. As I stepped onto the landing all I saw was smiles and bemused looks as we all made our way downstairs. All was quiet as no-one wanted to be overheard saying anything for fear of being seen to gloat at the misfortune of another's demise, just in case Jamie's departure was only temporary as his Group members were within earshot. Everyone was tight lipped as we took our places waiting to hear what all the fuss was about.

As the room filled up Tony came over and sat by me and asked what the hell was going on. I said I had no idea as I hadn't spoken to anyone, with that we both sat back and waited for Smitty to enter the room. As is normal in these cases the Security Governor entered the room first followed by Smitty and the rest of the wing screws.

The whole room went quiet as Smitty said "it is with regret that I have to inform everybody that Albino Jamie and Mac have been moved out of the prison due to information received from Brian that inappropriate behaviour between Albino Jamie, Mac and Kat had come to light and also from today Kat will be suspended and will no longer be working at Grendon until an investigation has taken place". Then he went on to say that Mac went without any fuss but Albino Jamie had to be restrained. He also said he was sorry if it had caused any concern to anyone on the wing. He then asked the room if anyone had any questions.

The first question was from Sean the armed robber on my group, who was a good friend of Albino Jamie. He asked when Brian had first made these allegations, was it before Kat accused him of touching her up in the office or after and was that the reason he was moved to F-wing 3 weeks ago? Smitty said that Brian was moved because of the allegations he had made, he also said "however it was nothing to do with him touching Kat". I then said "yeah we all believe that one". I then asked "if you already knew about the allegations then why did you give Albino Jamie the Chairman's job knowing full well that you were moving him this week? Also, whilst we are on the subject if the allegations are true about Kat and Jamie, which we all know are not as Brian is just lying to save his own skin, then will you bring Gary back and if not, why and will you amend his reports?"

Smitty went a bit red in the face at these questions and stated that wing jobs are nothing to do with him and Albino Jamie got the job on his own merits. I said "that's not the question I asked you. I asked you if you knew about the allegations before you gave Jamie the wing Chairman's job?" Smitty just said "I have answered your questions Terry" and went on to say if the allegations were true he would be writing to Gary and that was all he was going to say on the matter.

Mick asked where Jamie and Mac had been moved to. Smitty said Jamie had been moved to Bullingdon and Mac had been moved to HMP Woodhill, which meant that they had known for weeks about the moves as all lifers had to get permission from Whitehall and that takes weeks, if not months. So, Smitty was lying to us all and now he had just been exposed.

This was typical of Smitty and typical also of the way he did things, he was useless in these situations, and we could see his own behaviour as underhanded and devious. This sent out a signal to the deviant brigade that if your back was up against the wall then blame your way out of it, which is exactly what Brian had just done. We were to find this out when he finally came back to the wing a few days later as he had to explain his actions. He told the wing that Mac and Jamie had been acting strange and that was why he believed they had a phone on them. Also, he had been standing outside the office when Jamie and Kat were in there and they were laughing and joking, which in his book meant that they were having sexual contact. This was a fucking joke and we all said so.

We asked him if he had seen a phone, he said "no he hadn't". He also said that in the past when people had phones on the wing they had acted like Mac and Jamie which in his eyes meant that they must have had a phone. This was the evidence he had brought to Smitty and the rest of the Governors. Smitty however thought that the allegations were serious enough to get the Governor involved and also suspend Kat and move the boys without giving them a chance to defend themselves. It was all a fucking joke.

We, as a community, all felt that it was ridiculous as we could clearly see that Brian had done it out of revenge. He was showing all the behaviours of a deviant with nowhere to go as Kat had already put him in the book for trying to molest her. His actions were because like most deviants they can't control their sexual perversions, so had reached out and touched her arse. A seemingly innocuous action as it isn't the crime of the century but to a deviant lifer in for killing his Mum and Dad it's a serious setback which could potentially be irrevocable as far as Brian getting out of prison was concerned. He acted out the same criminal behaviour he had done when killing his Mum and Dad which was plain to see.

He was also an accomplished liar who had convinced his then girlfriend that he was a professional tennis player and had even talked her into going to America with him. So, with Kat on holiday he had taken his chance to kill her, at the same time taking down Jamie and Mac who were in fact his friends as I had seen him over the last year going in and out of their cells, giving him the perfect opportunity to concoct this story, which was actually so full of holes that you could have driven a bus through them. He said that he hadn't seen a phone and that he only assumed Jamie and Kat were looking at her tattoo, so his whole evidence was based on the fact that he thought they had a phone and also that he thought Jamie and Kat were up to something. Smitty had taken that to the bank and deposited it as fact and now Brian was back on the wing we could all see the game he had just played and subsequently got away with. There was nothing we could do though as Smitty had said Brian shouldn't speak any more about the situation until the investigation was over which could take months and with that he brought the meeting to an end.

Terry Ellis

Three people's lives had just been destroyed all because Smitty couldn't see further than the end of his nose when it came to a master manipulator like Brian, or did he just want Albino Jamie and Mac gone?

We found out a few days later that Kat was working over at Spring Hill as she had sent a message over to us that Brian had touched her up as he squeezed past her and because she had caught him red handed he had made the whole story up. She also said that she couldn't believe Lord Smitty had backed a deviant like Brian over her. That was Grendon for you.

However, the Officers were not too pleased with the way Smitty had backed Brian over one of their own and had spoken openly about the fact that they would do their best to keep Brian locked up for the rest of his life if they had anything to do with it. This was fed back to the wing on the next community meeting by Lewis as he had overheard Dave and John the 2 Officers speaking in the office about it. However, they both denied it and the matter was swept under the carpet.

This double standard behaviour wasn't setting a good example but we were told that whatever happened on the wing shouldn't be a distraction from the real reason we were all here in the first place which was to work on ourselves. So, it was back to therapy as normal and by the weekend the whole episode was just a blip on the therapeutic journey.

I had learnt a valuable lesson as Brian's actions had shown me how cold and calculating another human being could be, as even by my own standards he made me look like a little kitten and I classed myself as a hard man. He had shown me a side of the deviant I had never truly appreciated as I saw most of them as insignificant cowards but the way he had gone about the destruction of Kat and the others brought home to me how insensitive and cruel they could be and any doubts I had about seeing the deviants as weak had just been diminished, as the blackness I had seen in Brian and the rest of their eyes was there for a reason, to show us all that the darkness was their friend and the light was ours. I also noticed on many occasions when talking to Brian and the other murderers that their eyes betrayed them as I could see their true nature from the darkest recesses of their eyes as even acting all sweetness and light couldn't hide the fact that they were lost souls and no amount of subterfuge or therapy could bring them back, or was ever going to change the fact they belonged to the dark side and were abomination to the values held by me and most of humanity. They were a race of their own, a race of evil and to trust any of them would only end badly, as Kat, Jamie and Mac could testify to as Mac had helped Brian on many occasions with his university degree by studying with him, also helping him to research. Also, Kat was always there for him with a shoulder to cry on but he had snuffed them all out like he had done his Mum and Dad like they were human cockroaches, a mistake I would not make. So, another lesson learnt.

Terry Ellis

CHAPTER TWENTY-SIX

The next day Stutter Andy, my next-door neighbour who had killed the old man with a concrete slab, was also moved to Bullingdon as he'd had enough of therapy and had refused to go to his small Groups. Also, Leon, 2 doors up from me was going, as he too had put his papers in as he also couldn't take any more shit. Which left a gaping hole in the community as Mac, Gary, Jamie, Stutter, Leon and a young guy called Richard had also left, which meant we would be getting new community members on the wing.

However, we were all a bit apprehensive as we had heard that there had been quite a lot of inmates coming to Grendon over the last 3 months from one of the dangerous severe personality disorder units that had been shut down and by all accounts they were deviants of the worst kind. All of them had been in therapy for years and had mastered the art of manipulation and were all in control of their own emotions and were seen as more dangerous and had only been sent to Grendon to be deprogrammed, which was a complete U-turn from what they had been taught for years, as it had been proven that the therapy they were receiving had in fact made them unpredictable. Good old Grendon though had thrown them a lifeline believing they could change the nature of the beast through kindness and the odd family day, as the only other option was to admit that the years of championing the therapy that had been taking place in the units were a waste of time and tax payers money, they would never let that happen. Plus, the take up of offenders had fallen off from main stream prisons and Grendon needed bums on seats, so they welcomed this new strain of manufactured therapeutic deviants with open arms as they were seen as being more manageable and also the safer bet as the funding which had been dwindling at Grendon would now be ringfenced to save the powers that be the embarrassment of having to admit failure where prison therapy in the past was concerned.

Before the new arrivals came onto the wing my door burst open and Tony came in with a face like thunder and just collapsed onto my soft chair with his head in his hands, he looked up at me and said "you won't believe this". I asked "what?", but then he said "I can't tell you as you will only take the piss", so I gave him a sincere look and said "I won't mate", he then blurted out "you know that queer git Adam who came to the pink party with us, he has just used his Group and told them that I had tried to come onto him". He then said "you wait until I see that cunt". He then looked at me for support but I couldn't help myself and shouted "who are yer, who are yer Tony?" which sent him into one as he just sat there and buried his head in his hands and called me all the cunts under the sun and said that he knew he shouldn't have told me. I laughed my bollocks off crying on the bed as Tony now looked a broken man and over the next few days or so I ruined him with every sarcastic remark in my armoury. The lesson Tony learnt from these malicious lies was to own his own shit in the future and admit the fact that he hated Scottie and didn't like gays as it was against his religious beliefs which he was entitled to, but he wasn't entitled to call them names because of their sexual orientations, as the lie of pretending he was OK with it had backfired spectacularly. A mistake he would never make again and one I would never let him forget. Even Bilal was now looking at Tony funny which only compounded the situation adding another big fat King Edwards onto poor old Tony's shoulders giving him the new name of 'Mr Attitude".

True to form, over the next few days we had an influx of scum, the likes of which I'd never seen before on C-wing which sickened me to the core and unfortunately resulted in me being put on 2 commitments and falling out with members of my Group

I also met an old friends son, Bill, who turned out to be a proper deviant and I could see why his Dad had never mentioned him to me before.

First though we had to be introduced to 7 new members of the community which brought about in me a new hatred of everyone deviant, which I found hard to control as it became one of my biggest tests to date of my tolerance levels so far and a battle I had to win or I would end up killing someone. But, the lessons I learnt over this period would be the most beneficial as every coping strategy would be called upon if I was ever going to survive the battle of the beasts.

The first deviant to come onto the wing was called Gavin who was about 35 years old, 5' 9" tall, skinny and reminded me of a weasel. He came onto the wing like a whirlwind using his Group that very first day, leaving his Group members to pick up the pieces as when they had to do their feedback they were visibly shocked and at one stage Medication Mark who had killed the special needs kid, broke down in tears and another member had to take over but he too couldn't finish. Gavin stepped in believing he was saving the day by starting from the beginning which did nothing to endear him to the rest of us, in fact the opposite was true as there were a lot of sad looking deviants who saw his crime as the worst of the worst and to see him tell it without so much as a tear or a flicker of emotion was enough to light the fuse that brought about a barrage of questions once he had finished. This was also the catalyst for me to go on one as my reaction was one of pure hatred that would spiral out of control over the next few weeks. But, first I had to listen to Gavin.

Gavin explained that he had been having difficulties with his wife as they were going through the process of splitting up and were going through the family courts. He said his wife had started to have an affair with the judge in his case, making him really resentful towards his wife as he was still living at home with her and their 2 kids. One night he had decided to kill himself and decided the best place to do it was in the kitchen while his wife and kids were asleep. After they had gone to bed he started drinking and taking pills and in his drunken stupor he had inadvertently woken his daughter who was only 6 years old. She then came downstairs and upon seeing her Dad upset she asked him why he was crying and he told her that he was going to heaven, she asked if she could go with him and he said yes. So, they played a little game with the pills by pretending they were sweets saying "one for you and one for me" which went on until she passed out but she was only unconscious, so he got a plastic bag out of the cupboard and put it over her head and held her down as she kicked and scratched him until she was dead. He then drank some more and popped the rest of the pills until he also fell unconscious.

It was not until he woke up the next morning that he said he realised what he had done but by this time the 9 year old daughter had woken up and upon seeing her little sister dead on the floor with the bag still on her head started screaming for her Mummy who then came down to see what was going on and upon discovering her daughters lifeless body and fearing for herself and the other daughter, she picked up her baby and ran out of the house screaming for help and for someone to call the police.

After he had finished talking I just sat there as I couldn't understand what sort of man could do that to his own little girl, an angel. I then turned to him and said "once you realised you were still alive why didn't you kill yourself so you could be with her, as then she wouldn't be all alone you fucking piece of shit?", but he just put his head down. I told him I had 3 girls of my own and if anything ever happened to one of them I would kill myself and join them because I couldn't let one of them be on their own. As I was saying this I could feel the tears rolling down my face, so I had to stop myself. Then I asked him did he really expect anyone to believe that she had any perception of heaven or even dying. I then called him a fucking degenerate cunt, but once again he never answered me, he just lowered his fucking head so I just got up and walked out as I needed to get back to my cell.

Living amongst the beasts: The rise and fall of the Grendon experiment

Once there I sat with my back to the door and just cried for that little girl and my own kids for all the years that I have not been there for them. This was also the day that broke me as I couldn't take it anymore but I would carry on for now as I told myself that sitting through this shit would help me as it made me reflect over my own kids and family, but it didn't make it any easier.

A few days later when I was sitting alone in the dining room Gavin came over to me and said sorry for what he had done. He added he didn't set out to kill her, it just happened that way and he wasn't a bad person, otherwise why hadn't he killed his other daughter? Upon hearing this I sat back and looked him in the eye and said the reason you never killed her was because she was 9 years old and knew fucking better. He then went on to say that he loved her and started crying, but I couldn't feel sorry for him, in fact I wanted to punch his fucking face in. It took all my strength to hold back, so I just sat there not saying a word then got up and walked back to my cell wondering once again what I would do if anything happened to one of my babies. I started crying again at the same time kicking myself for being so soft but I just couldn't help myself. It only reinforced my own opinion of Gavin that he was a scumbag as how could anyone do that to their own daughter, the self-righteous weedy little prick, that's all he was. He should fit right in at Grendon as he was just as manipulative as the rest of the scum here. Also, he actually saw himself as a victim in all of this. He would be a Psychologists wet dream because he had just the right amount of shame to keep him in line, making Lord Smitty's job that bit easier.

I was still feeling pretty angry a few days later when Medication Mark came over to the Pod and said that I should take it easy with Gavin and maybe I should back off as he was in his Group. Gavin had asked Mark to have a word with me thinking that because he was 20 stone and 6' tall and thinking himself as a bit of a chap that I would back off but I just looked at him and said "why don't you fuck off you fat ugly cunt?" This sent him into a bit of a rage and he started swearing at me calling me a bully which I thought was a bit rich coming from him who had killed a little kid. I said "come in the pod and I will show you who is a bully you fat prick". James the old man killer who was one of his group members then came over trying to hold him back but I said "let the fat mug go" and with that he pulled him away and I thought that was the end of it.

The next day they tried to put me in the book for a commitment vote but Smitty said we had to have a sit down first. A time was set for that afternoon, so I asked Sean my Group member to come with me thinking as he was a robber and the best choice, as the rest of my Group was full of wankers, he did join me, so we went on the sit down which would be facilitated by Smitty and one of the screws, Dave. We spent about 40 minutes arguing and telling our sides of the story. James on Marks side and Sean backing me up. However, Sean the shit cunt said that I had been upset all week and he thought that I had taken it out on Mark, so by the end of the sit down we were both put in the book thanks to Sean stabbing me in the back as he was sitting on the fence as normal. Also, James was lying his bollocks off but it didn't work as I kept my cool and baited Mark a few times which made him really angry and he just got up and walked out. Smitty said that we were both to blame as we were both volatile and for that reason he was putting us both in the wing book for a commitment.

When I came out of the room I was still fuming inside as I felt that Sean had betrayed me but I would leave it for another day as James the old man killer was now my top priority. As we queued up for tea he kept looking at me but Mark had told him to calm down and thinking he had got one over on me started looking at me as if he was a bit of a geezer. I kept my cool and waited for the screw to leave the dining room before I said at the top of my voice "I am not an old man you can intimidate" and smiled at him. He went bright red in the face and just like the coward he was he hid behind Mark saying he was going to put me in the book for using his offence against him, but I just winked at him and smiled while Mark asked him to calm down.

After I got my food and sat down he kept looking at me thinking I would back down as I was already in the book but I just looked over at him and mouthed "you little poof" and winking at the same time but he didn't bite. He just got up and walked out and brought one of the screws back with him saying that I was calling him names, which of course I denied, then I went back to eating my tea making a mental note to fuck him up the next chance I got.

When I went to bed that night I couldn't sleep as I felt that rat Sean had let me down. I also reflected over my day and I could see that I had over-reacted in the way I had spoken to Mark as he was only trying to help and because I was angry with Gavin and all the other shits on the wing, I had taken it out on him, bringing about the escalation of all the other madness I was going through. This was all because I couldn't control my anger which nearly brought about my downfall.

At least now I understood why I had done what I had done, so this meant that I would work on my temper in my Group and hopefully not make the same mistake again. But, even though I knew where I had gone wrong I was still going to give it to Sean the next morning, then I would start afresh after that. Another lesson learnt. Revenge was still on my mind regarding James and Sean but I would make an effort in the morning to bury the hatchet as I could see Mark didn't want this getting out of hand.

CHAPTER TWENTY-SEVEN

The next morning I was up bright and early and caught Mark in his cell. We had a chat and by the time we had finished talking we were the best of mates. Also, I had a better understanding of him, so we both agreed to call a truce, so by the time I made it to my small Group the boys were already there, also Monkey Boots.

I said my good mornings and waited for my chance to say my piece with Sean and by the time they had all finished their minutes Sean asked me how I was feeling which was a big mistake as I told him what I thought of him for about 20 minutes calling him all the cunts under the sun, which didn't go down too well with the Group as I also turned on all of them for being spineless pricks and before I knew it the room was full of screws. I calmed down and kept my cool for the rest of the Group and just as we were leaving Sean apologised. I then shook his hand but the damage had already been done and he knew it as it was the last time I ever spoke to him apart from saying good morning when I came on the Group, this was for the benefit of Monkey Boots and the rest of the Group.

Just when I thought things couldn't get any worse Mick took the day off and Lewis took his place and as he was a stroppy little fucker by the end of the day he had got right under my skin saying something sarcastic to me, saying I was a cockney gangster, this coming from a low life like him who had killed an old man. I took it the wrong way and whispered in his ear that he was an old man killing poof who if I ever saw on the outside I would cut his throat. With this he ran out of the pod to get one of the screws and Smitty telling them I had threatened him. He then stormed out and by the next morning he was trying to put me on a commitment with the help of Play Station John, who was a cockroach and a member of Lewis's group, he even said he had heard me threaten Lewis which was a fucking lie as I had whispered it in his ear.

Living amongst the beasts: The rise and fall of the Grendon experiment

I asked Martin if he would come to the sit down with me as he was working in the pod and had heard everything. Also, being a mate he would back me up so I didn't have too much concern when we went on the sit down the next morning.

We had our sit down but this time Miss Piggy and Jamie the lying screw who Mac had put in his place was facilitating. We both went at it arguing the toss about who was right and who was in the wrong for about half an hour whilst Miss Piggy wrote everything down. Meanwhile Martin was backing me up and John the cockroach was backing Lewis up lying saying that he had overheard me say that I was going to cut poof bollocks' throat, so I gave it to John and after a few minutes he walked out leaving Lewis to fend for himself. He then made a fatal mistake by telling the truth by saying I had whispered it to him in his ear and that's why Martin didn't hear me threaten him. I said "if that's the case Lewis then why did John just say he heard what I had said from the corridor?" This left Lewis with egg on his face and well and truly in the shit for lying. This got me off the hook s Miss Piggy had wrote everything down. I just smiled at the deviant prick and mouthed 'nice try you little cock sucker' and with that he started crying and ran out of the rooms screaming the odds but I had come through it sweet as a nut with my reputation intact and still one of the good guys.

The funny thing was if Lewis had just told the truth then he may have been able to beat me at my own game as everyone knew I was spilling out all over the place that week but because he was a spoilt little prick and needed to win at any cost even by lying, he had fucked himself up which just goes to show you shouldn't lie especially when it comes to trying to fuck someone like me over as I have been a career criminal all my life and manipulating situations is my game, especially when it comes to winning an argument with 2 little deviants as there is really no contest as I treat every situation like a bit of work and am able to think quickly on my feet. To lose is not an option that I relish especially when it comes to battling with the beasts as losing to them I saw was unacceptable as I was the good guy and they were the darkness and plus, the only way I would be leaving Grendon would be on my own terms and not by the hand of some deviant who had killed an old man.

This was the second time I had been on a sit down with a deviant and as much as the idea in principle was for reconciliation, it actually was and felt like a battle ground as the potential for being put on a commitment and voted out could be the eventual outcome. So, instead of me owning my own mistakes and dealing with them I had to consider the consequences that my deviant enemy had more support due to his own manipulative behaviour and would be making deals and as I had just proven this with Lewis and Play Station John, who had joined forces to bring about my demise by collaborating with each other. So, with this is mind and the way the Small Groups stuck together I saw the reconciliation process as a battle for survival which brought out your primeval instincts to fight the good fight as the embarrassment of having to walk the therapeutic plank with a misfit smiling behind you wasn't a good look or an option that I was willing to take.

Like the rest of the deviants, I acted out the need to survive as there was no other way out, which in turn created an atmosphere of infighting between the Small Groups as these hidden conflicts overshadowed any potential for real change. All because the reconciliation process was seen by us all as not fit for purpose as the real objective had been lost. To admit you had made a mistake would resort in you being voted out of Grendon, so instead of resolving these difficult situations we sometimes found ourselves in the reconciliation process only perpetuated this bad behaviour of one-upmanship, which in turn brought the Small Groups into conflict with each other as the victim and the victor would both profess their innocence, this would then spill over into the rest of the Groups. Alliances were then formed and strategies against said perpetrator would be put into action so as to antagonise him into making a mistake as his friends, the silent assassin waited in the shadows under the guise of being a supportive member of the community to bring about his demise. which once again only antagonised the other side to do likewise and retaliate and that's why reconciliation did not work on these so-called sit downs.

Also over that week our small group acquired 2 new Group members, one of which was Gordon he was in his late 50s and was like the rest of the guys who had come from the Dangerous Severe Personality Disorder units that week from F-wing.

Gordon started off by saying that this was his second life sentence. The first was when he was 17 and dressed in his scouts uniform. He had gone round to his teachers house who he said he loved as a father figure, however his teacher was out so Gordon had decided to wait. A car pulled up with his teachers wife in it so he asked her how long her husband would be, she replied that he wouldn't be back all weekend This information pissed Gordon off so he followed the teachers wife round the side of the house and smashed her over the head with a flower pot knocking her out, he then raped her. Afterwards he tied her up and dragged her back to the car where he punched her in the face and ripped her knickers off so he could gag her, as by now she had started screaming and was struggling to get out of the car.

At this point Simon the screw who was facilitating our Group asked him if she had any kids, with that Gordon went quiet. He then uttered 'yes', she had 2 little girls, one aged 5 and the other was 6 who were both sitting next to her in the back of the car. He then added that they were both OK as he never touched them. As Gordon finished his sentence I said "let me see if I heard you right, you raped their Mum on the floor and then dragged her back to the car, punching her in the face and ripping her knickers off and gagging her so she would shut up and you say her kids were OK. You fucking scum bag". After my outburst Gordon didn't say anything else as he said he was scared to say anything else in front of me.

If I'm honest I don't know if I could have taken anymore as I'd had enough of all this shit. I was questioning why the fuck I was still putting myself through this. After a few minutes I said I was sorry and Gordon carried on. I promised I would stop my outbursts as I was disrupting the Group, so he carried on where he had left off.

Smitty had told me that week that he knew how hard it was for me to listen to the rest of them, but if I could just keep it together it would be my biggest test and would be an example not only my Group but to the rest of the community. So, with his words still ringing in my ears I sat there and tested by resolve to the max and gained another weapon in my armoury to fight the beasts.

As Gordon continued he said he then got into the car and drove about with the girls and their Mum for about 40 minutes looking for somewhere to dump them but was seen by someone in his village which made him panic, so he just parked up and got out of the car and ran home. He was arrested a few days later and banged up for rape.

The story did not end there as the last time Gordon was released he met and married a post mistress who he said was domineering and reminded him of his Mum, who he said was cold and that's why he hated her. Then 6 months after being married his wife started taking charge of his finances which meant she made him sandwiches every day and only gave him enough money for petrol, this made him resentful and he became withdrawn. Then 2 years into their marriage he decided to fight back and regain control of his life.

He planned what he thought was the perfect murder and nearly got away with it but like the rapist he was, it was ill conceived as Gordon wasn't the cleverest of guys.

He said he came home one night and they ate their supper together as normal, then after she asked him to do the washing up which he resented as he had been at work all day. He just snapped and strangled her, breaking her neck in the process, which he said felt like a release after all the years of her berating him. Also, it was payback for all the times his Mum had never shown him any love or affection. The euphoria didn't last long though as now he had a dead wife on the kitchen floor.

Terry Ellis

He then hatched what he thought was an audacious plan to cover up his deviant act. He popped out to the garden shed and got himself a crowbar and jemmied his own back door open to make it look like they had been broken in. Next, he put her body in the boot of his car and drove it to the wife's post office where he stole £15,000 out of the safe and at the same time left the safe open and also the back door hoping that someone would notice it. Then he drove her body to a layby where he dumped the body hoping it would be found quickly, it was now about 1 o'clock in the morning. He then went home and tied himself up. The 'perfect' crime he thought as it looked like someone had broken into the house, tied him up and kidnapped the wife so she could open the post office safe, then on their way out of town the kidnappers had thrown her out of the car accidentally breaking her neck. Job done, case closed he thought.

However, like most ill- conceived deviant plans they never work out as no-one noticed the back door to the post office was open and also her body wasn't found until 3 days afterwards which left Gordon in a state of panic as for the first 2 days he had tied himself up and was waiting for the police to come round but no-one came. So, on the third day he untied himself, took a shower, had a shave and made himself something to eat, then once he had done this he tied himself back up.

Half an hour later the police came knocking at the door and upon seeing Gordon tied up on the kitchen floor they broke down the door. He then gave them his spill telling them that 2 robbers had broken in through the back door as he and his wife were eating tea and then tied them both up. They then took his wife with them to open the safe before supposedly releasing her, which he presumed was why the police were now here. He then faked a few tears for good effect. The 'perfect' crime he thought.

What Gordon didn't count on was that the sharp- eyed copper had noticed he had washed up after eating, as the plates were still wet. Also, why was he clean shaven if he had been tied up for 3 days. So case closed. Gordon got another life sentence; however he still went not guilty and for the past 18 years maintained his innocence. That was until a few days after our small Group when he went to Smitty's office and confessed all and at the same time getting maximum brownie points by admitting he had killed his wife and to prove it he asked Smitty to phone the police so he could tell them where he had hidden the £15,000 in his loft as he had always used the fact that the money had never been found to cast some doubt on his original conviction for all those years, which he had been using to maintain his lies.

Living amongst the beasts: The rise and fall of the Grendon experiment

As he had only been in therapy for a few days I had to ask myself why he had decided to come clean after being on the Dangerous Severe Personality Disorder unit for 18 years. My only conclusion was that he was still a manipulating deviant and was only using Grendon as a stepping stone for his eventual release, as why else would he come clean after supposedly working with the best Psychologists for years on the unit. Also, our Group hadn't put him under any pressure yet as he had only been in the Group for a week, plus he had never shown any shame in what he had done or any empathy let alone mentioned he was sorry for the rape or the murder.

It seemed the only reason he was coming clean was for the benefit of the parole board as if you don't admit your guilt, whether you are guilty or not, you will not be released. This made people act out this manipulative behaviour which wasn't real change but a by-product of the stupid red tape laid down by the law and the establishment as most innocent prisoners will tell you that if you don't admit your guilt you are still considered as dangerous, which puts you in a Catch 22 situation. Admit to something you have not done and you will get out, or maintain your innocence and stay in prison, so what would a lying rapist murderer like Gordon do when put in the same situation, because I'm sure he wouldn't tell the truth would he? That's how I saw Gordon, just another deviant playing the therapeutic game.

CHAPTER TWENTY-EIGHT

It was now 3 weeks until Christmas and I had already been here 18 months. I was told by Smitty that this was a milestone in my therapy and a significant stage in therapeutic terms as everything I had been learning would start to come together. This was true in some respects as my eyes were now wide open when it came to spotting behaviours in the deviants before they happened. This was a tool I had acquired in dealing with them, helping me to calm down as every incident and confrontation by others and myself had been a learning opportunity which I had subliminally grasped with both hands, as I was now intellectually operating on a different level which was perplexing for me as I hated everything therapy stood for when it came to the deviants and the way they manipulated their surroundings.

All this had made me resentful of therapy but because I had continued to participate in it I had incrementally soaked up all therapy had to offer me and more as I had now become fascinated with the mind, especially criminal psychology, which in turn made me focus not only on the deviants behaviour but also my own criminal behaviours. Who else apart from myself could understand the complexities of the criminal better than me, yes me who had been a career criminal most of his life. So, with this new found understanding I had gained the tools to self-analysis and evaluate my own weaknesses and strengths to a far better degree than any Psychologist ever could.

I started to focus more on my past behaviours and my thoughts and feelings and tried to forget what the deviants were doing. Now I had to concentrate on myself which meant asking myself some searching questions and answering them in a way I could never have done in the past let alone in my Small Group or for that matter any of the Psychologists at Grendon as the only person I trusted was myself.

I decided to use the guinea pig approach hoping it would open up Pandora's Box as lying to myself was not an option if I was ever going to understand the intricacies of my own mind. The therapy I'd been doing for the last 18 months had taught me that the answers that I'd been seeking were in fact all within me and it was just a matter of interpreting them through this self- introspection now I had the tools to make sense of them.

As I tried to comprehend what Smitty had told me it felt like he had just off loaded the burden of therapy from himself to me as the onus was now on me, thus taking any responsibility away from him if I now failed to reach my objectives. This felt like an anti-climax and the only analogy I could come up with was it felt like reading one of those self-help books that go on for about 300 pages which says everything but at the same time says nothing, as once you have read it you are left more confused than when you started. The only difference between them and me was I was in the living book which I was now hoping would be more rewarding in terms of self-enlightenment. Just like the book I would not know the truth until I got to the end.

All that aside I still had to make it to Christmas which meant 1 more week in therapy in my Small Group listening to the next deviant who would come into our Group, Jeff, before we broke up for that magical time, Christmas. I hoped this would give me some time to recharge my batteries as I was sick to death of Group therapy and also the monotonous day to day bollocks of having to sit through feedbacks as the deviants regurgitated aspects of their lives to elicit sympathy and portray themselves as the victims, hoping in some way it would absolve them from the guilt of their crimes in the eyes of the community and the Psychologists alike. This constant drive by the deviants for atonement of their sins was to show themselves in a better light, this was all they were interested in, this was their only goal and it was driving me mad as I could see right through their subterfuge . Also, I was starting to see therapy as a waste of time.

Having to listen to Gordon and now Jeff felt like dèja-vu times a million. I just smiled and said good morning as another beast Jeff took to the stage to try and convince us and Monkey Boots that he also was yet another fucking victim.

Jeff was a big black guy, 6' tall, 18 stone and a serial rapist. He came across as calm as a cucumber as he had been in therapy in his previous prison for 8 years in the Dangerous Personality Disorder unit, where he had, like the other beasts, learnt to control every aspect of his personality right the way down to his emotional management, which was spot on in front of the cameras but unfortunately for him it wouldn't last long as he was just another lying deviant.

Terry Ellis

He had come into our Group and explained the reasons for the rapes and gave us the normal run down on them, obfuscating any real detail as is common amongst the rapists. He just said the first girl he had raped he had met in a night club. He'd slipped a drug into her drink before taking her home.

The second rape was a woman he knew. One night he had decided to go round to her house. He knocked on the door and when she opened it he put a knife to her throat and threatened to kill her and her 2 little children if she made a sound. He then went in her house and raped her all night while the 2 little girls slept in the other room. He thought this would keep her calm and more compliant, which it did.

Jeff came across as cold and calculating and never once mentioned the names of the girls he had raped. He also showed no emotion apart from when he said that his girlfriend had cheated on him whilst he was in prison when he was younger. So, he now believed this was the reason he hated all women, as he thought it was her actions that had turned him into a rapist, as he had lost all trust in women blah, blah, blah.

We thanked him for being so honest with us and welcomed him into our Group of mixed misfits. I even patted myself on the back as I hadn't had a go at him. This was hard for me as he had mentioned the 2 little girls, I remained calm as I was on best behaviour still, also I knew he would keep for another day. I really hated rapists and now there were 2 in our group. Happy fucking Christmas I thought.

CHAPTER TWENTY-NINE

Christmas at the monster mansion was now a reality and living around them was not getting any better. Even with 18 months under my belt, all the coping tools I had acquired along the way would have to be used if I wanted to make it through this period of living amongst the beasts.

That same afternoon I was sitting in my cell when Bilal walked in and said he knew Jeff when he first came to prison and believed he had changed his deviant ways and also added that he was a good bloke and an asset to the wing. We talked for about 15 minutes regarding what had been said by Gordon and Jeff on the Group and by the end I just happened to mention to Bilal what Jeff had said to me about not reading any porn magazines and what he now felt about them and their use. This brought about a puzzled look on Bilal's face as he started to twist it up, so I asked him what was the matter. He told me that only yesterday when he was having tea with Jeff, Jeff had asked him if he had any porn or as he said it had actually asked Bilal if he had any dirty ladies to look at, which was his code for a porn magazine. I asked Bilal if he would repeat what he had just said to me in front of the Group and Jeff himself as I needed Jeff to by taught a lesson.

I then called a Group special and asked Bilal to come as he could do my bidding by confronting Jeff regarding his manipulating behaviour.

The next afternoon we all assembled in Group 3s room, Daryl, Terry P, Jeff, Gordon, Sean, Dan and myself also Monkey Boots and my star witness Bilal. Once the room had settled down Monkey Boots asked me what the problem was so I said I'd had a chat with Bilal yesterday and a certain subject had come up regarding what Jeff had said in our Group yesterday which had contradicted everything he said to us and as Bilal had the conversation with Jeff I had asked him to come and repeat it to the rest of you. Also, just to keep Jeff on his toes I asked him if he had ever lied to us since he'd come into our group, with a bemused look on his face he said "no". So, with that I asked Bilal to take

Terry Ellis

the stage and repeat what he had said to me. Five minutes later Jeff's jaw hit the floor as he squirmed in his seat as his manipulative behaviour had just been exposed, when he looked at me I just smiled which sent him into a deviant rage as he protested his innocence. He then tried to wriggle out of it by saying Bilal was lying and he didn't know why he would say these things, but his mask had well and truly slipped off as we could all see and feel his embarrassment at being caught out lying on his 'first' Group. Not a good start for Jeff I thought but at least he would think twice before lying again.

As I had been the one who exposed the rapist scumbag the pleasure was all mine, which only reinforced in me that no amount of therapy could change a deviants nature as even 8 years in therapy by Jeff had proved that. It only taught him and other deviants to manage and modify their behaviour in front of the cameras. Their cloned conformity was the only change they were actually making which was not real, just a therapeutic mask and a substitute swap from who they really were, beasts, and not what they were trying to portray now, which were wolves dressed up as sheep.

Like most deviants caught with their pants down, Jeff denied it until he was blue in the face but we could all see he was lying, but he wouldn't let go and he just kept saying and pleading with Bilal. He said "Bilal why are you doing this to me?" and "what have I ever done to you?" over and over again thinking that repetition of his denial would change the fact that he was a lying deviant. Bilal didn't back down and by the end of the meeting Jeff looked a broken man so I gave him a little smile and a wink for comfort and said maybe he should rethink his use of porn mags as it would be better for his victims in the future as it might stop him raping them. I then got up and went back to my cell.

On Friday we broke up for Christmas, however it was tinged with sadness as Smitty informed us all that x2 Steve had been diagnosed with cancer, so all morning everyone gave him words of comfort as he sat there with his tracksuit bottoms pulled up to his neck like Simon Cowell with his man nappy hanging over the sides. As for me I couldn't help but smile and at the same time thank God for the misery that he had just bestowed on this deviant rapist, which in some respects renewed my faith in God as seeing Steve sitting there in pain was payback for all the lives he had destroyed. However I kept to Grendons script like everyone else and faked sincerity by wishing him well and a speedy recovery at the same time acknowledging the fact I too was able , like the deviants, to show empathy on the outside but inwardly I was wishing Steve a painful death.

All this was evidence enough to me that the skills I was learning here at Grendon could be used for good and evil. This tool or mask I felt could also benefit the deviants in their pursuit to manipulate new victims on their eventual release as it would help them to integrate better. This churning out of master manipulators to go back into society to rape and pillage again was somewhat disconcerting. However, it was overlooked and was seen as a by-product of therapy as it was far better for the deviants to go undetected back into the real world giving them a fair crack of the whip to change their ways, but I thought it was a calculated gamble never the less at the expense of their next victims lives. So, with this charade of empathy out of the way the wing meeting was called to an end and we broke up for Christmas.

The Christmas break gave me a chance to catch up with Tony as he wanted to tell me about the new fella on his group called Kevin, who by all accounts was a first-class deviant who just oozed slime.

Kevin always walked around with a book in his hand to stop anyone talking to him which was characteristic of a few of the deviants, as they thought it gave them an air of superiority but to the trained eye it was seen as a defence mechanism of the passive aggressive to keep everyone at arms- length and as Kevin was a deviant of the worst kind, I could see why he used it more than most.

His story a one of the worst acts of depravity I had heard so far whilst at Grendon. He had told his group that he had been arguing with his wife as she had found out he was using crack cocaine and watching child porn, so she had decided to leave him. While she was making up her mind she went and stayed at her Mum's house for a few weeks leaving Kevin alone in the house. To blank out the pain of his impending divorce he went back to watching child porn on the internet while at the same time doing crack cocaine. One night when he was out of his head he went and found a prostitute that he knew and being high on drugs he couldn't get it up so he took all his rage out on her by hitting her over the head with a hammer until she was unconscious. He then got on top of her and put a plastic bag over her head so he could watch her die while she carried on looking at him.   When she was dead he raped her dead body, buggered her and did other despicable things to her with implements in the basement of his house. Even when his wife came back and forgave him, he still kept the dead body in the locked basement so he could visit it

After a few weeks his wife smelt something funny, so when Kevin was at work she phoned her brother who came over and broke down the door and discovered the decaying corps bound and wrapped in a St Georges flag, she then phoned the police. However like most self-serving deviants he blamed his wife for grassing him up saying if she really loved him she would have kept her mouth shut. He even blamed the girl he'd murdered for being a prostitute and even said she tried to nick his drugs. When Kevin was asked about kiddie porn on his computer, he said he was looking at it by mistake and the police had made it more than it actually was in court to reinforce their case against him.

By the time Tony had finished telling me all this shit about Kevin we decided to go down for tea and once again as I looked over at another deviant rapist murderer I couldn't help but notice how normal he looked, which made what he had done even worse, giving me another reason to hate his guts but at least he wasn't in my Group.

This only left Alex the ex-old bill who had moved into Pete's old cell opposite mine and Wayne who had moved into Stutters Andy cell next door to get the lowdown on before my nightmare was complete. First, I had to wait for Tony to finish his tea as he said he didn't want to put me off my tea as Wayne's story was a bit gory. With that we both laughed as making light of what we heard was our only form of defence and a way of coping with the enormity of the situation we found ourselves in.

Alex was in for killing his girlfriend who was a police woman. Alex came across as a shy guy, also weak but like the rest of them he was very manipulative through his acts of self-harm. He had only been on the wing a week before he started self-harming by rubbing salt into his eyes which got him moved downstairs to one of the observation cells which were nearer to the main office as it was easier for the Officers to check on him every 15 minutes throughout the day and night. Also, I think he felt safer on the ground floor, especially with him being ex-old bill and all that.

If I'm honest none of us really cared one way or the other because in my eyes he was just like the rest of the scum here who enjoyed beating up women and also like the rest of them he thought he was the victim as he said he found out his girlfriend was having an affair with a few of his old bill mates, which he only found out the night before they were due to marry and this was the night he actually killed her. He said they had started arguing and she tried to hit him over the head with a hammer but he took it off her and beat her with it, killing her outright with 20 blows across the nut. Upon realising what he had done and to cover his tracks, he put her in the car and drove it into a tree trying to make it all look like an accident as it was raining. The normal story blah, blah, blah. However an examination of the body determined the real cause of death and he was exposed, this was very embarrassing for him as his best man had to arrest him.

We later discovered that Alex was gay and had been having an affair with one of his colleagues which was the real reason he had killed her. His shame of being found out that he was gay was common amongst the young guys which says a lot about the society we live in where guys would rather kill their partners than let them expose them for being gay. Pride, ego and also shame was the biggest contributing factor in most of the killings of old gay guys and their wives. In general, if not all the acts of depravity that had been perpetrated by most of the deviants at Grendon apart from the rapists and paedophiles who were just scummy predators and evil by their nature.

This leads me onto Wayne my new next- door neighbour. He was a little guy in his 30s and a Scouser, he came across as one of the boys as he was always joking and like the rest of them it was him who was the victim as he said the prostitute he had taken home tried to rob him of an ounce of crack cocaine, so to teach her a lesson he cut off her head and dismembered her body, he then put it in bin bags and got rid of it bit by bit around the town where he lived. The body and head have never been found but Wayne had taken photos of himself waving her arm about in front of a mirror as if she was waving at him. There were also photos of her head on the kitchen table, but as I said he was a funny guy who had a good sense of humour. As the body had been cut up and thrown away, any deviant sexual acts he may have done to her had been lost for ever but nevertheless I could only assume like the rest of them it was sexually motivated and the cause of her demise.

With the last few cells now occupied the wing was back to full capacity as we broke up for Christmas. At least this year I wasn't singing in the choir which was a blessing as last year it had ruined my street cred. Also, I had got out of working in the Christmas cafe as my team would be cooking over Christmas, which was a bit of a pain as I would be working all over Christmas, even Christmas morning when I should be on the phone with my kids. So, I would just have to see how things panned out.

Being in the kitchen though would keep me out of trouble as most of the shit that happened on the wing was brought about by boredom which lead to piss taking and playing jokes on each other. This was then taken out of context by members of the community to get their own back on each other This sort of behaviour happened all the time but this year I hoped I would be well out of it and true to form the shit started 3 days into the break.

Jamie and Lewis, the old man killers, started taking the piss out of x2 Steve as he had been walking about in his man-sized nappy which could be seen over the top of his tracksuit bottoms. Jamie and Lewis were both overheard saying x2 Steve stunk to high heaven, which he did but because they had said it as they passed Steve in the queue it was seen as bad taste. This was my way to get my own back on Jamie as this rank opportunism was what Grendon was all about if you had the bottle to use it and I did, so I put them both in the book for bullying. Also Bilal and Derek put them in the book as

Terry Ellis

Jamie and Lewis had been bullying them which lead to both Derek and Bilal staying in their cells all over Christmas.

I went to see them both and explained my plan to get rid of Jamie, with their help of course, reinforcing my plan to get them both on a commitment vote after Christmas. My aim was to kill 2 birds with 1 stone but as luck would have it Bilal made a big song and dance about Jamie, Lewis and Cockroach John taking the piss out of him by standing behind him with their thumbs pointing upwards and at the same time saying "friends" and pulling silly faces. This resorted in a wing special being called and as Bilal had called it I was now off the hook but I would say my bit to help the matter along. With nothing to lose I sat back and enjoyed the show.

Bilal started off the special by breaking down and crying and after a few more tears for good effect he started to spill his guts.

Next it was time for x2 Steve to take to the floor. He talked for what seemed like an age but it did have the desired effect as the whole room was up in arms at Jamie and Lewis's behaviour, which only left Derek to say his bit and I had spoken to him just before we came down to let him know that he had my protection if he opened up with both barrels, which he did. This only left me to finish Jamie off and of course that little prick Lewis.

I took a deep breath and asked to take a minute. I started off by saying that "it wasn't bad enough that they were both in for killing old people but now they were picking on 2 old men in the community and as x2 and Derek were of similar ages I could only assume they were both still re-offending in their own heads by trying to humiliate Derek and x2 for their own inadequacies. I also feel they are trying to demonise Derek and x2 to make them look like devils to justify their own actions in killing those 2 old people that they were both convicted of, as by humiliating them in this way they would somehow redeem themselves in the eyes of the community, which couldn't be further from the truth as taking the piss out of x2, who had cancer, just showed how low they would stoop in their pursuit to minimise their own deviant actions and behaviours. I for one think they should both be put up for a commitment as their behaviour was despicable".

I also felt that Cockroach John and anyone else involved should put themselves in the book for a commitment vote. I then looked over at Jamie who now was bright red as I had well and truly covered all the bases on his and Lewis's deviant crimes and behaviours and there was nothing they could say or do apart from say sorry and put themselves in the book, hopefully followed by Cockroach John who had kept rather quiet for a change, but I let it go as I wanted Jamie, he was my number 1 target. If I had my way today he would be gone, which would teach him a lesson not to fuck with a proper criminal. I never smiled or winked like I would normally have done as I wanted to keep the high moral ground if I wanted to have the backing of the whole wing. I had to make it look like I was fighting for a just cause and who better to defend than Bilal, x2 and Derek if I wanted to achieve my aim of getting rid of Jamie, also at the same time make myself in the eyes of Smitty look like a changed man and of course the saviour of the persecuted deviants.

It was mission accomplished and all it had cost me was a few days sitting with x2 who I hated and also Derek and Bilal to show the wing I was on their side when it came to bullying, which in some respects was true as I hated bullies. Plus, over the year I had seen Lewis bully Pete out of Grendon and Jamie bully Derek. Just by the nature of Jamie's and Lewis's offences on the old men they deserved all they got. Also, Jamie did side with fat Mark against me so he was fair game as far as I was concerned. So all in all Christmas had got off to a good start.

To say Jamie took it bad was an understatement as over the next few days he went into melt down smashing a window then punching a hole in the pool room wall, which got him put in the book for 2 more commitment votes by members of his own Group who he turned on by threatening to kill them. This sealed his own fate as Smitty deemed his behaviour as unacceptable and for the safety of the staff and inmates alike Jamie was moved to Bullingdon. JOB DONE.

The funny thing was we hadn't even eaten our Christmas dinner or even opened our presents yet.

Terry Ellis

CHAPTER THIRTY

It took a few days for the wing to mourn Jamie's passing as I could see by Bilal and Derek's reactions as they sang their hearts out on the karaoke machine and seemed happier than I had seen them in quite a while. They danced the days away as Cockroach John and Lewis sat in their cells plotting their revenge as their leader had just been dethroned by his own immaturity and of course a little help from me, so it was game over.

On the morning of Christmas Day I was up bright and early and made my way down to the kitchen where Mick and Martin were hard at work already preparing the roast potatoes and traying up all the chickens before they put the veg on. I chucked the apple crumble in the oven and made the custard before I jumped on the phone to the family and kids, which set me up for the morning.

Mick and Martin were on good form as we were all laughing and joking with each other. We gave each other Christmas cards which took our minds off the fact that we were all missing out on another year away from the people we love, but like most guys in prison this time of year we just made the best of a bad situation and pretended that we were all enjoying ourselves as we made small talk and prepared for the onslaught of hungry deviants who would be making their way down in a few minutes. This gave us enough time to lay out the hot plate and put the custard on the side.

Adam came down first with his budgie Sproggit on his shoulder both wearing Christmas hats and smiling while wishing us a Happy Christmas as we filled his plate with Christmas cheer and then sent him on his merry way asking him to call the others down.

Before we knew it there was a queue of smiling deviants backed up to the door all wearing Christmas hats and wishing each other well, putting aside any grievances they may have had with each other. One by one they thanked me and the boys for giving up our morning to slave over a hot stove just so we could give them all a taste of home cooking, which would transport them back to happier times. This brought about an atmosphere of jocularity as the room seemed to come alive with laughter and goodwill to each other as they all took their places. They were all opening up bottles of coke and Pepsi and sharing their ketchup.

When the boys and I cleaned everything away we joined them all in the Christmas festivities and to my surprise I was actually enjoying myself. Also to my surprise fat Mark gave me and the boys a card wishing us well, which brought our own hostilities to an end. This would come in handy for when we both went up for our commitments as we had now agreed to put a good word in for each other which would help us both survive the vote as our prospective Groups would vote in our favour. With the burden of our impending doom now averted I could now start the new year with renewed optimism that no-one would be knifing me in the therapeutic back, leaving me and the coming year to consolidate all I had learnt. This would mean being off the radar and pulling my socks up as I had decided to give it another 6 months as it was time for me to move on and regain my sanity but that was 6 months away and anything could happen in the meantime but at least I would have made it to the 2- year mark and in the eyes of the therapeutic community that was seen as a triumph in therapeutic terms.

This was further than I could ever have imagined I would have come considering all the scum I was surrounded by and all the shit I had listened to but nevertheless I still had a glimmer of change in me and I was still optimistic that coming here wasn't a complete waste of time. So, to carry on would be the smart move if I was going to give myself the best chance of never coming back to prison again. As the new year approached I reminded myself that I was not only doing this for myself but I was also doing it for my kids as they more than anything else were my driving force behind me doing therapy in the first place and I didn't want to let them down as failure is not an option for me.

CHAPTER THIRTY-ONE

The new year started off with a bang as we were all told that Smitty was on a one-man crusade to eradicate all forms of bullying. He had decided to call a wing special to explore his theory that there was a subculture operating on the wing which had now got out of hand and needed to be curtailed as it had the propensity to become systemic, which we were told would not be tolerated and as the Christmas break had shown us all, there were certain members on the wing who were complicit in this behaviour whose names had been brought to his attention.

Today he would give them all a chance to own their behaviour by putting themselves in the book for a commitment vote so that they and the wing could explore their behaviour. So, with these words ringing in everyone's ears we all took our seats in the community room and as I looked around it was plain to see that Bilal had been talking to Lord Smitty and had spilled the beans, not only on Cockroach John and Lewis but everyone who had taken the piss out of him historically over the year. Which meant most of the wing would be shitting themselves as most used him and his offence as a topic of ridicule, apart from me that is, I had always kept him close as I'd always known what a vindictive prick he could be as he used to be on my Group. I never openly said anything about anyone for fear it would be repeated as I had seen it so many times before on the wing over the last 18 months, I knew that I was in the clear.

So I sat back in my chair and waited for the fireworks to begin which didn't take long as Lewis was the first to put his hands up and say that he stood behind Bilal and took the piss out of him by putting both thumbs up and mouthing 'friends' knowing full well it was a derogatory expression used by his gang, but then added that it was only friendly banter. Bilal jumped in and said he didn't find it funny as the expression being used meant he was a retard. Lewis then added that there was no harm meant by it and it was only meant as a joke, then added Bilal had used the same derogatory expression himself on many occasions when messing about with Pete who used to be on the wing, so to now say that he felt bullied was a fucking joke. With this Cockroach John joined in and said he had also seen Bilal use the same word and expression and thought it was seen by him and everyone else who had used the word 'friends' with the thumbs up as a joke.

Smitty asked Bilal if he had ever used the term they were talking about in the same way. This seemed to shock Bilal as he had to admit he too had been complicit in the past. He then quickly added that it had been a joke as everyone was involved but this time it was different as he wasn't friends with Cockroach John or Lewis and their gang, also adding that what they were doing behind his back was hurtful and who were they to use him as the butt of their jokes? As Smitty was never one to miss an opportunity he jumped on the word 'gang' and asked Lewis who else was in their gang and party to their joke. As it was honest hour he pointed to Steve and Neil who both went red in the face as they had just been grassed up, which was the aim of therapy to show everyone there was no hiding place when it came to criminal loyalty on the wing as every action had a consequence and now they were up to their necks in shit. So, both had to admit their parts and say that they were sorry. They were then asked if anyone else in the room was involved and they each pointed to Anwar and Billie. Billie pointed out Alex and Scottie who then in turn pointed out Tony, Cockroach John, Dave and Jamie (the 2 wing screws) had also participated in the joke. They both denied this until Bilal said that he had seen Dave do it, which put Dave on the back foot so he then said he could remember doing it once but didn't know the significance of the joke, which was par for the course as far as screws were concerned or admitting anything.

This put Smitty on the back foot as he tried moving things along by saying that those who have admitted their part in the joke should take it to their Groups and work on it before putting themselves in the book which didn't go down too well with the guys as now they would all miss their family day, as anyone on a commitment vote wasn't allowed to go for backing for family days if they were in the book. Which was a bit of a disaster as there was now 17 commitments in the book which would take months to sort out. This in turn pitted the guys against each other as they resented the fact they had been grassed up by their own so-called friends which in turn provoked anger towards each other.

This was the other aim of therapy as you had to manage your emotions as the person you felt vengeance towards would still be on the wing or even a member of your Group. But that was confrontational therapy for you and the purpose of the wing special in the first place was to make you think before you acted as every action had a consequence whether it was intentional or not. So another learning lesson brought about by a few idiots who belittled Bilal, who himself was put on a commitment for his past behaviour, which showed the whole community once again that there was no hiding place when it came to historical bullying. Even if you were the victim your past always caught up on you and the only way to avoid that was to never join a gang or joke as the only person you could trust on the wing was yourself. This would make you think about every action microscopically before you said anything or joined in or ever opened your mouth again. Which hopefully brought about real change, or it made you a smarter manipulator of your surroundings, which was normally the case.

When I spoke to Tony afterwards he was fuming as now he would miss his first family day. He also wanted revenge on Bilal as he now blamed him for being a prick for stirring up all the shit in the first place and vowed never to talk to him again. But, once I explained to him that his own actions were the reason he was put in the book, he calmed down and learnt from his mistake.

Over the next few months he could see that what I said was valid as time and time again he saw the results of not thinking before he spoke. A perfect example of this was on Friday when Dan one of the guys on my group was put forward for the pod job and like an idiot he declined the job, adding that if he was forced to take the job he would poison the whole community. This brought about gasps of indignation from the wing as one by one they tore him a new arsehole and by the end of the meeting he was put up for a commitment vote for threats to kill. Anywhere else this idle threat would have been seen as a joke, but not in Grendon as every little thing you said was blown out of all proportion to teach you to think before you spoke. When you considered Dan was doing 8 years for an imitation gun and threats to kill, it would be in his best interests to learn to keep his mouth shut before he condemned himself again as another conviction in the future could result in him being given a life sentence, all because he wasn't bright and just a silly little boy who had not grown up and couldn't keep his mouth shut.

This was another case of not thinking. Terry P was another one of my Group members who believed he could spend 2 years in therapy and try and lie his way through it. He had just been knocked back on his re-categorisation as he had said his then girlfriend was only slightly burnt, when in fact the real truth was that she had spent months in hospital after he had set her alight. By minimising his offence the Psychologists had decided he was still a danger to the public, which was a massive blow to him and he handed his papers in straight away pulling out of therapy all because he couldn't admit that he was a low-life deviant as the shame he felt was holding him back. When you considered he had been the Wing Chairman and also had been one of Grendons biggest proponents lambasting everyone in therapy over the last 2 years under the guise of helping others, then you could only imagine that he had been playing a game all along just like the rest of the deviants. I thought he was playing a game as many a time he had slipped up in our Small Group. Most deviants learnt that to lie on the Small Groups was futile as the Psychologists knew all there was to know about us from our reports and even our history before we came here.

So to see Terry P knocked back for lying was a joke as now he had well and truly been kicked off the therapeutic pedestal and was suffering the shame of being winged. This only reinforced in us that lying was not an option as his downfall was spectacular, as to see him walking around with his head held down and ostracised in such a public way taught you a very valuable lesson, never to lie.

I saw lots of examples of lying on the Group and the wings, but when it happened to our Small Group it was harder to accept as you had to trust the guys in it as we shared a lot of dark secrets also our thoughts and feelings with each other, so trust was paramount.

When 'on-the-fence' Sean came to the Group one morning and said he now believed his best friend, who he had mentioned a million times before in therapy, was actually a figment of his imagination, or in his own words 'an imaginary friend' my jaw hit the floor as he was definitely playing a game without a doubt. What made it worse is that I believed all that he had said for months, so my trust in him was now gone. Just like Terry P and Dan, also deviant rapists Jeff and lying Gordon who were all fucking born again deviant liars.

Just when I thought it couldn't get any worse in our Small Group Daryl slipped up by saying his girlfriend believed he was doing a life sentence for self-defence instead of telling her that he had killed the guy whilst robbing him. He had lied to her for the past 6 years to keep her onboard as he didn't want to lose her. So, with him now a paid-up member of the lying brigade, my whole Group was filled up with a bunch of misfits and any respect or trust I had in any of them was now gone forever.

I should have known better as my original assumptions of them all was spot on. Deviants never change their ways they just learn to adapt but a least now I knew they were all playing a game as all were doing life sentences, so for this I couldn't really blame them but as far as trusting them ever again was concerned that was well and truly over. So now I would just do my own work in therapy and disregard anything that they said because if I'm honest none of them were that bright anyway and most of their advice was not worth a wank. Also, if they couldn't be honest with themselves then how could I really take any of them seriously as honesty worked both ways. Even the screws couldn't admit their own shit regarding taking part in the jokes about Bilal. Their hypocrisy in the whole

Terry Ellis

situation was laughable but I had to carry on as in between all the bollocks there was still learning opportunities, which I hoped would add up to change.

CHAPTER THIRTY-TWO

At the end of January I was sitting in my cell minding my own business and watching TV when Derek rushed into my cell looking all pensive as if he had the weight of the word on his shoulders. He told me he had just received a letter from the police saying they wanted to interview him regarding a letter he had received from Levi Bellfield, a guy he had befriended at his last prison. Levi had written Derek a letter saying 'Derek we are good friends and I know that you would never betray my trust'. This sounded like a warning to Derek to keep his mouth shut about something.

After I read it Derek told me that Levi was the guy who had killed a young school girl on her way home from school and was also responsible for a number of other attacks on women with a hammer and by all accounts he was a proper deviant scumbag. As he was just about to go up for his retrial the police wanted to know if Levi had confided in Derek about any more of his crimes, so they had booked a visit to see Derek. Derek didn't know what to do as he said that he was scared of Levi as he had a big family and was worried they might come after him if he talked to the police. He asked me what I would do, so I told him that the guy had killed a young girl so to me it was an easy option, I would just see the police and put the cunt right in it as Levi should be taken off the streets for the rest of his useless life as he was a sexual predator of the worst kind. If his family had any respect for themselves they would understand that Derek was doing the right thing for the greater good, plus it might help him in the future when he went up for his lifer board. I told him that he should look at it as an honourable thing he was doing instead of looking at himself as a grass.

This seemed to have the desired effect on Derek as he said I was right, he said that he was going to spill the beans on Levi as he knew a lot about Levi that might be of interest to the police. With that he asked me not to repeat our conversation and that was the last I ever heard of it.

Terry Ellis

The next day on our Small Groups we were informed that Smitty wanted everyone that was seeing Sam, the drug, alcohol and dependency support worker, to stop seeing her as he would rather they worked in their small Groups regarding such matters. While he said he respected the confidentiality agreement between her and the inmates, he also felt that the guys on the wing had an obligation to discuss and disclose the work they were doing with her as it was part of their therapy. So for the benefit of the community he was now asking all inmates on the wing to comply with his request, which to me seemed a reasonably fair demand.

However to most of the guys seeing her they thought that she was doing an invaluable job, which was also confidential. This brought about outrage and demanded to see Smitty after their Groups to discuss the matter but he had refused their request. So they asked to see Sam who came over that afternoon and to the guys surprise she told them that she was unaware of what was going on and as far as she was concerned Smitty had overstepped the mark and was talking out of his arse as there was nothing he could say or do regarding them seeing her as the work she was doing was independent of therapy. She demanded a sit down with Smitty who refused point blank to see her but she waited outside his office while talking to the guys until Smitty came out.

To say he looked a little perturbed was an understatement as he went bright red as he himself was caught out by his own arrogance to control every aspect of therapy on the wing. By doing this he had shown us all that he didn't even have the decency or guts to have spoken to Sam beforehand. He had just tried to implement his own dictatorial regime, which really showed a lack of honesty on his part and a great deal of manipulation which wasn't setting a good example to us as we all looked at him as a role model as his own mantra was honesty was the main goal of therapy. So to see him embarrassed by his own lack of honesty was a therapeutic nail in his coffin and as he had pushed by Sam refusing to discuss the matter her, we then saw him and his actions for what they really were, dishonest.

However, by the Friday the matter was put on the back burner as it had been discovered that Cockroach John had evaded a commitment vote over Christmas as Smitty had decided to handle the situation himself behind closed doors which didn't go down too well with the staff as one of them told me that they felt John was a danger to the community as he had been found up on the 3s landing with a sock with 2 tins of tuna in it, apparently waiting for x2 Steve to enter the room so he could beat the shit out of him. So me being me, I asked Smitty why he hadn't brought it to the community but he refused to discuss the issue as he said he had already dealt with it. However, me and the wing persisted and eventually I was allowed to carry on so I asked Smitty if any of the staff had informed x2 Steve about what had happened up on the 3s landing and he said he had informed the senior officer Miss Piggy and that she was the one who had informed him. I said that was a lie as I had spoken to x2 Steve myself this morning and he had told me he never knew anything about the situation and was unaware of what I was talking about, also he was visibly shocked. I said someone is lying and it is not me or Steve but I said I wouldn't dwell on it as I'd made my point. However I would like to know why the community was not informed as if it had been me, Mac, Jamie, Eugene, Gary, Tony, Mick or even Martin we would have been kicked out of Grendon straight away no questions asked, so why was he still here I asked? Anyone else in the past who had made threats would be gone or put on a commitment, like Pete or Gary as we had seen over the last few months. Even Bilal was put on a commitment vote for saying he was going to smash up the office, so to see Cockroach John had actually waited with a sock with 2 tins of tuna in it and was still here was a joke, it's like you see his actions less serious that anyone else's. I find it totally unacceptable as Cockroach John actually acted out his behaviour.

Furthermore the only reason we are not here today talking about x2 Steve's murder is because Steve was too ill that day to work as he had cancer so couldn't walk up the stairs to water the plants and to add insult to injury x2 Steve and the rest of us were not even informed so that we could keep an eye on John and the situation. Which, in my view, would have been in the best interest of the whole community and the staff, as why else were we informed in the first place by one of your staff if they were all in agreement with your decision.

Smitty knew he had well and truly fucked up and to make it worse for him it was one of his staff that put him in it as even Miss Piggy had perpetuated his lie and now looked a right lying Pratt. I had said my piece now so I sat back while the rest of the wing went to town on Smitty and Miss Piggy who now both looked broken as they both had to defend the indefensible, which was my intention all along to show the whole wing the hypocrisy of the whole situation, as there was one rule for the deviants and one rule for the robbers such as Mac, Albino Jamie, Gary and Eugene who were all robbers and had been kicked out of Grendon at the first sign of trouble, as we had all seen over the last year but the deviants got their shit brushed under the carpet.

However by the end of the meeting Smitty and Miss Piggy were left smarting as they both sneaked back to their office. I had to let it go though as I knew how vindictive they both could be, plus I had enjoyed it as I was learning to play him at his own game by articulating my arguments instead of swearing which was the aim of therapy in the first place. So, if I'm honest it was ever so rewarding.

Terry Ellis

CHAPTER THIRTY-THREE

That afternoon though I was called down to the office by Miss Piggy and Smitty and told I was becoming a disruptive influence on the community and at the same time they asked me what member of their staff had told me of the incident between Cockroach John and x2 Steve but I wasn't having any of it. All I said was "remember it was one of your own staff who thought it was serious enough to tell me that both of you have tried to cover it up and had even lied about it. This was seen today by all of us and secondly I can't remember which officer told me of the incident". With that I asked them if there was anything else they needed from me.

Before I left I said "I can't believe the hypocrisy of this fucking place, you drum it into us every day to speak our minds and be honest with ourselves, then you fucking lie to us and when you are found out you act like I am the one to blame, typical of you fucking lot". I then smiled and walked out.

I now knew that my time at Grendon was numbered as Smitty and Miss Piggy had both been humiliated in here today, not only by me but also by the rest of the wing and their own staff and if I knew them then they were not prepared to take it lying down.

I was then informed at teatime by John the Screw that my commitment vote had been brought forward by Smitty to Monday. He suggested that I had better watch myself, which I thought was par for the course as under all the psychological bollocks Smitty was just like the rest of us, a vindictive prick. But, two could play at that game and plus I had all the weekend to manipulate the game in my favour as no-one else knew that I was up on my commitment vote on Monday. So I would go on another charm offensive which would be easy as most of the wing had seen what I had tried to do on their behalf regarding Sam the drug worker and also what had just happened with Cockroach John.

Living amongst the beasts: The rise and fall of the Grendon experiment

I told anyone who would listen what the situation was and what John the Screw had told me about my coming commitment. Also I added that Smitty had warned me not to defend x2 Steve or Bilal or anyone else on the community ever again. Upon hearing this most of them promised me that if Smitty tried to get rid of me they would then back me to stay. I still had reservations though as there were still a number of deviants on the wing who would like me gone for no other reason that I was one of the good guys and not one of them, a deviant. Also I was seen by most of them as someone who had a controlling influence over the wing. So I spent a restless weekend wondering how it would all turn out.

On Monday morning a few of the guys came to my cell to see me. I acted surprised that Smitty was being so underhanded by bringing my commitment vote forward but I said I wasn't worried as Tony, Mick and my Group had given me their word that they would support me.

So I wasn't too worried when I made my way downstairs to the community room, even though I knew I had enough votes to keep me in the game and this would be just a formality, I still felt that Smitty would try his best of get rid of me for no other reason than I had embarrassed him over the last couple of weeks. However it would give the whole wing the chance to see him for the imbecile he really was, just another Psychologist playing God in his own poxy little world who could be beat I hoped. So, as soon as I took my place I looked around the room I wondered who would stab me in the back and who would surprise me.

Smitty then entered the room and nodded to me so I smiled back as he made his opening gambit. As usual he did not disappoint, he said that my behaviour over the last few months showed that I was out of control, not only on the wing but in my Small Groups as I had been reprimanded on a number of occasions not only by him but also by Monkey Boots. This had left him with no other option other than to vote me out.

Cockroach John and Lewis said their bit but it only came across as sour grapes, then fat Mark who I had the original altercation with said his bit and true to his word he said that it was his fault, saying that it was he who had over-reacted in the first place and that he was now sorry that he had been in the wrong place at the wrong time. This seemed to do the job as it knocked Smitty off his pedestal and made me for once look like the victim in all this and not the aggressor as he had been trying to say I was. However, as he had gone straight for the jugular in his opening gambit he now looked a bit of a Pratt with egg all over his smug face but he still took it to the vote. One by one the guys voted for me to stay apart from Cockroach John, Lewis, golf club Chris, cricket bat Brian, Scotty,

Terry Ellis

Gordon and Dan my two-faced Group member, which surprised me but was to be expected because my honesty meant that there was no hiding place for the deviants, especially on my Group, so he probably thought that he had no other option but to get rid of me even if I was the victim on this occasion.

The next morning I was told by John, the same member of staff that Smitty was livid when he came out of the meeting and now had it in for me. He said I should try my best and pull my horns in as he wouldn't put it past Smitty to use my security issues against me under the guise of therapy and the greater good to get rid of me. I promised John that I would behave myself and thanked him for telling me about Cockroach John and x2 Steve.

The next few months seemed to fly by without too much fuss as I kept my nose clean and worked in my small Group to the displeasure of Gordon and Dan who I constantly took to task over their deviant pasts. I kept it real though and stuck to the therapeutic script which got me promoted to the Facilitators Rep where I came into contact with the Governors on a regular basis to the displeasure of Smitty as Nick, one of the Governors, had asked me to do a recital of Hamlet at the next charity event. As I was asked by the Governor it meant that Smitty had to play second fiddle and bide his time if he ever wanted to get me out of here.

I had also been signed up to do the charity rowing competition where we came third as a wing, just about beating the Jimmy Saville wing to fourth place as most of the guys on my wing were not that fit. But we persevered and triumphed over the evil and had our photos taken for the Inside Times where I hid behind Mick so no-one in the system could see that I was at Grendon.

CHAPTER THIRTY-FOUR

It was now April and things were going well for me as I had once again slipped under the radar as Smitty was preoccupied with a spate of self-harm incidents and one attempted suicide on the wing as Wayne and Alex seemed to be having a competition of who could cut the deepest as their arms were constantly being bandaged up.

Smitty had called a wing special to discuss the matter which resulted in both of them being put up for their commitments. I said this was a bit harsh as I had spoken to Alex and Wayne who both told me that they had been self-harming for years, so it was a behavioural problem and not a crime and shouldn't be treated as such.

Smitty was having none of it though and said they both needed to be punished by way of a commitment vote and if the outcome was against them or for them they would both have to do forfeits or leave which would have to be decided at a later date, but for now both will be put in the book for their commitments if it's agreed by the whole wing. He then asked the wing to take a vote on it but I said if you put them in the book and it takes months for their book issues, it will only lead to more stress for them and I should know as I have been on two commitment votes myself and I can tell you I felt on edge all of the time as the pressure of being voted out put a lot of shit on my shoulders and my anxiety levels went up. So, for that reason I will not be voting for them to be put on a commitment.

Once again Smitty said that it was for their own good and he for one believed they would both benefit from it. So he took the vote and one by one all the deviants sided with him apart from Tony, Mick and myself but Smitty had won again and just to rub salt in the wound he asked the Chairman how long it would be until Wayne and Alex were up for their commitments. The chairman said it may take 6 or 7 months as there were 17 book issues in the book, which meant more anxiety for Alex and Wayne. This was Smitty's intention all along as he believed this sort of anxiety was good for you as it made you reflect over your behaviour, which was absurd.

Terry Ellis

There was nothing I could do as it was written in the Constitution which Smitty had written over the years to cover every angle so as to give him absolute control over every aspect and everyone on the wing which resulted in him having a God complex as he thought he was never wrong and he bent the rules when it suited him and just like in the meeting today he revelled in the fact that his word was final as he knew the deviants wouldn't go up against him as most, if not all, were lifers and knew the pen was mightier than the sword. I knew better though as I saw him as just a power-crazy mug as I had been in care homes and prisons all my life and knew he was just abusing his position and sooner or later he would slip up and someone would end up getting killed, just like what had happened on F-wing. I just hoped I was not here to see it.

To take my mind off the situation I carried on learning my lines as I had promised the Governor I would do a reading of William Shakespeare's Hamlet (To Be or Not to Be). I had told him that I would memorise it and act out for the best effect as it would have more of an impact than just reading it out of the book.

I had learnt it by heart and was actually looking forward to it as there would be about 120 people there, even a few of my mates from other wings who would be surprised to see me up on stage in the first place, let alone doing Hamlet. Also, most of the seats would be taken up by the friends of Grendon who were roughly made up of 60 or 70-year old birds and blokes, all of which were ex-magistrates and do-gooders. There would also be tea and biscuits served into the mix and I hoped it would be a good night.

For now though I had to learn my lines and Tony helped me. I also perfected my acting skills as I really wanted to ham it up and show the guys that there was more to me than just being a cockney robber. I thought that I had the potential to hit the stage when I got out.

Enough of the sycophantic flattery as tonight was my big night. I made my way over to the conference hall with butterflies in my stomach wishing I'd never volunteered to put my head on the Shakespearean chopping block because it could all end in tears as the apprehension I was now feeling at the prospect of performing to a big crowd was causing me to forget my lines. However that all changed when I met my old mate Craig who called me over as he was queuing up at the entrance which seemed to take the edge off my fear of failure as he too was as nervous as me. He told me too he had volunteered at the nights event regarding his own experiences at Grendon over the last year or so. As we shared our doubts about our impending performances, the foreboding we both felt was

Living amongst the beasts: The rise and fall of the Grendon experiment

replaced with humorous banter which we both hoped would be enough to get us through this night.

However as we entered the theatre of dreams we were met by the Jimmy Saville brigade who ushered us to our seats and at the same time they handed us our programmes of the night events which would detail the order that we would be performing in. I quickly perused mine to find out where I was on the list as I was hoping that I would be first so that I could get it over and done with so I could settle down and then enjoy the evening. To my horror though I was second to last which meant roughly a 2 hour wait for me, 2 hours of anxiety which I hoped would enhance my performance, or it could turn me into a blathering ignoramus to a baying mob of deviants which didn't help my nerves.

I sat there nervously biting my nails, at the same time trying my best to look as if I was up for the job as everyone was now coming in and taking their seats. Even the blue rinse brigade of ex-magistrates looked a bit fearsome.

I took a deep breath and went through my lines in my head as the Governor took to the stage to a warm applause as he introduced the band of Stuart Hall look a likes, with fat Mark on the drums singing 'don't let the sun go down on me' while a Michael Jackson impersonator danced around banging his tambourine in the background. This brought everyone to their feet as they danced and sang along as if they were at a musical performance of Annie in the West End to the delight of the band as they hammed it up hoping there may be a scout hidden amongst the assembled spectators who might be working for Simon Cowell.

As they came to an end the brass band of the Salvation Army stepped forward from the side lines as no gathering at Grendon would be complete without the God squad being there to deliver us from our sins, as faith in God played a big part in the lives of the deviants whose sins were overlooked by the do-gooders as most of them were nearly at the gates of heaven and saw the help they gave the Grendonites as their passports to that place in the sky as atonement for their own sins. This brought good and evil together like a coalition of the grotesque and the sublime, leaving both sides none the worse for their brief encounters.

The deviants confidence was boosted by their interactions with the blue rinse brigade who themselves received reparation through their donations, which was a win-win situation as far as Grendon was concerned as their benefactors used their influence to muster support for their shared ideology through their contacts in Whitehall, who in turn continued to fund Grendon in these times of austerity.

Terry Ellis

Once the brass band had finished it was then time for Grendon to bring out the big guns. There were 3 secret weapons one of whom was Craig whose stories of change due to his stay at Grendon were paramount in his own conversion from the dark side back into the light.

One by one they recounted their life stories to the now stunned audience who sat there in silence wiping their tears away as they listened to the childhood abuse and the horrors the guys had suffered throughout their lives. But, now thanks to Grendon through its' therapy they had found salvation which brought about rapturous applause and a standing ovation. This was the cue for the brass band to start up again, belting out all the old classics much to the delight of the old dears who were now grabbing their cheque books and waving them in the air.

This was the signal to the Governor to make his move with a 20- minute speech thanking them all for coming and their money, also thanking them for their help over the years. He ended by saying he had a special surprise for them all, a rendition of William Shakespeare's Hamlet by no other than Terry Ellis from C-wing. This brought about another round of applause as I made my way up onto the stage wishing I had brought the book with me instead of trying to do it from memory.

Then the lights went down and the spotlights were on me, which actually helped me as I couldn't see anyone. So I took a deep breath and got into character. For the next 10 minutes I brought the house down with my cockney version of Hamlet which was word perfect, thank God.

By the time I had finished Tony and the boys from my wing were up on their feet, this encouraged the rest of them to do likewise as I received a standing ovation, which I milked for all that it was worth. After I had taken a bow for the 10th time, I left the stage and returned to my seat as Tony and Mick slapped me on the back congratulating me on what they said was the performance of the evening. We all laughed and joked before the Vicar took to the stage to end the nights entertainment with one more encore from the band.

The lights then came on and everybody made their way over to the tea and biscuits stand, which was now mobbed with handbags as thirsty ex-magistrates guarding their position from marauding inmates intent on getting to all the fairy cakes first under the guise of an orderly queue. Then with their belly's full, the blue rinse brigade fanned out to interrogate their minions at will thus ensuring their own peace of mind that their money was being spent well.

Living amongst the beasts: The rise and fall of the Grendon experiment

As the well- rehearsed inmates spilled their propaganda like a congregation of the faithful under the watchful eye of the Governors and their well -placed henchmen disguised as Psychologists with their pen swords at their sides waiting to wave them at you at the first sign of any indiscretions. Then the 5-minute call went out meaning we would be returning to our cells. So we said our goodbyes and promised the old dears that we would keep up the good work until we met again. The doors then opened and we were off again back to the belly of the beasts lair.

CHAPTER THIRTY-FIVE

The following week I was told to attend the diversity meeting that was being held on the Jimmy Saville wing as there were people from local charities and also theatre workshops who wanted volunteers from each wing to record interviews for a radio programme they were doing.

Grendon jumped at any opportunity of publicity as all publicity is good publicity as far as they were concerned, This brought all the Governors out in force on their best behaviour as they were all self-publicists at heart as most loved the sound of their own voices anyway.

So, all attended thinking they might get their 15 minutes of fame. It was also the first time I'd seen so many Governors on the diversity meeting as usually the meetings only consisted of 1 Governor, someone from I.M.B., the canteen reps and the odd screw, also 2 inmates from each wing. Today though there were an army of Psychologists and Governors all hoping to get on the radio programme as we were told it would be played nationally also on Brixton radio which was hoped would entice new recruits from the mainstream prisons towards Grendon.

However todays objective of the meeting was to discuss the content and what wings would be participating with the exception of C-wing as we had already taken a vote some months earlier not to take part in any more publicity especially after what had been written about Brian the rabbit killer. So D and B-wings were chosen to represent the Grendon massive, which left the Jimmy Saville wing with egg on its face as they were voted 51 to 1 not to partake as most, if not all were kiddie fiddlers , which showed them that democracy only worked on their wing and not in the real world, sending them all running to the phones to ask Max Clifford to represent them, but he himself was out being charged with 11 indecent assaults at his local police station with his old pal Rolf Harris in tow.

Living amongst the beasts: The rise and fall of the Grendon experiment

We carried on regardless and by the end everyone was still smiling as we rounded off the meeting with words of comfort from the Governors regarding all the self-harmers and attempted suicides on our wing hoping I would return the favour in front of the programme makers. However, me being me I took the opportunity to go Smitty bashing by saying that C-wings policy for anyone caught self-harming was to punish the individual concerned as it is written in C-wings Constitution as being an act of physical violence, so this automatically puts you on a commitment vote by the community putting your place at Grendon in jeopardy. Sometimes it is dealt with by way of an I.E.P. and even an adjudication which only puts more pressure on the self-harmer to hide their behaviour instead of working on it in a therapeutic supportive environment so they can address their behaviour as the threat of de-selection only makes them more introverted which has been the case on C-wing as far as condemning them is concerned when really, we should be helping them. However Smitty says it is for their own good that they are punished and as you know his word is final on our wing.

This brought about a gasp out of the mouth of the Governor and also the other Governors as one by one they all said that I must be mistaken as this was the first time that they had heard that someone at Grendon was being punished for self-harming. I asked them all to come over to my wing if they didn't believe me and see it for themselves as they could hear it first-hand from Smitty, adding I had seen it with my own eyes only the week before when Alex and Wayne had both been put on a commitment vote for self-harming and just so there was no doubt in what I was saying was true, I also invited the I.M.B. who I asked to accompany me back to the wing to verify my account, which he accepted and did.

I hoped the Governor would be forced to take action and change C-wings Constitution which I knew would infuriate Smitty who would definitely take it personally, but there was nothing he could do. Also, this would be my parting gift to him.

CHAPTER THIRTY-SIX

First though I had to lay the ground work for Monday by bringing it up again on the community meeting, hopefully giving him just enough rope to hang himself with as I knew if I asked him to change the Constitution in front of the whole wing for the wellbeing of the self-harmers, he would make a song and dance about it proclaiming the benefits of keeping it in the constitution. I would then drop the bombshell on him by saying the Governors had asked me to do it, hopefully knocking him off his pedestal, which cheered me up as I could almost imagine Lord Smitty's reaction as he choked on his own self-importance.

On Friday morning I got up bright and early as I wanted a good seat opposite Smitty as these moments only came round once in a blue moon, so I wanted the best seat in the house to see him squirm as he had nowhere to go on this one, which meant checkmate to me.

It was now 5 to 9 so I made my way down to the community room taking the seat directly opposite Smitty and waited for the room to fill up and for the games to begin, which was only moments away.

Then the big cheese entered the room with Cry-Baby at his side as normal, also Miss Piggy and the 2 screws, Dave and John, who I hoped afterwards would share the good news amongst their colleagues that there was a new Sheriff in town who was changing the law for the good of the community who went by the name of T-bone Tel. The room went quiet as one by one everybody took their minutes, until it came to me.

I looked at Smitty and said I'd been thinking about the effects of punishing the guys on the wing for self-harming and felt it really was not conducive to helping them. So today I want to ask the whole wing to take a vote on it being removed from our Constitution, as no other wing in Grendon uses punishment to cure someone of self-harming as what they really need is compassion regarding their behaviour as it would be better served in these cases.

This seemed to hit a note with all the guys as everyone agreed with me, apart from Smitty who said it was in the Constitution and basically that was the end of the matter and that we should all move on.

So, I had no other option but to inform him of the conversation I had with the Governors on the diversity meeting. I also asked the guy from I.M.B. to reiterate what had been said, which he did. This sent poor old Smitty into melt down as he said he would take it up with the Governors but as far as he was concerned the punishment would stay and that was the last word on the matter as he didn't want to discuss it any further. I said that he might not want to discuss it with me or the wing, which is fine , but the Governor will be coming over on Monday to take it up with him and from what the Governors had said to me I could only assume that it would be the last time anyone on this wing would ever be put in the book for self-harming. I then gave him a little smile and we carried on with the meeting.

He had been beaten fair and square and everybody knew it, even the screws looked at me and smiled their approval and by the end of the meeting I could gauge by the looks on most of the guys faces that they too had enjoyed the moment when Smitty fell off his therapeutic pedestal as all gave me the thumbs up, especially Wayne and Alex who were both smiling from ear to ear.

On the Monday we were informed that Wayne and Alex would be taken out of the commitment book, rightly so I thought, and given the real help they needed and so rightly deserved.

As for me I carried on with my therapy without any more run-ins with Smitty. However the therapy I was now doing was becoming tedious as I was constantly being asked to consolidate my work which meant going over the same old shit time and time again, hoping repetition of my thoughts and feelings would somehow give me a better insight into myself. This only prolonged the agony of being on the Group with the misfits and the 2 fucking rapists, as I saw the use of consolidating my work as a way of keeping me on the Group and a way of making me work for my keep, as the knowledge I had learnt was now being used to bring along the others, which I was starting to resent as I'd had enough of listening to the rapists telling me that they were all victims and that their crimes were the same as mine.

Terry Ellis

This was a step too far one morning as I completely lost it with Jeff and Gordon and the rest of my Group as I told them they were being delusional if they imagined for one second that our crimes and victims shared any similarities. Their crimes destroyed not only their victims lives but their whole families, which in most cases lasted for years and even ended in suicide, which was a consequence of their despicable deviant crimes as both also involved kids. So in my eyes they should both be put down as they were the scum of the earth and if I ever saw them or ever heard where they were living I wouldn't hesitate to put them both out of their misery when I got out. Then I character assassinated both of them for the next 15 minutes before I was asked by Monkey Boots to calm down which sent me into one again as I told him to fuck off as he was only a deviant loving cunt who was too soft on all of them because it was better to pander to them all than do any real work that might change their fucking lives as they were all fucking scum.

This didn't go down too well as he went red in the face and nearly had a heart attack as he told me to get out of his Group, which I was only too happy to do and I fucked off back to my cell.

That afternoon I was asked into the office for a sit down with Monkey Boots, Smitty and the rest of my Group which ended in me being put up for a commitment vote, which was par for the course, as I told them they were all scum and no amount of therapy would change any of them. So I was now on a commitment vote as Smitty and Monkey Boots wanted me out as I had no shame and couldn't be curtailed like the rest of them.

As soon as I came out of the meeting I went sick as I was going to play them at their own game so I convinced the doctor to sign me off for the next 2 weeks with a chest infection and a bad back, which I hoped would give me enough time to decide what I wanted to do with my commitment which wasn't for another 6 or 7 months as there were so many book issues.

I booked a visit with the kids to ask them what I should do as they had all been on at me for months to leave Grendon as they could see that being around all the deviants was doing my head in.

We all agreed enough was enough as I had tried my best to change and I had gone as far as I could go as far as therapy was concerned. Living amongst the beasts was starting to be counter-productive, so we planned my exit strategy as I didn't want to be hanging around for months waiting for a prison to take me as it would mean I still had to listen to all the community meetings for months and I couldn't take that shit anymore.

Living amongst the beasts: The rise and fall of the Grendon experiment

That night when I got back to the wing I phoned Terri and as planned I asked her to phone a reporter she knew and ask him if he would be interested in me writing a book about my stay in Grendon and just to juice it up a bit I gave her the title over the phone which we both knew would be picked up by the security department as they listened to all our phone calls. I also knew Smitty would have something to say about the matter and knowing him he wouldn't wait 6 or 7 months, he would in fact react straight away as calling the book "Living Amongst the Beasts' and saying I was going to write about everyone here would be the last straw for him, I hoped.

The name was also very apt as most of the guys on my wing were cold blooded murders and low-life scum who I hoped would never be allowed out. So with my fate determined by a phone call, the weight of the last couple of years was lifted off my shoulders and as there was no going back now and if I did it right I would be out of Grendon in the next couple of days or weeks I hoped. So I used the rest of my time to say my goodbyes to Tony, Mick and Martin. I had also written down all that I had learnt, hoping it would add up to change and not the waste of time my family and friends thought.

I still had one more visit with the kids, who bounced onto the visit happier than I had seen them for months as they all knew once I made up my mind about leaving that I meant it. This was music to their ears and made for one of the most productive visits we had ever had as we spoke for 2 hours about the pros and cons of therapy and the book I wanted to write, which got me to thinking why I had come here in the first place. I also thought about the benefits I had gained from the experience.

First though I had to get out of here if I was going to give myself freedom to write without the constraints and the interference from Lord Smitty and the screws who were now constantly monitoring me.

As expected my commitment vote was brought forward and before I knew it I was walking into the lion's den for my last community meeting and as I sat there with my thoughts waiting for Smitty to enter the room, I knew today had to end with a bang. I wanted them all to remember me as someone who left with his head held high and not whimpering like most of the mugs that left here begging for forgiveness, because that wasn't my style. Plus, I told Tony there was going to be some fireworks in here this morning so I couldn't let him down.

As I watched the usual suspects enter the room, Smitty followed by Cry-Baby, Parrot Face Sue, Miss Piggy, 4 screws, Dave, Jamie, John and Simon, also the old guy from I.M.B., Ann from the Chaplaincy, Miss Hitler from security department and Nick the

Terry Ellis

Governor, this indicated to me that they knew about what I had said on the phone as this was the normal routine when something was said on the phone that they didn't like, which was supposed to intimidate me but it did not. It actually made me more determined to say my piece as I now knew they were going to come at me.

I waited for the room to settle down, looking at Smitty who was now looking at me intently like a paedophile in a sweet shop on his way to the playground. I returned his gaze with a smile and a wink which took him by surprise as the realisation that I knew what was about to happen dawned upon him which took away his power of surprise but he masked it well. However I could see he was flushed as he went red and crossed his legs and arms in a defensive posture which he always used when going on the attack, which I had seen a million times before.

He then played what he thought was his ace card by asking me if I had anything to say to the community regarding writing a book and could I tell them what the title was going to be? This suddenly brought everyone in the room into the game as none of them knew what was going on, but now all their eyes were focused on me and thinking I might back down under the weight of the occasion like most I'd seen in these situation over the last 2 years, but not me. So I fronted it out and said yes you are right, I am writing a book and the books is aptly titled 'Living Amongst the Beasts' which is going to be an honest account of my time spent here and will cover every aspect of my stay and the work I've done in my Small Group and also on the main wings, which I hope will be an interesting read and hopefully give the outside world a better understanding of what therapy is all about and the way it's run. Also, it will be about the people I have met. Surely you have not got a problem with that or the truth have you Smitty?

This sort of threw Smitty as he was expecting me to be sarcastic with my response so he could take the moral high ground but I had been a good student and had learnt from my mistakes so I wasn't going to give him the satisfaction. He then changed his tact and said the title was very offensive, so I stated it's not really offensive as you will find it in most daily newspapers to describe most murderers of kids and women, also rapists so I don't honestly see a problem with it.

He then asked the wing what they thought about me writing a book about them and added that the whole ethos of therapy is trust. So he said "don't you think Terry that you would be breaking that trust by writing a book?". Once again, I stated "no not really, as I've always told you, it's about my experience here not theirs, but I will be saying what they are in for and what I think about most of them as I'm entitled to my own opinion as all their offences are in the public domain". Then a few of the guys said they wouldn't be

Living amongst the beasts: The rise and fall of the Grendon experiment

happy about me putting it in a book, so I said "I don't give a fuck for one, and two I never signed a confidentiality agreement and just like their victims life can sometimes be a bitch". This brought about a response from Sue who was from Art Therapy, who was aptly named Parrot Face Sue as she always repeated what Smitty had said and today was no exception as she asked the wing what they felt about being called beasts, which brought about the biggest laugh of the morning as Wayne, who had chopped up a woman said he thought of himself as a beast. Bill then said the same as he had killed a young kid. Mick and Tony then joined in by saying they were beasts for their crimes, even Kevin the necrophiliac said he thought of himself as a beast followed by Anwar and Nigel who was in for murder and kiddie porn.

So to say the question backfired was an understatement. I then turned to Parrot Face Sue and said "does that answer your question darling?" at the same time I gave her a little wink. I then said "the only surprise in here today is that the rest of you haven't owned your shit for being deviants". It was now my turn to go on the attack, I said to Scottie "you are a murdering rapist, don't you think you are a fucking beast? And you Jeff and Gordon and let's not forget you Bilal, Brian and Cricket bat Chris", but none of them said a word. So I repeated the same question to fat Mark and Cockroach John, then to Lewis and x2 Steve, then the last person on my list was Gavin who had killed his own little girl but he like the rest of them said nothing

Next, I said "there is going to be a vote in a minute asking whether I should go or stay and I want you all to know that I want you to vote me out, even you Tony and Mick as I want to go so look at today as you doing me a favour". I then turned to Smitty and said "I know you are just doing your job but you should take your own advice and take the ego out of your job and stop taking things personally". Then I smiled and got up.

I looked around the room for the last time, then I thanked Tony and Mick and said "it's been emotional", then I walked back to my cell and packed my things.

Half an hour later Tony and Mick walked into my cell looking sad as they said they had some bad news for me. They said that I had been voted out which brought about fits of laughter from all of us as we fell about laughing.

-THE END-

Terry Ellis

Living Amongst the Beast

The day I left Grendon was the day the weight of years of division lifted from my shoulders. It felt so good to finally be away from therapy and the minefield that was conflict resolution.

My anxiety levels immediately started to dissipate and were replaced with a more self-confident me. My eyes had been opened as I could now see everything before it happened. Peoples behaviours started to shine brightly in technicolour, exposing their hidden personalities. This eureka moment was the start of the realisation that living amongst the beasts had actually worked.

I was now free from the constraints that had shackled me for years. Free from anger, free from the misery that had been my pathetic life. It was now all gone but, thankfully it had been replaced with a renewed optimism for the future and a self-belief that I had changed for the better.

I could now try and make amend for all those wasted years separated from my family.

It's been 4 long years since I left Grendon, a time for readjustment and reflection, but above all it's been a time for me to evaluate my stay there and the pros and cons of living in its therapeutic community, and if you've read this far, you should also now have a better understanding of who I am and the sequence of events that brought me here in the first place. You've read my journey and you obviously know my views on its deviant community. So all that's left for me to say and write about is what I actually got out of it.

But first I have to admit I was wrong as the whole experience did change my life and continues to do so in so many ways. It has made me a more balanced individual which is excruciating for me to say on so many levels, as even by the nature of therapy it was never designed to work within a prison environment. But it did and I'm testament to that.

I came to Grendon to find some answers as I was curious about why I am the way I am. So what better opportunity for someone like me to take, than to come to Grendon and find out more about my thoughts and feelings and challenge them and my behaviour.

Yes, it's been hard at times, as trying to find straight forward answers has been almost impossible, as I'm a complicated person with so many issues and trying to identify cause and effect has been at times a difficult process. But, if I am honest it is still an ongoing exercise but coming here gave me the chance to question every aspect of myself and personality. This process has been instrumental in the way I now live my life and the way I treat and view others. I can't change my past but I will and can shape my future and with the love of my family and Grandkids, 5 of them, I will get there.

Cognitive Behavioural Therapy is used for many different types of psychological problems. You could say at Grendon CBT is used to rehabilitate the mind. The techniques used are specifically designed for better mental and emotional health on our journey towards becoming self-therapist of our own minds as Grendon sees emotions as interconnected with thoughts and behaviours. So it follows that if these thoughts and behaviours are targeted for change, a change in emotions will come about. That's why I was asked to keep a thought diary as it helped me understand the functions and consequences of my behaviour in the context of emotional problems. It helped me see that my thoughts and beliefs were somewhat off-key and by me seeing this on a daily basis it was helpful as it pushed me to find more helpful alternative belief systems, also coping strategies.

Grendon used many CBT therapies rather than a single approach. Here are just some of the types I believe were used on me throughout the period of my stay at Grendon.

In no specific order:
Cognitive Therapy (CT) was founded by Aaron T Beck who believed using thought diaries and behavioural experiments (CT) focused upon uncovering unhelpful thoughts, rules and assumptions, beliefs aiming to replace them with more helpful alternatives.

Behaviour Therapy (BT) is most often associated with exposure, the therapeutic use of facing your fears. Another key contribution is to understand the functions and consequences of our behaviour in the context of emotional problems.

Rational Emotional Behaviour Therapy (R.E.B.T.) developed by Albert Ellis. R.E.B.T. is philosophical in promoting flexible thinking, high frustration, tolerance and self-acceptance behaviour. Change is seen as acting upon and therefore strengthening healthy beliefs.

Acceptance and Commitment Therapy (A.C.T.) was conceived by Steven Hays. A.C.T. tends to focus more upon acceptance of your current reactions, mindfulness of the present moment, identifying your valued directions (what you are really about as a person) and committed action.

Metacognitive Therapy (M.C.T.) was founded by Adrian Wells and Gerard Matthews focused upon the thoughts we have about mental processes, such as dwelling on the past, focusing on future threats, confidence in our memory and where we focus our attention. M.C.T. also tackles practices that are backfiring as coping strategies and which therefore keep the problem going.

Compassionate Mind Training (C.M.T.). Developed by Paul Gilbert. Focuses upon the importance of shame and self-criticism in emotional problems. It encourages people to become warmer and more compassionate to themselves by using a variety of imagery, attention and behavioural strategies.

Behavioural Activation (B.A.). Most often associated with Christopher Martell. B.A. is a treatment for depression. B.A. helps patients activate themselves out of a pattern of inactivity and avoidance driven by depression.

Psychodrama was another complementary therapy in which volunteers form a group to talk about and re-enact scenes from their lives and offences that they have committed with particular significance for them.

Art Therapy was another complementary therapy by which a man can express himself through art.

Empathy and Communication are two of the most important things that those in therapy should strive for. To articulate your thoughts, feelings and emotions so as to feel empathy for others is the key to Grendon and its continued success.

The kind of strategies that may be causing you problems and that you may be using to cope with problems include:

- Avoiding situations that get you into trouble. Also situations that trigger anxiety
- Withdrawing and isolating yourself
- Dwelling on and reviewing past events
- Repeatedly seeking reassurance
- Criticising yourself or others in your mind
- Comparing yourself with other people
- Analysing what people say about you
- Reviewing interactions with other people
- Using alcohol or non-prescribed drugs as a treatment for your problems
- Over planning and preparing for future events in your mind.

Also other things you should be looking for: has your mood become low, neglecting yourself and your home, changing your eating patterns, feeling anxious when in social situations and anxiety

- The ears hear
- The eyes see
- But the head can't make sense of it

Terry Ellis

Why Grendon works.

It worked because Grendons foundation is built basically on trust with staff, as it is of vital importance if we were ever going to make any inroads, especially when it came to changing our behaviour. Most of the men who came to Grendon have spent years being abused in the so-called care system by organisations that represent the establishment, like prison officers who have dealt out beating over the years whose cruel and violent assaults have left us scared and resentful of anyone in authority. That's why it was imperative that the first lessons we learnt were to break down the barriers of resentment and mistrust by talking to the screws on those little trips into the office under the guise of reading the papers on the induction wing, as they were fundamental in humanising them. Which was the start of the psychological process towards repairing the damage that years of so-called institutionalised rehabilitation through a good kicking had built up within us. Even eating together was an innocuous first step as we saw the act of eating along as another barbaric punishment for our crimes, so to finally be able to sit at a table with others was seen as an end to this anachronistic behaviour and the start of the second stage of our social development back into the human race and away from the subspecies that they the system had created from years of eating alone.

Step three on the induction wing was the small therapy Groups as it was the first time any of us had ever openly opened up in front of anyone else about how we really felt regarding being away from our families and the despair we felt. Just talking this way helped us release years of spent-up anger and frustrations as we had never been given this opportunity to express ourselves this way before, as I like many of the guys could only express my emotion through anger. We found this new way of articulating our thoughts and feelings brought about a new awareness of our past juvenile behaviour, which in turn stopped us from reverting back to type in times of stress. We started using words to express ourselves instead of profanities or our fists, which in turn brought about a more mature approach in our mental and emotional development as most of us had all the adult characteristics of a grown up but due to not being able to express ourselves properly, we hadn't developed the skills to function like adults in normal situations like most people who have been nurtured in childhood and who are encouraged in their development with hope and belief and even ambition, but most importantly through education, as we were brought up on feral council estates or in the good old care homes where the mantra was to separate you from your family and beat you into submission. This is turn made us hostile to anyone in authority making the state our life long enemy which only reinforced in us our antisocial beliefs, hence I was now in therapy being reprogrammed.

For me those first few weeks on the induction wing helped me shed some of the baggage I had been carrying for years, armour I had put in place to protect myself, which I now saw as a hinderance when it came to my mental development from childhood to adulthood. I believe this was because my only role models growing up were other kids, so instead of learning to formulate measured responses to given situations like any normal grown up, I always go back to acting like a pubescent delinquent because that's all I've ever known. This I believe, was due to me being placed in care as a child. This realisation was another insight on my journey to address my shortcomings and the start of bridging the gap back emotionally to adulthood through therapy.

These epiphanies were the cornerstone that made Grendon unique as seeing these behaviours played out on a daily basis reinforced in me that what I thought was normal was in fact holding me back, as I could see I had been a moron masquerading as an adult. These insights brought about by realisation instead of being told or lectured to help us to slowly bridge the gap back, which had a humbling effect on us all over those first few months, as I for one saw my past behaviours for what they were, moronic.

That is why the small Groups worked so well, because we could all see similar traits in each other, this mirroring effect of seeing behaviours played out in this way help us change our behaviours incrementally through self-realisation.

The other important lesson I learnt over these 2 years was to let go of my ego. It's a small word but ego is responsible for so much in our lives and letting go of a super-ego like mine was my biggest battle. It made me an arrogant self-opinionated prick, so letting go of it was a massive step. If I ever wanted to free myself, letting go of my ego would be the first step and I can't stress enough how imperative the part of letting go of the ego played getting through therapy.

Terry Ellis

Embarrassment like ego was another monumental hurdle to overcome as it's probably responsible for the majority of killings by inmates at Grendon, so learning to deal with it by doing the Small Groups and seeing the others on a daily basis talking about their offences regarding their sexuality and sexual abuse and all the other subjects that we brought up, we soon learnt that embarrassment wasn't a life or death situation and could be overcome by rationale thinking. We soon understood that our own embarrassment was our biggest obstacle and because we could now feel it if for what it was, just another emotion that could be overcome, we began to realise it couldn't physically hurt us. So instead of using violence to mask our embarrassment we learnt to embrace it by channelling our anger through conversation and articulation.

Anger through our inability to argue verbally was another stumbling block we had to overcome but thankfully once again through our weekly community meetings and infighting we were able to perfect our arguing skills. Not only did we learn to manage our anger we also learnt to control our adrenaline rushes as far as flight or fight was concerned as we began to articulate our arguments. We learnt to feel and understand the process that our mind and body went through in those times of stress. The signals were slowly being replaced with common sense, a better weapon to defend ourselves with, without crossing the line that brought most of us into conflict with our peers and authority, which only reinforced in us that violence was no longer the answer to those situations we found uncomfortable. This freedom through self-expression was liberating, helping us believe we were not beyond the realms of help as we had all thought. This enabled us to struggle on in what felt like an exploding minefield of reality checks put there by the Psychologists like a mirror of our imperfections. This was a humbling experience because for the first time in our lives we realised that the defences we had put in place to protect ourselves were now useless. These new feelings of vulnerability helped us to understand that we were the masters of our own environment, which meant not being aggressive 24-7, as all that did was push others away. It also stopped us from communicating and functioning like normal human beings.

Another contributing factor of why most of us were at Grendon was boredom which for years we had all overlooked but actually it played a big part in our lives. The more I heard the word used as an excuse by the child killers, the rapists and the guys who had killed old people because they said they were bored with their lives, or because they never had any money, it dawned on me how pathetic it was as I'd even used it for my past actions. So learning to deal with it and understand the consequences that idle minds and hands have was another important lesson we had to deal with through the jobs that we were given on the induction wing in those first 12 weeks, it was fundamental if we were ever going to turn our lives around.

Sexuality is also responsible for people killing as peoples own misplaced shame, ego and fear of being labelled by others means more to them than taking someone's life. Most of the guys I met saw their sexuality as abnormal so covered their tracks by beating their conquests to death, it was called 'gay rage', this somehow made it right in their own minds, which was a shame for them and their victims. Their fear of being labelled was their own bigoted view and theirs alone, which I saw as a sorry indictment in today's society. But all that aside, I saw that once they embraced their sexuality they were happy within themselves and became happy and less argumentative and less confrontational. Their self-esteem grew and blossomed in a more promising healthier ways which was liberating to see as they became the people they were supposed to be. Seeing their fears of being gay dissipate through being honest with themselves made their past behaviour seem all the more absurd and a waste of their victims lives and their own, and hopefully a lesson to anyone who reads this.

Misplaced anger was also rife within the walls of Grendon and the more I saw of it the more transparent it became. It was normally because someone was unable to communicate properly or articulate themselves, so they would use whoever they were arguing with offences against them to justify their bad behaviour believing their primitive approach would win the debate. This sort of behaviour only happened when someone new came on the wing as they still had their prison heads on, but if they thought they would get away with it they were mistaken as the guys on the wing were aware of this technique as they themselves had all been using the same behaviours for years to justify their own bad inadequacies. So the newbie would receive a berating by the whole wing making him think twice before ever using that method again to win an argument. For the newbie it was the start of the long therapeutic process in learning to always think before you spoke. Even though this is a very basic example of misplaced anger, we as a community learnt to read the many signs and signals in which misplaced anger was used, so instead of reacting likewise to someone offloading in this way we saw it for what it was, which in turn gave us a better understanding of our own shortcomings bringing the use of it to an abrupt end as far as using it to express ourselves or justify our bad behaviour. This is what made Grendon unique when it came to understanding our own actions, which in turn made us want to learn more, so we invested not only our time but blood, sweat and guts in every issue we were tasked with until we were proficient enough in our own abilities not only to read body language but to show restraint when needed. We learnt to spot a liar as soon as they opened their mouths, also identify our own triggers in high risk situations so we could put coping strategies in place and we built stronger support

Terry Ellis

networks with family and friends. But our number one priority along with taking responsibility for our actions was victim awareness and empathy. We learnt to apologise for our pasts which in turn made us less self-opinionated and more tolerant of others and their opinions.

Misplaced loyalty and other imaginary criminal codes became a joke and I started to see how pathetic it was. I started to listen more and take advice onboard and state my opinions in a calm and reasonable manner, also to be more assertive which gave us the confidence to speak up on the wing community meetings which made us more approachable and less intimidating. Sarcasm and humour were no longer used as a weapon or a defence mechanism. We learnt about relationships and actions on others, this made us look at ourselves in a way that made us ashamed of who we used to be, which again reinforced in us all that the work and changes we had made were the right ones. We became better at decision making, interpersonal problem solving, critical reasoning, moral reasoning such as fairness and exploring links between our values and behaviours. The list was endless.

The penultimate lesson and absolutely essential if you were ever going to make it through Grendon was conflict resolution, as it started that first day. The day you met your fellow Grendonites who one by one introduced themselves to you by revealing who they really were by their crimes and acts of depravity, which in turn was the start of your internal conflict that would rage within you until the day you left. But, before that day came you would experience conflict on a daily basis on your Small Groups, the verbal clashes we had on the community meetings, the discussions by the Small Groups and the whole community, hostility, antagonism, feuds, every conceivable conflict situation imaginable would eventually be played out in front of you, or by you, perpetuated by the Psychologist and staff who thrived on it, but it eventually made you skilled in the art of conflict resolution which in turn kept you safe. The practicalities of putting us in these situations meant our involvement through doing rather than hearsay brought about in us a more measured response. This only worked through repartition as we were dealing with many conflict situations on a daily basis that we found ourselves in. But, practice did make perfect and I assume was the most valuable lesson Grendon had to offer if we were ever going to function as productive members of society every again.

Grendon will always have its detractors as they believe the money spent pandering to the deviants is a futile exercise. This is due partly to the fact that by the nature of their crimes they are beyond the normal realms that govern civil society and I for one totally agree with them, as no amount of therapy could ever change their behaviours. I more than most can again totally understand this line of thinking as I've experienced it first-hand by living amongst the beasts. I've experienced their manipulation and all their deviant behaviour, so I understand the detractors concerns as my own perceptions of Grendon are the same.

However, it does work for a recidivist like me on so many levels, I only hope that after reading what I've had to say they can understand this too, as I believe there are many lessons to be learnt from both sides. I also have to believe that one day soon the Psychologists at Grendon will give up on the idea that they can change a deviants nature, just like they gave up years ago on the idea that electric shock treatment worked and the idea that they could change a homosexuals sexuality through aversion therapy, because it didn't work then and it doesn't work now.

However therapy does work and my only hope over the coming years is that all prisoners get the same opportunities that the deviants have had for years, to change and understand and interpret their own behaviours for what they are. Hopefully then, like me, it will free them up so they can go on to reach their full potential.

A few lessons I've learnt at Grendon that might help you if you are prepared to make some real changes in your life:
1. Stop people pleasing
2. Learn to say no
3. Control your anger
4. Take people's opinions into account
5. Tolerance
6. Think before you speak
7. Articulate your words
8. Don't swear when arguing
9. Listen
10. Stop being self-opinionated
11. Understand criminal values for what they are
12. Criminal associates
13. Support networks are important
14. Take yourself out of harmful situations
15. Learn from your own mistakes
16. Learn from others mistakes
17. Empathy
18. Treat others how you expect to be treated
19. Never lie to prove a point

20. Stop using sarcasm
21. Know when to stop
22. Learn to talk about your thoughts and feelings
23. Become a better communicator
24. Work at building a strong relationship
25. You will start seeing situations before they happen
26. Peoples behaviours become transparent
27. Stop using humour as a defence
28. Learn to debate as you will learn to control your anger through repetition
29. Stop being the life and soul of the party
30. Learn better social skills
31. Stop ruminating
32. Look at your behaviour and actions on others
33. Patience
34. Willpower comes from therapy, stop smoking
35. Write a book
36. Gain real confidence
37. Stop blagging it
38. Learn to accept the things you cannot change
39. Learn to take no for an answer
40. Turn the other cheek
41. Accept feedback constructively
42. Accept responsibility for your own actions
43. Learn to sit with your thoughts and emotions
44. Stop being passive aggressive
45. Stop isolating yourself
46. But, most of all learn to love.

Dedications

I would like to thank a few people:

First of all, I would like to thank the most wonderful woman in my life, my soul mate, my best friend and the most beautiful girlfriend I could ever wish for Anna Wheatley.

Anna, your love and support has been immeasurable, your warmth and generosity has been overwhelming since day one. You have allowed me the latitude and time to fulfil my dream bringing my book into the light, without your words of encouragement I would have fallen at one of the many hurdles I have encountered on this journey.

I thank God every day for sending an angel to guide and look over me, I have been truly blessed to have found true love and happiness.

Thank you so much, Anna

I would like to thank Melanie my Psychologist, who I had the good fortune to meet in Pentonville in those early days. I would like to thank her for her cards and her follow up visits at Grendon, and always being at the end of a phone when I needed her. She is responsible for pushing me towards the light.

Thank you

I would also like to thank Kelly, who is funny, witty, sarcastic and the Mother of my girls. She is generous, loving and I love her and the boys for always being at the end of a phone when I needed them.

Thanks Kelly

Terry Ellis

I would like to thank my Mum and sister Tracy for always being at the end of the phone when I needed them. My Mum's cards and letters have kept me going and kept me strong.
Thank you both

The next two people in my life are my Step-Mum Eileen and my Dad. Their support and encouragement over the years has been extraordinary and greatly appreciated. Also my Step-Brother Jonathon for always being at the end of the phone.
Thank you

A special thanks to Ann Alston, Ann painstakingly went through written manuscripts and voice recordings to get the book into its first digital format, a task that was promised by so many but only delivered by you.
Thank you, Ann

And to Chris Alston, the editor. Without you the book may never have seen the light of day, between us we took hand written piles of paper and formulated it into a book, plus you always let me steal your words on Facebook and pass them off as my own!
Thank you, Chris

I would also like to thank my son Kyle for his visits, phone calls, letters, cards but most of all his support. He has shown strength of character by giving me a second change to be his dad. He continues to make me proud of his achievements and the way he lives his life. He has stood by me at the darkest times, making it possible for me to see the light
Thank you, Son

The same should also be said for my other son Tony, who too has given me a second chance. I would like to thank him for his cards, letters and phone calls and also for letting me be part of his girlfriend Natasha and their daughters life.
Thanks Son

There are not enough superlatives to thank the next three people in my life, Charlene, Terri and Chloe.

Living amongst the beasts: The rise and fall of the Grendon experiment

They have been there throughout the hardest time of my life. Their visits, love and support have been invaluable and have kept me going. Their strength of character and tenacity throughout has been amazing. Their letters, cards and emails have brought me back from the edge of the abyss more times than I care to remember. They're my inspiration, my life and the reason I stayed at Grendon.

All my life I've been missing something, but in them I've finally found it. Charlene has given me two beautiful grandsons and Terri a handsome Grandson and a beautiful Granddaughter. Chloe continues to make me so proud. Also she has given me a beautiful Grandson. I'm a very lucky man.

Even good men sometimes take the wrong road in life.

There's a reason why there is no data on reoffending by ex-Grendon inmates or any other psychology-based prisons in England or Wales

Terry Ellis

C WING COMMUNITY - CONSTITUTION

"WELCOME TO C WING"

By choosing to come to Grendon and joining the C wing community, you are committing yourself to a therapy process that, depending on your efforts and contribution, will help you change attitudes, offending behaviour and lead a law abiding life when you leave prison. The community will maintain high levels of decency and mutual respect, irrespective of sexual orientation, age, race, colour, ethnic background, religious beliefs and offence behaviour.

1. <u>COMMITMENT PERIOD</u>

Men are required to continually demonstrate their commitment to therapy and the community throughout their time on C Wing. The first three months on the community is the first part of this commitment requirement. New arrivals will undertake wing based jobs and will not be able to go for backings for off wing activities. The exceptions will be to attend religious observances, the gymnasium and approved diversity activities. The three month commitment period is completed once the initial assessment has taken place.

2. <u>COMMUNITY MEETINGS</u>

Community meetings or 'wings' are held twice weekly on Mondays and Fridays. Attendance at this is **<u>compulsory</u>** for all members of the community.

The wings provide an open forum for communication. Community members can raise minutes, seek backings and debate the standards and expectations for the wing. The Cleaners Foreman and Pod Workers report weekly to the wing. The wing is also an important clinical meeting: individual assessments are fed back and discussed; Psychodrama and Art Therapy are also fed back.

You are accountable to the community for lateness, failure to attend or walking out during a meeting. If you leave the meeting you will not be allowed back into the meeting. If you are late you will not be allowed into the meeting or at the discretion of the chairman. You will explain your actions to your group and the wing when asked to do so. Each absence is recorded - if the absence is not acceptable you will be given a "strike". Two "strikes" leads to an automatic commitment vote. You can also be give a "strike" if you walk out of wing meetings.

Once men leave wing feedback/wings it is unlikely they will be allowed back. In some circumstances it may be necessary: wing specials or in the best interest of the community. It is down to the discretion of the chairman if they are allowed back into the community room. If a man has a medical condition that necessitates he leave the community room he can then return - this has to be supported with a medical certificate.

3. THE BACKING SYSTEM

C Wing aspires to operate as an open and transparent therapeutic community. The community residents and staff - operate a backing system. All issues that are related to your therapeutic work, sentence progression and to the activities on the community eg: to have visitors attend Family day, be considered for art therapy and psychodrama therapy, re-categorisation issues or to attend an off wing event - are in the first instance taken to your small therapy group to be backed. You will be asked questions about the issue and backed by the group if a good case has been made. The backing is then taken to the community meeting and the same process is repeated. - you will be asked questions and if a good case has been made you will be backed. A wing backing is based on a majority vote. The backing is then considered at the staff meeting. You will then be informed whether you have been backed by the staff group. To be backed by the community and staff group is a positive endorsement and in turn is a demonstration of your commitment to the community. The backing process is suspended if you have been put in the "book" for your commitment to the community (in the community book). - when your place will be decided by a community vote (see section 9 below). Once the commitment issue has been resolved on the community you are then able to resume the backing process.

It is acknowledged in some circumstances, that a backing cannot be taken to the groups during group time. - i.e.: something has come up at short notice or at the weekend. In these circumstances, the matter should be firstly discussed with the wing chairman who can advise and gauge the urgency of the matter. If the issue is considered to be an emergency, then a group special should be called. If backed, the matter can be brought to the community at the earliest opportunity for wing backing before the backing request is put to the staff group. At all stages it is important to liaise with the wing chairman.

4. **WING BOOK**

The Community Book records the minutes of all community meetings and group feedbacks. A resident or staff member can also use it to log a book issue. A book issue is an inappropriate action or attitude by a community member of staff member.

Before putting an issue in the book, you should take it to your small group. The group can advise on the appropriate action. - whether to enter a book issue, a commitment issue or a sit down. The incident will then be explored on a wing meeting if it is either a commitment issue or a book issue or feedback slot if it is a sit down. It is an opportunity for the wing to consider what has happened, to challenge those involved and offer advice. When a man is OOT (out of therapy) and he wants to use the book, he should firstly discuss the matter with the Wing Chairman and the Vice Chair.

In exceptional circumstances and at the discretion and judgement of the wing chairman, pressing book or commitment issues can be prioritised and brought to the wing's attention e.g.: anything that undermines the safety of the community.

The community book is to be respected and not misused.

The protocol for using the wing book is in Appendix 11.

5. SPECIAL WINGS

Any member of the community, including staff may request a special wing but the issue must first be discussed with the wing chairman, vice-chairman (secretary) Officer I/C of C Wing, Orderly Officer and the therapist member of staff, All community members should attend and observe the wing's dress code for community meetings. It is acknowledged that Special wings are called sometimes at short notice and at inconvenient times of the day. It is at the discretion of the wing chair to allow a five minute window for late attendees - who may have prior appointments. The chairman also has the discretion, once the meeting has started to allow any community member who has to leave the room (in urgent circumstances) to return into the community room.

The rest of the community will then be informed if a special wing is called and notified of the time the wing is to be held. Please remember that special wings will only be called in extreme circumstances and only when other courses of actions have been exhausted or are deemed inappropriate. Once a special wing has been called, it is expected that every community member and staff on duty, attend the meeting. The wing chairman will ensure that the wing pod is covered during any meeting that takes place during the times of meals preparations.

This means that special wings will be the **exception** rather than a regular occurrence. Attendance at wing specials is recorded and any absence without a reasonable explanation will be given a "strike".

Whenever possible, a 'Group Special' should be called first. This may solve any problem that you are having and let the group know what is happening to you.

6. THERAPEUTIC GROUP

These are held three times a week on Tuesday, Wednesday and Thursday mornings at 0900 hrs - 1030 hrs. The community assembles at 10:40 - 11:00 for group feedback. Staff that facilitate the groups have a feedback meeting from 11:00 to 12:00. The member of staff who has manned the office during the group period will join the community for the feedback.

Like community meetings, groups are compulsory and lateness, failure to attend or walking out makes you accountable to the group and the wing. Therapeutic integrity is maintained by consistent attendance by all group members. If a group member suddenly stops attending groups he is liable to be put up for his commitment. If he continues to miss groups and does not communicate his intentions nor observe the ending process his IEP status will be reviewed in line with Grendon/IEP compact.

Group members are there to help you with any problems and dealing with offending behaviour; there are always others in similar or worse positions than yourself.

Absence due to sickness must be confirmed by healthcare with a sick note.

Group meetings help you settle into C Wing, get to know fellow group members and eventually other community members. You will be a member of your group throughout your time on the wing.

7. GROUP SPECIALS *(in agreement with staff held on the ground floor)*

You or other members may call a special 7 days a week for any reason that is troubling you; from receiving a bad letter from home, to having an argument with someone, be it resident or member of staff. All group members should attend and a member of staff should be present. These groups should be held on the ground floor in groups room.

A joint special involving more than one group may be called, if necessary, if persons from those groups are involved. Staff should be present.

As with the wing specials, all other avenues should be looked at before calling a special as a last resort. The group will be fed back to the wing at the earliest opportunity ideally by the person who called it. There may well be occasions when a group is called by a member of staff. Rather than delay feedback because the staff member might not be available, the group should be fed back at the next available wing by a group member.

8. LATENESS FOR WINGS OR GROUPS

Any resident of the community arriving late to either a wing meeting or small group will not be permitted entry **unless** they are returning from healthcare or reception. In these instances there will be a five minute window to allow both community member and/or staff to attend.

If a resident is late on more than one occasion he is liable to be put on the wing to have his commitment questioned.

If at any time a resident walks out of groups, wings, either a member of staff or a community member will follow to check on the resident's safety.

9. ART THERAPY AND PSYCHODRAMA

Art Therapy and Psychodrama are also part of Grendons therapy programme and are provided as part of the overall therapeutic regime. You will need to have been on the wing for 12 months before applying to join either group.

Groups and wings can, and should, recommend these to individuals if it is felt that the individuals concerned would benefit from participating in them. Individuals who feel that they will benefit from these additional complementary therapies can also put their own name forward.

Acceptance onto either art therapy or psychodrama is dependent upon group, wing, staff backing and successful interviews with the facilitators of these therapies. Both the Art therapy and Psychodrama groups are made up of men from across the whole community. Therefore at any one time, the membership of either the art therapy or psychodrama group is (6-8 men) will consist of a maximum of only 2 men from the same small therapy group. If a space is not immediately available your name will be placed on a waiting list. Please refer to the backing procedure flow chart - appendix 5.

Art therapy and psychodrama groups work alongside the small therapy groups. These groups will help you to explore your family and personal relationships, emotional states and offending behaviour, using artistic and psycho dramatic methods. The work undertaken on art therapy and psychodrama is fed back to your small group and the community meeting each week.

It is only possible to be a member of either art therapy or psychodrama at any one time. Once you have successfully completed one of the therapies you can apply to do

Terry Ellis

the other. Psychodrama meets on Tuesday afternoon between 2:15 and 4:15 pm. Art therapy meets on Thursday afternoon between 2:00 and 4:00 pm.

If you are accepted you will have to make the same commitment to them as you do to your own main therapy group. If you fail to attend, walk out, arrive late, leave without reasonable cause or prior discussion with whichever of these two groups you are taking part in, you will be expected to explain your behaviour.

Both Art Therapy and Psychodrama are fed back to the wing on a weekly basis.

It is the responsibility of all community members to respect both groups - no noise/interruptions whilst they are running.

10. **COMMITMENT VOTE**

Any member of the community (including staff) may put another member of the community up for the commitment vote if commitment is in question. Please see section 3 of The Wing Book for guidance.

This could result in the resident being voted out of Grendon by the wing, and the recommendation being then put before the staff group for a decision to be made whether he stays in therapy or is deselected from HMP Grendon.

A commitment issue can be challenged to confirm that it fulfils the stated criteria. This can be raised on a community meeting when the matter was due to be heard. The community will then ask questions and fully explore the issue. The community will then vote whether a commitment vote is still appropriate. If this standard is met then the community will proceed to a commitment vote.

Some of these reasons apart from those already mentioned are:

- Threatening Behaviour
- Consumption of Alcohol
- Drug Abuse - illicit or prescribed
- Inappropriate Sexual Behaviour
- Theft
- Violence or Verbal Abuse

- Being absent, late or walking out of groups and wings
- Bullying Behaviour
- Gambling
- Racism
- Non Engagement with Therapy
- Non Compliance with the Constitution
- Throwing articles out of the windows
- Provocative behaviour
- Breaching the confidentiality of the wing - taking off the wing.

Remember these are voting issues and can cost you your place at Grendon. <u>The final decision will rest with the staff group. Please see appendix 3 for an outline of the staff voting procedure.</u> Any individual put up for their commitment and subsequently voted to remain in the community will be expected to fulfil a service for the benefit of the wing - all forfeits to be relevant and reasonable. This will be decided by the whole community and your progress in completing your commitment tasks will be fed back and monitored by the community. If this involves working in the pod or any change of labour job, the usual backing process is then followed and supported by the staff group.

Commitment times will be determined by the community - possible guidelines are:

First commitment vote - 6 weeks (dependent upon the seriousness of the issue)
Second commitment vote - 3 months
Third commitment vote - 6 months.

11. <u>VOTING GENERALLY</u>

Voting issues take place on the community meeting. A community member up for his commitment must give reasons to the wing shy he should be allowed to stay. The member putting him up for the vote must say why he has done so.

A vote is then taken, EVERYONE must use their vote on any matter brought to the wing and anyone abstaining is liable to have **their own** commitment questioned. ALL community members are expected to participate in community matters. The only exception to the non-abstention rule is new members during their first week on C Wing. Staff do not vote on the wing.

12. CONFIDENTIALITY

There is **NO** confidentiality within the community and anything that is heard, said or known about you may be fed back to the groups and wings.

Malicious or secret gossiping, snide, racial or derogatory remarks are not acceptable and any member who indulges in this will be challenged and may also have their commitment questioned. This includes staff.

To maintain the integrity and safety of C Wing, you must not repeat off the wing, anything said on groups and wing meetings, or treat members of the community outside the wing with disrespect.

To be respected by others you must give respect to them. **To breach the confidentiality of the wing is a commitment issue.**

Anyone who is aware of a breach of these rules should raise the matter on the community. In this way, we keep things in the open and avoid the unpleasantness and bad atmosphere caused by gossip that undermines the trust and confidence that sincere community members strive to attain as part of their therapy.

13. WORK ON THE COMMUNITY

New community members commitment will start the day that you arrive on C Wing and you will initially work on the wing as a cleaner for a minimum period of 3 months. This will allow them time to settle on C Wing, get to know fellow community members and also get to be known. Poor performance can lead to the commitment period being extended.

After your initial assessment, if the community (including staff) think that you would benefit in a job off the wing then this will be backed on educational or development grounds. You are however expected to continue in your present job until such a time that a space becomes available in your requested position and a replacement has been found for your job.

You must have been in therapy for 12 months before applying for a Red band position.

You must have been on the wing 6 months before applying for a pod job.

All members of the community will be encouraged to try all wing based jobs.

All full or part-time educational courses and jobs being applied for must go through your group, wing and staff for backing.

Work is part of the therapy programme and all work will be advertised so that anybody who feels it will benefit them, and are able to do the work, can apply for the vacancy. No application for a job or job change will be considered unless you have group, wing and staff backing. This also applies to filling a job or reps position on a temporary basis - you will require formal backing (emergency backing would be considered).

All community members are expected to work in a job for a minimum period of 3 months. If you are voted out of therapy or terminate your therapy without following the ending protocol, you will be only eligible to attend education or be employed as a wing cleaner. Where possible, any subsequent forfeited job will be offered to those engaged in therapy at the earliest opportunity.

All off wing jobs will be reviewed after 6 months.

14. RESPONSIBILITIES - REP JOBS (appendix 4)

Undertaking a rep job is an important duty to perform on behalf of the community. Every community member should be encouraged to undertake positions of increasing responsibility.

A chairman and vice chairman are elected every 3 months by the community and at the time of the election, the candidates must have spent at least 9 months in therapy.

At the same time, the community will elect other responsible jobs, with the successful individuals either representing C Wing at various prison wide meetings or fulfilling other wing positions.

These jobs are intended for therapeutic reasons they should be taken seriously. Other community members may put individuals forward for these jobs, or they can put themselves forward. The therapeutic reasons for these must be discussed. It is very important to fulfil your commitment to these positions. If people drop out or fail to perform to the expected standard they are answerable to the wing.

In line with the 3 month commitment period, off wing rep jobs are confined to those who have completed their three month initial assessment.

The safer custody rep is considered to be a very important position. Men selected to undertake this role have to display a genuine interest in safer custody issues. The position cannot be filled as a result of a commitment issue. Please see appendix 13 for details of the role and responsibilities of the safer custody rep.

15. DRUGS

All community members have a contractual agreement to co-operate with the Compliance Drug Testing Programme, which means giving a urine sample under the supervision of staff. Any missed CDT, a positive test or refusal to comply will be communicated back to the community and may result in your behaviour being challenged and your commitment to Grendon being questioned.

C wing has a very robust attitude towards maintaining the community as a drug free environment which allows all community members to address and confront their former drug and alcohol dependency, in a safe and supportive environment. The community operates a zero tolerance approach to the supply, distribution and use of illicit drugs. Anybody who is discovered to have engaged in or encouraged illicit drug misuse will be automatically put up for their commitment and are at serious risk of losing their place in HMP Grendon.

It is now accepted in HMP Grendon, that in some circumstances, men in therapy who experience a down turn in their mental state can be prescribed with appropriate psychotropic medication for either the short or long term alleviation of their presenting symptoms. Whilst confidentially is respected, community members are under an obligation to discuss and disclose to their groups and the community any prescribed medications. This openness allows for transparency, support and an understanding of the difficulties experienced by community members.

It is also acknowledged that in some circumstances, men may be prescribed opiate based pain relief to treat physical injuries or complaints. Hopefully alternative medications or other remedies are considered first and community members are encouraged to discuss the options with healthcare and the prescribing GP. Community members are also obligated to inform their group and the community when such treatments have been prescribed. It is not necessary to disclose details of the medical complaint (a voluntary option). It is important for the community to know when a treatment commences and when it has come to an end. Anybody who is discovered to be misusing, trading or concealing prescribed medications will be automatically put up for their commitment and are at serious risk of losing their place in HMP Grendon.

It is in the interests of every community member to preserve C Wing as an actively drug free environment, with the two limited exceptions: psychotropic and opiate based prescriptions which are managed and acknowledged through open communication on the community. Many members of the community have former serious drug and alcohol problems. These substances have often been used to excessive proportions and at times of extreme stress whilst undergoing therapy, the cravings for drugs and alcohol may re-emerge. It is important that these strong urges are safely addressed in a drug free and therapeutically supportive environment. THIS IS EVERYBODYS' RESPONSIBILITY.

16. SEX

It is not acceptable to have sexual contact with anyone on the wing or to be in possession of unacceptable or offensive material contained in: magazines; DVD's; computer games.

Grendon does not seek to change anyone's non-deviant sexual orientation, but as each member of the community is viewed in a therapeutic role for everyone else, it is expected that everyone behave in an appropriate and responsible manner. It is recognised that sexual feelings are normal, as is sexual attraction. It is encouraged that these feelings be explored and examined within the small groups.

17. VIOLENCE

Terry Ellis

Anyone who commits an act of physical violence towards another person is accountable to the community and will be automatically put up for their commitment to the community and are at risk of losing their place in HMP Grendon. The resident can also expect to be dealt with through IEP scheme and adjudication process.

The 'No Violence' rule is one of the most important in providing a safe environment for therapy to take place at Grendon without fear of 'systemised pressures' and must be strongly upheld for the common good of all community members. All areas surrounding violence will be looked at thoroughly.

Acts of violence include:

- Any attack on another person
- Deliberately provoking someone into violence
- Causing an object to strike another person
- Spitting at or threatening another person
- Being verbally threatening, abusive or offensive

Each of these acts triggers a commitment vote

18. SOCIAL EVENINGS AND FAMILY DAYS (see appendix 7)

The wings hold two social afternoons (June and December) and two family days (March and September) each year. Everyone in therapy is expected to participate in some way towards these social occasions, which are a community activity. You are expected to attend as part of the therapeutic programme, even if you do not have guests yourself - remember you are part of the community and your attendance is a valuable contribution towards successful social events for the community. Anyone not attending is accountable to his or her group. community members can invite their probation officer and others involved in their sentence and onward progression. Group, wing and staff backing are required. men who are OOT and maintain an active engagement with the community - attending wing meetings on Monday and Friday, are eligible to invite their probation officers or other relevant professionals.

To qualify for a family day you have to be in therapy or have successfully completed your therapy and are awaiting a progressive move and continue to also attend wing meetings. You require group and wing backing and you will have been on the wing for *three months.* There is a limit of two guests. It is recognised there may be circumstances when a third or fourth guest is considered. This request also requires group, wing and staff backing.

All members of the community are expected to wear appropriate clothing during social events. No-one is to wear shorts, flip-flops on either the ground floor or landings.

You are not entitled to have a family day if you have been de-selected from therapy by the community and staff group - even if you continue to attend wing meetings.

The wing social evenings and family days are a privilege that may be withdrawn if misused.

19. YOUR OWN DECISION TO TERMINATE THERAPY (see appendix 9)

Anyone deciding to leave Grendon before the completion of their therapy is allowed a reasonable time to reconsider.

The transfer papers will only be accepted by the staff, once they have been discussed by the group and raised on the wing. Once the papers have been completed they are '"non-negotiable" and transfer will take place. Individuals who withdraw from therapy are still subject to the rules and standards of the community with the expectation that they maintain

pro-community attitudes and behaviour. Although leaving therapy is your decision it is beneficial that you negotiate your ending.

Anyone who withdraws from therapy will be required to be in-cell during all periods of therapeutic work, i.e. groups and wings. Attendance at community meetings is nevertheless encouraged for men who decide to terminate their therapy. Continuing to attend community meetings is important: to feel part of the community; have knowledge of what is happening on the wing and around the prison and it continues to be a place to express concerns and resolve disputes.

Terry Ellis

Anyone who wishes to return to wings after an absence of a significant amount of time should give notice of their intention to return beforehand to the chairman. The man should then come to the community to make his case to return. Thereafter there is then an expectation that the man attend every wing meeting.

Members of the community who have been successful in gaining a progressive move should refer to appendix 8.

20. THERAPY TIMETABLE

- **GROUPS**

Tuesdays, Wednesdays and Thursdays 09:00 to 10:30. Extensions will be granted only under exceptional circumstances and with support of the group facilitator.

After each small group session there will be a period of group feedbacks commencing at 10:40 prompt until 11:00 when all groups come together in the community room. Group members take it in turn to feedback their group to the community. Once a new group member has read his initial assessment to the community (usually after 6 months on the community) he can then start to feedback his own group to the community.

Feedbacks allow all community members to learn about each other. Listening to other's problems enables all community members to become more aware, to be sensitive and give support to those who may need it. It also enables people to share in any good news.

Attendance at feedbacks is *compulsory* - failure to attend will result in gaining a "strike" - 2 accumulated strikes lead to a commitment vote.

- **WING MEETINGS**

Monday and Friday mornings at 09:00 to 1030. All community members are expected to attend, Any extensions to this time will be put to the community for a vote, and are the exception rather than the rule.

- **ASSESSMENTS**

Group assessments start at 10:50 to 11:45 on Mondays and on Friday between 10:40 and 11:35. All group members are expected to be in attendance. Prior to the assessment, individual contribution sheets will be circulated for completion, to be fed back on the
assessments. These will be issued at least 48 hours before the assessment. All group members to complete the assessment forms. Noise outside the assessment room is to be kept to. minimum - this includes: staff; guests; community members - the assessment is very important and this time needs to be treated with respect. The assessment documents will be completed ASAP. The completed assessment is taken to the small group to be read before being read out to the whole community. The wing chairman will prioritise initial assessments being read to the community at the earliest opportunity. Interim assessments are also read out to the community.

You are not able to undertake any off wing activities (except gym, diversity events or religious) until you have had your initial assessment. <u>This is scheduled to be held approximately three months after your arrival on the community.</u> The dates are posted in group 4 room.

The annual sentence planning review is now combined with a therapy review and is held on either the Monday or Friday slot in the times outlined above. The meeting is jointly chaired by your offender supervisor and either the wing therapist or another member of the C Wing staff group. Unlike other therapy assessments, group members do not attend this meeting. Usually this is a meeting your offender manager should attend if possible. Two sets of paperwork are completed: Firstly, your offender supervisor will complete an overview of your sentence plan, reviewing targets and if necessary setting new objectives. Secondly, the wing therapist will review your therapy targets and the therapeutic work you have undertaken in the past 6 months. The comments and observations of your group are important and will be recorded in the therapy review paperwork compiled by the wing therapist. Both reports will be produced within good time for comments and agreement.

21. <u>LATE UNLOCK</u>

Terry Ellis

There will be occasions when the wing is unlocked later than the standard opening time in the morning 08:15 am. This is usually the result of operating difficulties in the prison. It is acknowledged that time is required to have breakfast and prepare yourself for the groups. On the occasion of a late unlock that exceeds 8:25 am a maximum window of 45 minutes will be available before the commencement of groups or a community meeting.

22. APPLICATIONS

These must be made before evening "lock up" both during weekdays and at the weekend, and placed in the applications box which is located on the wall outside the wing office. Staff will then process these - a white copy is placed in the incoming mail box for distribution the following morning. Applications are then sent to the relevant department for consideration.

23. MAIL

The mail box is emptied in the evening or early morning. Incoming mail is dealt with by security and it arrives on the wing after 3:30 pm. However, this time changes because of variable postal delivery times.

24. ROLL CHECKS

It is the responsibility of each community member to attend roll checks between 16:30 and 16:45 Monday - Thursday. Even if you are not collecting your meal, you must still report to the office for the roll check.

Failure to do this may result in you being made accountable for your actions.

25. SMOKING

In line with national policy, C Wing is a non-smoking area. Those who wish to smoke can do so in their cells with the door closed. This requirement safeguards the health safety of the community - if a member of the community smokes outside of their cell or with their door open, they are liable to be put in the book, or put up for their commitment to the community. Continued infringement could lead to you being adjudicated.

26. LAUNDRY DAYS

Between Monday and Friday, the laundry is managed by the "laundry man". Two members of the community are responsible for the management of the laundry during the week - they cover the laundry on alternative weeks. Laundry access is provided:

Monday	-	group 1
Tuesday	-	group 2
Wednesday	-	group 3
Thursday	-	group 4
Friday	-	group 5

Saturday and Sunday are a "free for all" - Do it yourself - laundry bags are placed in order of arrival in the laundry - Please do not jump the queue.

The laundry rules are posted in the laundry room.

27. MEALS

Sandwich and soup is served: Monday - Thursday from 12:00 - 12:30 and a hot meal is served Monday - Thursday 4:30 - 4:50 pm.

Friday: A sandwich and soup lunch is provided from 11:15 am. An evening meal is served at 3:45 - 4:15.

Saturday and Sunday: A cooked lunch is served at 11:30-11:50. A sandwich pack is available from 4:00 pm.

POD workers to be dressed appropriately at all times whilst working in the pod.

It is the responsibility of each community member to inform the Pod workers of whether or not he is having his meal, in accordance with health and hygiene requirements, meals cannot be saved on the hotplate. There is a 20-minute serving window for all meals.

Plates and cutlery are allowed to be kept on dining room tables, but at your own risk. Sauces and items that require refrigeration are to be stored in the fridge in the dining room. Please leave other people's property alone, unless the owner gives you permission. No dirty plates, bowls etc are to be left in either the dining room or in the sinks.

All <u>main meals are to be eaten in the dining hall</u> from Monday to Friday. Meals can be taken to cells on a Saturday and Sunday if so desired, but this is not encouraged. In everybody's interest please observe the dress code.

The Pod Workers will feed back at the Monday's community meeting any problems or difficulties they experience in the preparation and delivery of meals/food. They will also feedback any problems, conflict or difficulties they experience with community members.

28. **CELL MOVES**

C Wing does not operate a policy of casual cell moves. The cell you are allocated upon arrival on the wing is the cell you will occupy throughout your time on C Wing. On the 1's landing cells have been identified which fall into the category of a priority cell. These cells are situated near the landings recess area or the stairwell. The 1's landing: 101; 102; 103; 109; 110. Men who are allocated to these cells have the option to move to another cell - when vacant. Only one chance of a move will be offered and a move can only be exercised once. Other cell moves can only be considered on medical grounds and this requires group, wing and staff backing supported by healthcare information.

New community members can have a choice of which cell to occupy, only if that option is available at the time of his arrival on the wing.

If the ground floor cell is used other than for a medical reason, the occupant has the option to move upstairs onto the landings when a cell becomes available.

29. QUIET HOUR

Quiet hour will be during lunch time bang-up (weekdays) Monday - Thursday 12:45 - 14:00. Fridays 11:50 - 13:00 and Saturday/Sunday 12:15 - 13:30. During these times, electronic devices to be kept low and Hoovers' are not to be used. This period of time is for therapeutic reflection. If you disrespect the quiet hour your behaviour will be challenged on the community.

Please use the time after your small group and the feedback session for therapeutic reflection.

No general enquiries at the front general office between 11:00 - 12:00 after groups and 10:30 - 11:30 after wings.

On weekends throughout therapy breaks and Bank Holidays, noise levels to be kept to a minimum. No Hoovers, stereos or loud talking or use of the games room before 10:30 am.

30. MUSIC, TELEVISION AND CONSOLE GAMES

All TVs and stereos are to be turned down to within the confines of cells from 22:00. This applies to all nights except Friday and Saturday, where an extension until 23:00 is allowed.

If your music is unacceptably loud to someone and they ask you to turn it down, please adhere to their wishes.

31. DRESS

Members of the wing are expected to be appropriately dressed at all times.

***** *In the interest of hygiene - please observe the dress code* *****

- **MEAL TIMES**

Terry Ellis

A choice of shirts t-shirts jumpers and trainers or shoe must be worn in the dining room during meal times. Shorts may be worn instead of trousers etc. No capped or sleeveless shirts or vests are to be worn.

Pod workers - anyone working within the Pod should be dressed appropriately, this includes Boots and Whites.

- **SHOWERS**

At least shorts or dressing gowns are to be worn to and from showers *(not just towels).* Also please note that showers are not to be used on night-san.

- **GROUPS, WING MEETINGS, WING SPECIALS AND INTERVIEWS**

A choice of shirts, t-shirts, jumpers and trainers or shoes must be worn together with trousers, jeans or tracksuit bottoms. No hats, caps or shorts are allowed.

- **GROUND FLOOR**

There is to be no nightwear or dressing gowns on the ground floor during the core day, i.e. 09:00 to 17:00.

- **THE WING OFFICE**

No general enquiries in the morning between 11:00 - 12:00.

Please dress appropriately at all times - no vests, capped or sleeveless shirts, shorts, slippers or flip-flops. Please also note that food and drink are not to be consumed in the office.

32. **GENERAL HYGIENE**

C Wing members are expected to help keep the wing and their individual cells clean and tidy. Although we have dedicated wing cleaners it is everyone's responsibility to use the ashtrays and rubbish bins provided. **Throwing rubbish out of cell windows will not be tolerated and will lead to the person being put up for his commitment.**

33. GYM FACILITIES

The use of gym facilities can be suspended up to a period of one month (4 weeks) as the result of a commitment vote and subsequent forfeit recommended by the community. You will nevertheless be allowed one session that will be allocated to you by the gym rep.

34. PERSONAL ITEMS AND BELONGINGS

All belongings, articles of clothing and all footwear must be kept in your own allocated cell at all times. At no time should there be any personal items left on the landings either on the floor or hanging up.

35. GENERAL RULES

Cells should be of a reasonable standard.

Pool is not to be played when groups/wing meetings are on or when either art therapy or psychodrama sessions are in progress.

No talking in the community room if this is requested by any member of the community during a TV programme.

No smoking - except in own cell.

No swinging from pipes or other fittings.

No feet on chairs or tables.

No one other than Pod workers, in whites, to be in the pod at any time.

All areas and rooms to be accorded the utmost respect and left clean and tidy.

Terry Ellis

The TV, Ariel and remote control are not to be removed from the Community room.

REMEMBER WE ARE ALL ACCOUNTABLE TO OTHER COMMUNITY MEMBERS AND MUST TAKE RESPONSIBILITY FOR OUR ACTIONS THAT MAY AFFECT OTHERS. YOU MUST EXPLAIN YOUR BEHAVIOUR IF YOU ARE ASKED TO DO SO.

This community works best when it is working together. It will not always be easy and there may be times when you feel like giving up. Your group, other community members and staff are here to help you and give you support.

Appendix 1

Grendon
C Wing Community

Hello there . . . .

We would like to welcome you to Grendon and more particularly to C Wing. You are probably wondering what to expect from C Wing? Don't worry too much. There will be a reasonable period where you can settle in and acquaint yourself with the wing. Most of the lads here are more than happy to help you settle in. We've all been through the Induction Process and know how difficult it can be at times to adapt to the therapeutic regime.

You will eventually be allocated to a permanent group; 1,2, 3, 4, or 5. These are held three times a week; Tuesday, Wednesday and Thursday, which you must attend as well as the two big wings on Monday and Friday. Only appointments and illness will be excused. Any other reason you will be asked to explain.

We have our own wing constitution which works alongside the main prison rules but doesn't substitute them. We are all answerable to them both. Any person can be challenged on these rules and have their commitment questioned.

You will be given a commitment job of cleaning for at least three months when you first start on the wing, you will be able to move from this job once a replacement has been found (this applies to all wing based jobs). This gives you a chance to prove your commitment as well as a period to stabilise yourself within your own therapeutic journey.

Terry Ellis

You will get opportunities for the gym and other activities and later on you can apply for jobs around the prison.

C Wing is an open community that encourages people to mix and form supportive relationships. Grendon tackles all of our lifestyles in different ways. It can be a very challenging experience to be in therapy, listening to other people's lives and sharing your own.

Don't forget that you're not alone on C Wing, there are always people at hand; staff and lads that can help and support you.

C Wing offers a real opportunity to change your life for the better. The more you participate and put in the more you'll get out of your time here.

We hope this letter helps put you at ease. We look forward to working with you.

All the best from the Lads and Staff of C Wing

Appendix 2

REP JOBS

Chairman

- The role of the chairman involves conducting all regular wing and special wing meetings.
- Organise the agenda and the order in which it is presented. Attend meetings with the staff group to discuss matters relating to the community, ensuring that wing meetings stick as close to the subject as possible.
- The Chairman is the go-between with staff and community members and should ensure that any problems are dealt with in a speedy and constructive manner.
- Meet and greet guests to the community.
- Be aware of matters affecting the wing and, where necessary, seek assistance from members of the staff group.

Vice Chairman

- Responsible for the completion of the minutes of wing meetings and assisting the Chairman in conducting his meetings.
- In the absence of the Chairman, to take over his role.
- Attend meetings with the staff group to discuss matters relating to the community.
- Be aware of matters affecting the community and where necessary, seek assistance from the Chairman or the staff group.

Register

- Ensure that an accurate record is kept of those attending al community meetings, community feedbacks and wing specials.
- Inform the Chairman of any members absent and, if known, the reason.

Treasurer X2

- Keep track of all the community finances.
- Give a financial statement to the community monthly.
- Arrange for the completion of the necessary forms for expenditure of community funds.
- Along with the member of staff overseeing the event, ensure that all monies from raffles are properly accounted for.
- Keep all monthly statements from the Finance Department.

Sports and Gymnasium x 2

- Responsible for ensuring that the gym list is completed every week and is handed in on time.
- Liaise with the gymnasium staff regarding any issues that any member of the community may have with the gym.
- Ensure that if any member of the community fails to attend their allotted gym session that you are aware of the reasons for their absence.
- Ensure that the sports notice board is kept up to date and tidy.

Plants x 2

- Responsible for the maintenance and propagation of the plants around the wing including watering and taking of and caring for cuttings.
- Maintain the cleanliness of the plant store.
- Where possible make plants available for community members to have in their cell, reminding them that the plants remain the property of the wing and can be removed if not looked after.

Fish Tanks x 2

- Responsible for the upkeep of the aquariums located on the wing.

- The safekeeping/handling, in accordance with the manufacturer's instructions, of any chemicals used for fish keeping.
- An inventory of all electrical items used is kept and that these items are properly maintained.
- If any repairs are required of any aquarium item this should be done through the staff group.
- Maintain the cleanliness of the aquarium store.

Entertainment Rep x 2

- Responsible for organising events for the community such as bingo, quizzes and karaoke. Competitions for the community should be organised during therapy breaks.
- Responsible through the Treasurer, for arranging prizes for competitions.

Social Evening x 2

- Along with the member of staff responsible for social evenings ensure that all invitations are sent out in ample time to ensure security procedures can be followed.
- Arrange for the purchase of food and drinks for the event.
- Ensure that there are enough volunteers to arrange the wing and prepare food prior to the event.
- Organise volunteers to help meet and greet guests and look after them during the event.

Family Day x2

- Along with the member of staff responsible for family day, ensure that all applications are submitted in good time.
- Arrange for the purchase of food and drinks for the event.
- Ensure that there are enough volunteers to arrange the wing and prepare food prior to the event.
- Organise volunteers to help serve food and drinks.

Inter-wing x 2

- Responsible to the community for C Wing's interests on the inter-wing meetings.
- Ensure that the community are aware of all forthcoming meetings so that they have the opportunity to submit items for the agenda.
- Ensure that copies of the minutes are available to the community and that the community receive feedback about matters discussed from these meetings.
- Ensure that new members to C Wing are aware of your role.

Induction x 2

- Responsible for meeting with future members of the community on F Wing prior to their arrival on C Wing
- Ensure that new members are invited for evening meal prior to arrival in the community.
- Accompany new members on the move from F Wing to C Wing and be available to assist them if requested.
- Give new members a guided tour of all areas of the community.

Education/Library Rep

- Responsible for liaising with the Education Department and library over matters affecting the community.
- Ensuring that the community are aware of their library times, and if for any reason these sessions are cancelled, arranging an alternative slot for C Wing to use the library.

Race Relations (6 Months)

- Make themselves familiar with all aspects of race relations.
- Attend race relation meetings called by the race relation officer.
- Ensure that the community are aware of all forthcoming meetings so that they have the opportunity to submit items for the agenda.
- Ensure that copies of the minutes are available to the community and that the community receive feedback about matters discussed from these meetings.
- Act as arbitrator if race issues arise in the community and seek advice from the race relations officer if necessary.

Food Rep

- Responsible for liaising with the kitchen when dealing with food complaints from community members.
- To ensure that a meal is available for the pre-visit of new community members and that details of their meal choices is known to the POD workers.
- Brief new members on how, and where, to fill in menu choices.

Indeterminate Rep x2

- Responsible for representing the community on all lifer meetings.
- Ensure that the community are aware of all forthcoming meetings so that they have the opportunity to submit items for the agenda.
- Ensure that copies of the minutes are available to the community and that the community receive feedback about matters discussed from these meetings.

Catalogue Rep

- Responsible for keeping and distributing wing catalogues. Update any catalogues as necessary and maintain a record of loans and returns.

Healthcare

- Responsible for representing the community on any healthcare meetings.
- Ensure that the community are aware of all forthcoming meetings so that they have the opportunity to submit items for the agenda.
- Ensure that copies of the minutes are available to the community and that the community receive feedback about matters discussed from these meetings.
- Ensure that the healthcare notice board is kept up to date and tidy.

Works

- Responsible for reporting to Works Department problems with plumbing, electrics and machinery problems around the wing.
- Log the problems in Works book and follow up to ensure they are fixed.

OMU Rep/Determinates and Indeterminates Rep

Terry Ellis

- Responsible for representing the community on all OMU meetings.
- Ensure the community is aware of future meetings so members can submit items for agenda.
- Feedback minutes of meeting to the community and make a copy of minutes available to Notice board rep.

Facilities Rep

- Responsible for representing the community on all facilities meetings.
- Ensure the community is aware of future meetings so members can suggest additions/replacements to the approved facilities list.
- Feedback meetings and changes to the community.

Notice Board Rep

- Responsible for maintaining the group floor notice boards.
- Read out on wing meetings notices arriving in the wing office and then display on notice boards.

Canteen Rep

- Responsible for representing the community on all canteen meetings.
- Ensure the community is aware of future meetings so members make suggestions for the agenda.
- Feedback meetings to the community.
- Help DHL staff distribute canteen on canteen night.

Conference Rep

- Represents the wing as a member of the steering group that organises conferences.
- Responsible for attending meetings and promoting the conferences on the community.

Charity Rep

- Responsible for arranging charity raffles on Family Days.

- Prepare a charity letter asking for donations and send to companies and charities.
- Promote the raffle and sell tickets on the community.
- Present the cheque for money raised to the wing charity on Social Evening.

Visits Rep

- Responsible for representing the community on all visits meetings.
- Ensure the community is aware of future meetings so members can suggest items for the agenda.

Appliance Rep

- Responsible for cleaning and maintaining all fridges, kettles and irons on the wing.
- Report any problems or breakages to wing staff and if necessary to Works rep.
- Maintain the log of fridge temperatures and ensure it is countersigned by a wing officer.

BACO Rep (6 months)

- Responsible for liaising with the wing BACO representative and inform him of community members wishing to make an application.

Research Rep

- To represent the wing to the frequent professional/academics that carry out research in Grendon.
- To disseminate information through the community in the interests of transparency.
- To pass onto researchers feedback from the community and the names of volunteers willing to participate.

Drug strategy rep (12 months)

- To go to the induction wing to induct new men into the Grendon policy on drugs
- To support men when drug issues arise on the wing

- To liaise with the drug support officer

Safer custody Rep

- To actively support men who are placed on an ACCT.
- To attend ACCT review meetings - if required.
- To attend prison wide safer custody meetings.

Art Rep (6 months)

- To manage the art materials held on the wing, donated to the wing from various charities.

Menu Rep

- Write all community members name on menu sheet.
- Go around the community and get everyone to fill in their sheet by Friday evening.

Assessment Rep

- To maintain an accurate record of all assessments that have been completed: initial and interim
- To liaise with personal officers to ensure that assessment paperwork is distributed in good time.

Appendix 3

BACKING PROCEDURE FOR A COMPLEMENTARY THERAPY

Backing for interview discussed on group. If both art therapy and psychodrama are considered at the same time, then two backings

The backing(s) are brought to the wing

The backing(s) are considered by the staff group

Interviews are arranged individually with either Jo or Alun

If both art therapy and psychodrama interviews are backed at the same time - interviews are arranged with Jo and Alun. Both interviews should take place before a decision is made about which is the preferred option.

Terry Ellis

The backing is brought back to the group with the stated option

The backing to john either art therapy or psychodrama is brought to the wing

The backing is considered by the staff group

Arrangements are made to join either the art therapy or psychodrama group

Appendix 4

QUALIFICATION PERIOD FOR JOBS AND SPECIAL EVENTS

JOBS	PERIOD ON WING	COMMITMENT
Cleaners' foreman x1	6 months on wing	6 months
Wing painter. x2	3 months on wing	3 months
M1 cleaner. x1	6 months on wing	6 months
Education full time	not until initial assessment has taken place	3 months
Pod pan wash. x2	3 months on wing	3 months
Pod cook. x4	6 months on wing	6 months
Laundry man. x2	6 months on wing	6 months
Red bands	12 months on wing	12 mnths
Gym orderly	12 months on wing	12 mnths
Gardens	6 months on wing	6 mnths

SPECIAL EVENTS

Art therapy/Psychodrama	12 months on wing
Family Day	3 months on wing
Vice Chair	9 months on wing
Lifers Day	No time limitation
Children's Day	Via RAMP approval and three months on wing

Terry Ellis

QUALIFICATION FOR OFF WING EMPLOYMENT:

To qualify for off wing employment you must first have undertaken a wing based job e.g. worked in the pod, undertaken the cleaner's foreman duties, worked in the laundry etc.

THE POD:

To work in the pod, the job of the pan wash is viewed as a necessary qualification to then taking on the role of pod cook.

Appendix 5

RE-CATEGORISATION PROCESS

Re-categorisation is an important acknowledgement that a man is making process in his sentence and that he has been able to demonstrate that he is reducing his risk. In Grendon, this means fully participating in the therapeutic process and working hard on risk factors and the identified therapeutic needs and issues. The work is done on the group and supported by the overall community. Being supported in sometimes very difficult therapeutic work and being equally challenged and made accountable is the result of the support and efforts of group and community members - this is the treatment model.

Therefore when a man considers going for re-categorisation, the views and opinions of his small therapy group and the community are very relevant and influential.

The issue of re-categorisation is considered on the annual joint sentence panning and therapy review meeting which is jointly chaired by the wing OS and the wing therapist. The date for this meeting will be posted several months ahead. If a man feels he has done the necessary work to be seriously considered for re-categorisation, he should follow the process:

1. Rise the matter of re-categorisation on the small therapy group. Outline the reasons and describe in detail the work that has been undertaken to support a reduction in risk. Be open to being questioned and challenged by the group. If the group feels you have made a good case they will back you. This is the important first step. This can be followed up with a discussion with your personal officer.

2. Take your backing to the next available community meeting. Explain the reasons for seeking re-categorisation and outline the work that has been undertaken to support a reduction in risk. Be open to being questioned and challenged by community members and staff on the meeting. The community will vote whether they will back you for your re-categorisation.
3. Whatever the result of community backing, it will then go to the staff group who hold a business meeting every Monday afternoon. The staff will follow their consultation procedure: An e-mail is sent to all staff which seeks the views on the backing for re-categorisation in which they will comment and register their vote. This process takes 7 days. The result of the vote will be announced at the next Monday afternoon business meeting.
4. The views of the group, the community and the staff group will be recorded in the personal officer report to the SP board. The matter will then be discussed on the SP board.

This process is adopted on all communities in Grendon and is the expectation of the Grendon OMU. It maintains a close and collaborative relationship between sentence planning requirements and the therapeutic process.

This process should also be viewed as a good test for anybody advocating that they are progressing in their sentence - making your case with sound evidence to back it up, is good preparation for the ongoing challenges you will meet as you progress in your sentence either in Grendon or once you are in another establishment.

Appendix 6

HMP GRENDON THERAPEUTIC COMMUNITY

FAMILY DAYS AND SOCIAL EVENINGS

1. **FAMILY DAYS**

1.1 Family Days are restricted to family members or significant others only. Wings should interpret 'significant others' to include people each man considers as significant in their lives if they no longer have contact with their close family group. This is important as many of the men who apply to come to Grendon may no longer be part of a discrete family unit in the traditional sense. This does not include professional staff that my form part of the man's resettlement support plans.

1.2 The purpose of family days is to help the men to maintain contact with family members or significant others who may continue to support them emotionally on their release. Another aim of family days is to educate and inform family members or significant others of the nature of the men's offending behaviours and the strategies either in place or needed to maintain an offence-free life following release. Family members have the opportunity to learn more about what Grendon Therapeutic Community is bout and the challenges the programme produced for the men.

1.3 Process and procedures regarding family days:

The man must be on the wing for a period of three months or have had an initial wing assessment completed (whichever is first) prior to qualifying to apply for their family or significant others to visit on family day.

- There is normally a limit of two guests per man, however up to three guests per man can be invited if there are spaces or in exceptional circumstances for the man concerned and they have group/wing/staff backing for this.
- Names of family members or significant others must be agreed to by the man's small therapy group and the community, including staff.
- Invitations must be submitted to a designated officer, who logs, posts and tracks responses and checks, where necessary, with the public protection committee and security department to ensure that it is permissible for guests invited to visit on family day.
- During family days, cell visits must be fully supervised by officer, should occur during the afternoon period and doors to the cells must be kept open.
- Visitors are allowed to bring up to 40 cigarettes or up to 25 grams of hand rolling tobacco (allowance - per prisoner not per visitor) which can be smoked during the day. Smoking areas will be designated. There needs to be authorisation from the Governor if these are different from current approved smoking areas.
- Landings will not be locked off during the day.
- Men who wish to hand out items to their visitors on family day should apply to reception seven days in advance.
- All communities should consider how men not receiving visitors should be involved in the day. This should be part of community discussions.
- There should be a set time for photographs to be taken on the ground floor (not in cells) and men must apply for this prior to the day.
- Men must be enhanced on the IEP scheme prior to applying for their family or significant others to visit on family day.
- Raffle money should be collected by a member of staff from both visitors and staff. The maximum purchase per person is restricted to £10.
- There needs to be a confidentiality protocol in place regarding families' questions on men's progress in therapy so staff are clear what can and cannot be disclosed.

2. SOCIAL EVENINGS

2.1 The purpose of Social Evenings is:

- To provide the prisoner with the opportunity to interact on a social level with service providers and interested professionals

- To provide a venue where prisoners can gain knowledge of prisoner support agencies and charities available to them on release.
- To enable both prisoners and providers to network and have the opportunity to pass on and gain information of value to them on areas of concern, i.e. accommodation, substance misuse treatment, NACRO etc.

2.2 Communities should ensure that the invitations sent out for Social Evenings are to legitimate professional contacts. Ex-Grendon residents can be invited to share their experiences post-Grendon though numbers will be tightly controlled (there is no lower or upper time limit following transfer/discharge from Grendon - each case will be judged on its own merits).

2.3 Processes and Procedures for Social Evenings are:

- Men who apply for visitors on social Evenings must be enhanced on the IEP scheme and must have been on the wing for a period of three months or have had an initial wing assessment completed (whichever is first).
- Two guests are allowed per man unless there are exceptional circumstances for the man concerned and they have group/wing/staff backing for this additional guest.
- Guests need to be approved by group/wing and staff. The men should state why they would like to invite someone and what they hope to gain from the visit.
- Invitations must be submitted to a designated officer, who logs, posts and tracks responses.
- Cell visits are not allowed on Social Evenings.
- Structure of each social evening subject to community discussion.

Terry Ellis

Appendix 7

PROGRESSIVE MOVLEMENT AND ENDING THERAPY

How you end your period in therapy at Grendon is just as important as how you start and continue the journey during your time here. For a lot of men endings have been difficult and bring up a lot of feelings and emotions and these can be intensified after a sustained period of therapy. Therefore it is proposed that there be a clear procedure set out for ending your therapeutic journey.

The criteria that should be met in order to end therapy in a constructive and satisfactory manner should include having <u>confirmation</u> of re-categorisation and/or a <u>date of transfer</u>. The process of being re-categorised, particularly to Cat D is a long and stressful one and involved sitting in on interviews for many reports and appearing in front of a board. Also, transfer between prisons cans take some time and it is difficult for staff and management to risk assess for days out and ROTLs if a man is no longer taking an active part in community business.

Steps that should be followed by men wishing to end therapy in a constructive and positive manner are as follows:

Step 1: Go through the re-categorisation process and wait for <u>confirmation</u> of the decision.

Step 2: Once you have confirmation of your status and a provisional date of transfer to your next establishment, take your decision to end therapy to your small group and ask for backing.

Step 3: If you get backing from your small group then take your decision to the community for backing. The backing will then go to the staff group and the transfer paperwork is completed.

Step 4: You should now attend community meetings twice weekly plus wing specials, and still be held accountable for your behaviour like any other member of the community. Non-attendance of community meetings as you get close to your transfer date can be negotiated with the community.

Following this procedure will help to ensure a safe and stable environment for the whole community and allow individuals time to prepare for the next stage of the journey.

Appendix 8

DECIDING TO TERMINATE YOUR THERAPY

It is acknowledged that some men are not suited for therapy and may decide to terminate their therapy. This may be for a variety of reasons. It is important to end your association with your group in a constructive and courteous manner.

To end properly:

Step 1 - Inform your group - explain the reasons - and get backing to end.
Step 2 - inform the community - get backing.
Step 3 - The backing will then go to the staff group - if backed the paperwork is then completed - once this stage is reached the matter is non-negotiable.

Men are encouraged to retain an active membership of the community and to attend community meetings. This enables ongoing access to the wing's backing system; to be kept up to date with events on the community and across the prison and to have the support and guidance of the community. Men who decide to operate outside of the culture and boundaries of the community and who display negative and disruptive behaviour will be managed by the IEP and adjudication systems. Failure to end your association with your group and the community in the agreed manner will bring about a review of your IEP level in line with the Grendon/IEP compact

Appendix 9

HMP GRENDON

End of Therapy Process (C Wing)

1. Take issue of leaving therapy to your therapy Group for discussion and joint agreement. Identify the date of lending. Obtain backing to end.

2. Take issue of leaving therapy to the community meeting for discussion and agreement. Seek the backing of the community

3. The backing is discussed in the staff group. Transfer paperwork is completed and sent to OMU.

4. Arrange end of therapy case conference. Invite offender supervisor, offender manager, wing staff and members of the group (optional)

5. Continue to be an active part of the community. Work towards leaving the community - organise leaving event (optional).

Terry Ellis

Appendix 10

PROTOCOL FOR USING THE WING "BOOK"

STEP ONE:

- Community member feels that an inappropriate action/behaviour attitude has been directed at him. Men who are OOT need to discuss using the book with the Chairman and the Vice Chair before putting anybody in the book.

STEP TWO:

1. Take the issue to the group at the first opportunity. Group to consider the seriousness and possible action:

- A sit down between both parties
- A "book" issue
- A commitment issue

STEP THREE:

- Inform wing chairman and vice-chair ASAP

STEP FOUR:

- If book/commitment issue:
-
- Inform wing chair ASAP

- Enter in book
- Inform the other party

STEP FIVE:

- If a sit down issue - arrange with wing chair, group and staff to facilitate meeting.

STEP SIX:

- The "book"/commitment issue comes to the wing for consideration at the earliest opportunity

Terry Ellis

Appendix 11

STAFF PROTOCOL FOR USING THE WING "BOOK"

STEP ONE:

Staff member feels that an inappropriate action/behaviour has been directed at him/her or at another in close proximity.

STEP TWO:

Record in Observation Book and alert other members of staff on duty.

STEP THREE:

Take the issue to the next available staff meeting eg: if the incident happened at 3:30pm then to be taken to following mornings 8:30 briefing meeting. Staff assembled to consider the seriousness and appropriate action:

1. A sit down between both parties
2. A "book issue"
3. A commitment issue

If option 1 and 2 are chosen then an entry in the wing "book" is made by the principle signatory/originator of the concern which is made on behalf of the staff group.

STEP FOUR:

If a "book" or commitment issue:

Living amongst the beasts: The rise and fall of the Grendon experiment

1. Enter in "book"
2. Inform wing hair ASAP
3. Inform the other party

STEP FIVE:

If a sit down issue - arrange with wing chair and other party - another member of staff may assist if required.

STEP SIX:

The "book" or commitment issue comes to the wing at the earliest opportunity - the originator/principle signatory raises the issue on the community.

Terry Ellis

Appendix 12

SAFER CUSTORY REP - ROLE AND RESPONSIBILITIES

Safer custody reps play an important role in helping to maintain a safe wing environment. The reps work in collaboration with staff, groups and the community to support men who experience difficult periods when they contemplate an act of self-harm or in circumstances when a man has committed an act of self-harm. This can be difficult and stressful work and it is therefore important that the men who undertake the role of safer custody rep are selected in a thoughtful and informed manner by each community.

1. Suitability for the role of SCR:
   - To have been in therapy for 12 months
   - To be willing to be in the role of SCR for 9 months
   - Have a genuine interest in safer custody issues.

2. Role of the SCR:
   - To attend the prison's safer custody meeting and feedback to the wing
   - To go to F Wing on a weekly basis to talk to new prisoners
   - To be responsible for the safer custody activity box
   - To be able to advise men of safer custody options: Samaritans phone
   - To be involved in supporting a man through the ACCT procedures:
      a) To be notified by staff and ACCT assessor when an ACCT is opened
      b) To attend case reviews if requested by the man on the ACCT
      c) To attend post closure interview

3. Training and support
   - To receive ACCT awareness training
   - To attend monthly SCR business meeting - facilitated by SC manager
   - To attend monthly SCR support group - facilitated by staff
   - To use small group when required - to address feelings associated with the role
   - To see safer custody manager when required - to communicate concerns
   - To see wing staff when required - to get support and advice
   - To see healthcare staff when required - to get support and advice
   - At the end of the rep period - SCR to be de-briefed

4. Safer custody awareness on communities:
   - Know your safer custody rep - photograph of rep on each community

Safer custody tee shirt

Printed in Great Britain
by Amazon